LITERARY AGENTS

To Malcolm and Kitty Muggeridge,
who so much appreciate the novelist as spy

LITERARY AGENTS
The Novelist as Spy

Anthony Masters

Basil Blackwell

British Library Cataloguing in Publication Data
Masters, Anthony
 Literary agents: the novelist as spy.
 1. Spy stories, English 2. Novelists,
 English—20th century—Biography
 I. Title
 823'.0872 PR106
 ISBN 0–631–14979–1

Library of Congress Cataloging in Publication Data
Masters, Anthony, 1940–
 Literary agents.
 Bibliography: p.
 Includes index.
 1. Spy stories, English—History and criticism.
 2. English fiction—20th century—History and criticism.
 3. Novelists, English—20th century—Biography.
 4. Spies—Great Britain—Biography. 5. Espionage—
 Great Britain—History—20th century. 6. Espionage,
 British, in literature. I. Title.
 PR888.S65.M37 1987 823'.0872'09 87–12155
 ISBN 0–631–14979–1

Typeset in 11 on 13 pt Garamond
by Cambrian Typesetters
Printed in Great Britain by Billing and Sons

CONTENTS

FOREWORD

Having so much enjoyed Anthony Masters' previous work, *The Man Who Was 'M': The Life of Maxwell Knight*, which contained much surprising new material, I am delighted to contribute this foreword to his new book, *Literary Agents*. It is, of course, carefully researched and excellently written. With the deft skill of a conjuror, Mr Masters has painstakingly provided us with a chance to look at the Secret Services through the eyes of some of the most accomplished and amusing writers of this century.

I confess to not knowing much more about the British Secret Services than is contained in this book. But it tells us quite a lot. If its former members offer us the truth here – and it is difficult to believe that all of them are entirely wrong – Britain's security systems provide an abundance of material for plays, films and books for many years to come. You shudder? But read on. Here are characters no writer could invent, situations that even television producers would find too broad.

It is a particular charm of these various organizations that they are staffed almost entirely by the products of our most illustrious public schools and universities. This gives their adventures a tone that is convivial if not to say gay. Some of the ex-members of the security services sound critical but most – drawn from the same middle-class background as the fellows who run things – show a light-hearted indifference to the real world. In this book we often encounter the jocular attitude of the uncommitted onlooker. The participants frequently find it all highly entertaining, and so does the reader.

Here is an incongruous collection of bureaucrats: Malcolm Muggeridge, Ian Fleming, Dennis Wheatley, Tom Driberg, and more! Perhaps they are well advised to stress their detachment from the curious scenarios set up by the Whitehall mandarins.

What are we readers to make of this secret, sometimes rather squalid, world that Mr Masters guides us through so skilfully? Are Britain's security systems in good hands? Is this the best we can do? Are things changing, or is a real shake-up long overdue? I don't know the answers to these questions. But I don't think that anyone, after reading *Literary Agents,* could believe that those security services provide any sort of threat to our personal freedoms, and still less to our system of parliamentary democracy.

And for that may we be truly thankful.

Len Deighton
1987

INTRODUCTION

Spies have to be liars, thieves and sometimes even murderers. For a variety of reasons, writers often wish they too could function more successfully in these roles: as liars, because they are perpetually attempting the balancing act between satisfying their publishers and at the same time satisfying themselves; as thieves, because many of them fail to repay advances for commissions that they never complete; and as murderers, because they often destroy their characters in far more subtle ways than real-life practitioners. A highly developed fantasy life is one of the novelist's most important assets – which gives rise to the belief, on the part of many writers, that they would be extremely successful in the world of espionage. There are also certain technical and emotional affinities between the writer and the spy, for the writer is a natural spy, perpetually gathering intelligence and often living, as Graham Greene would have it, 'on the dangerous edge of things'. One part of the writer lives a normal life in society, while the other part observes, gathers information, and fantasizes.

During the First and Second World Wars, some writers naturally gravitated to the field of Intelligence. There were a number of reasons for this. Not all of these writers were of a military disposition, or mentally tough enough to drive a field ambulance or to survive the physical rigours of working on the land. Some were ideally suited temperamentally to working in Intelligence, others, though perhaps not so happy in the

1

business, were to find that they could make use of their experience later, in their writing. Some went into the Secret Service to escape their emotional problems and responsibilities, while a few were inspired by thoughts of loyalty and the fight between good and evil. The leading exponent of this latter school of thought, John Buchan, wrote of his own Secret Service experiences: 'I have some queer recollections of those days – of meetings with odd people in odd places, of fantastic duties which a romancer would have registered as beyond possibility.' In fact, Buchan encapsulates much of the schoolboy spirit that has lured many writers into the Intelligence world. And the attraction was mutual, for Intelligence was also interested in them and their imaginations.

This was the case with Buchan himself, as well as with Somerset Maugham, Compton Mackenzie, Malcolm Muggeridge, Graham Greene, Dennis Wheatley, Tom Driberg and John Bingham. All these men were approached because they had fertile imaginations as well as sharp and questioning minds. Buchan was made Director of Intelligence in the First World War, Maugham was sent on spying missions to Switzerland and Russia, and Mackenzie was sent to Athens. In the Second World War, Muggeridge and Greene joined MI6 and were sent to Africa, Wheatley hovered on the fringe of MI5, Driberg infiltrated the Communist Party of Great Britain and is reputed to have become a double agent, and Bingham became a case officer in MI5's counter-subversion department, presided over by the mysterious Maxwell Knight.

There were others, however, who were not recruited because they were already writers, but who drew inspiration from their work in the Secret Service when they became writers – with varying degrees of success. Ian Fleming, seconded to Naval Intelligence, went on to write the phenomenally successful James Bond Books; Howard Hunt, the veteran CIA agent, notorious for his involvement in the Watergate scandal, wrote dozens of spy novels that lauded the American Intelligence Services and were themselves approved by the American administration. The espionage novels of David Cornwell, better known as John le Carré, who was recruited into MI5 under John Bingham, have challenged the whole public conception of the Secret Service. In a category of his own is Erskine Childers, whose brilliant imagination it was that alerted England to the threat of German invasion. He had never been recruited by any branch of the Secret Service.

CHAPTER ONE

ERSKINE CHILDERS:
THE INTREPID SPY

Although Britain mounted Intelligence operations against Tsarist Russia in the late nineteenth century, the Secret Service was then a very amateurish operation indeed. Gradually the Victorian War Office put it on a firmer footing, while anti-Fenian operations strengthened its experience; an early version of the Special Branch emerged in the early 1890s. The earliest writer to claim – although this was never substantiated – to have Secret Service experience was William Le Queux. He asserted that he had been severely underpaid for his services, and that he wrote his thrillers to defray his Secret Service expenses. In his book, A Secret Service, *published in 1896, Le Queux warns of German invasion. From 1900 onwards this threat was taken seriously by Britain's Naval Intelligence Department, who even went to the extent of translating a novel by a French naval officer, entitled* La guerre avec L'Angleterre. *The translation was for circulation to British officers only. But the book about potential German invasion that was taken most seriously was* The Riddle of the Sands *by Erskine Childers.*

'One of those romantic gentlemen that one reads of in sixpenny magazines, with a Kodak in his tie-pin, a sketch-book in the lining of his coat, and a selection of disguises in his hand luggage.'
        An early twentieth-century Englishman's idea of a spy,
            from Erskine Childers' *The Riddle of the Sands*

Erskine Childers was a spy by chance – a private spy, not a member of any Intelligence organization. He was a man who observed, and who then used his observations to write a successful work of fiction. He did not try to alert the authorities in any official way, but the book was taken so seriously by them that professional agents were employed to continue his observations. He had all the inner characteristics of a Buchan hero, but he did not look like one: he walked with a limp and was short and unobtrusive. Yet his sailing exploits became legendary, as did his life's tragic end, when he was found guilty of gun-running and executed. His creative, fertile mind could appreciate a potentially successful strategy, but he was not involved in a fantasy world of spies and spying. Childers was a natural spy; unlike other writers such as Ian Fleming and Howard Hunt, he observed and wrote for patriotic rather than financial reasons.

Robert Erskine Childers was born in London on 25 June 1870, the second son of Robert Caesar Childers, an eminent scholar. It was from his father, who died of consumption at the early age of thirty-eight, that Childers inherited his intense powers of concentration. From his mother he inherited his equally intense love for Ireland. Educated at Haileybury and Trinity College, Cambridge, he took his law tripos and BA in 1893. Although Childers often seemed introverted, he was able to rouse himself to splendid oratory, and this he first used to considerable effect at Cambridge when he was put up as a candidate for the presidency of the University debating society, the Magpie and Stump. He was a clerk in the House of Commons from 1895 until 1910 – a period interrupted in 1900 when he became one of the first volunteers for the Boer War. He joined the Honourable Artillery Company, and was part-author of *The HAC in Africa*, published in 1903. In the First World War he joined the Royal Navy, and was swiftly promoted to lieutenant-commander. He was mentioned in dispatches and received the DSC.

Soon after he left Cambridge in 1893, Childers began spending holidays, either alone or with a friend, navigating small yachts through the English Channel or the North Sea and, in particular, along the complex and dangerous shores of the German, Danish and Baltic coasts. The most arduous cruise he ever undertook was across the North Sea, on the first of six voyages of slow discovery through the narrow and sand-locked channels of the Frisian Islands to the open Baltic Sea. During the course of these voyages he was to become familiar with the physical hazards, the bleak, haunting scenery, and a strange assortment of Dutch, Danish and German sailors and villagers. Slowly the weird landscapes and isolated peoples were to make a deep impression on his fertile and creative mind.

On 11 August 1897 Childers cast off alone on a showery, dull day, heading for Dieppe. There he picked up his brother Henry, and in easy stages they progressed through squally weather along the north-east coast of France and through the canals of Holland. Childers had never cruised under such appalling conditions, and his much loved boat, *Vixen*, was ungainly and difficult to sail. He wrote in his Journal:

> A low freeboard, a high coach-house cabin room, and a certain over-sparred appearance aloft, would unnerve the most honied tongue. In the 'salon' [the sailor] would find just enough headroom to allow him to sit upright; and before he could well help himself, the observation would escape him that the centreplate case was an inconveniently large piece of furniture. Confronted with the fo'c'sle, candour and humanity would wring from him a sigh of pity for the crew, but here he would be comforted, for there were to be no paid hands.

The two brothers crossed the Zuider Zee for Terschelling, and sailed through the desolate region of long, low, lumpy islands of white sand, which were separated from each other by difficult channels and tides. On 25 September Childers wrote in his log:

> We saw this strange region at its best this evening, the setting sun reddening gloriously over the great banks and

shining ribbons of water, and bestowing pink caresses on the distant sandhills of Rottum (inhabited, so we were told, by one lonely soul who had grown fabulously rich by the export of 'sea-bird' eggs), and the feathery line of the Frisian coast. At night we sailed off into deep water.

The intrepid pair were later towed by a tug through the Kiel Canal towards the Baltic. Then, 'the sun burst through and, unreal as a dream, after the silent expanse of the North Sea and the lonely levels of Friesland, there came the vision of a noble fiord, green hills and richly wooded banks, sloping to the blue, deep tideless waters, where, in a long, majestic curve, lay moored a line of battleships.'

In mid-October Henry had to return to England, so Childers was left to explore the fiords alone. This he did with considerable courage and independence of spirit. Although he enjoyed company in small bursts, he had enough inner resources to cope on his own for long periods. The next Easter, together with a hired hand, Childers crossed over to Holland and repeated his exploration. The journeys increased his ability for independence of thought, yet his greater confidence went unnoticed at the office as he was able to use his customary reticence as a convenient shell. But he had a special secret world – an increasingly strong inner resource – to fall back on, and he stood apart from the frenetic world of politics, which seemed to him to be dominated by egoists whose second-hand patriotic ideas and blinkered opinions deeply depressed him.

At this point he was seriously considering the possibility of writing a book about his Baltic cruises, although he had no notion at this time of an espionage theme. By January 1901, however, this strand had taken slight root, and he wrote to his Great-Aunt Flora, confiding in her the germ of a growing idea:

I'm on a week's visit up here, shooting with the Thompsons ... and a Miss Matthew, daughter of the Home Rule Judge ... I have not begun that book yet. I forgot before coming away to get the diary of that cruise from the flat. An idea has struck me that a story, of which I have the germ, might be worked into it as a setting. Do you think that would be a good plan, supposing, of course, that the story was a plausible one?

Despite encouragement from Great-Aunt Flora, Childers did not immediately begin the project; he wrote to her dismally a few months later: 'I have not begun the Baltic book yet. I fear it would be no good without pictures. I also fear the story is beyond me.' By the winter of 1901, however, he was more optimistic, and wrote to his friend and fellow House of Commons Committee Clerk, Basil Williams:

Oh, about my book, which you say I have told you nothing of. It's a yachting story, with a purpose, suggested by a cruise I once took in German waters. I discovered a scheme of invasion directed against England. I'm finding it terribly difficult, as being in the nature of a detective story there is no sensation, only what is meant to be a convincing fact. I was weak enough to 'spatchcock' a girl into it and now find her a horrible nuisance. I have not approached Reginald [Smith, of the publishers Smith and Elder] as yet.

Eventually, Childers did write the book, but was not optimistic about its fate. He felt isolated, his sisters (with whom he lived) were in Ireland and he was alone in the flat, trying to put the finishing touches to his book, at which he had been obsessively overworking – and as a result, he fell ill. Reginald Smith had promised to read the book on completion, but its author was clearly in a pessimistic mood. He was worried about the plot and style of *The Riddle of the Sands*; it was only the title he liked. Eventually, he sent the finished manuscript to Smith, who returned it, asking for drastic revisions. Childers set to work gloomily. He did not agree with all Smith's points but was prepared to work at an acceptable compromise, and this he achieved, after a great deal of painful rewriting.

Neither Smith nor Childers had the faintest idea that the book would turn out to be a great critical success. Much of this success was due to the obsession that had taken root in Childers' mind during his voyages around the sands and dykes of the Frisian Islands: he felt that Britain, once the heart of a great and prosperous empire, was all too vulnerable to invasion by sea, despite her still great naval strength. The plot of *The Riddle of the Sands* involves the accidental discovery by two English yachtsmen of German plans to turn the bleak and lonely expanses of the Frisian Islands into the springboard for an invasion of the unprotected east and south-east coasts of England. The story opens slowly, with Carruthers, an indolent young man from the Foreign Office, used to cruising in large yachts with an attentive and servile crew, joining the taciturn Davies on his small boat, the *Dulcibella*, a craft not unlike Childers' own ungainly but much loved *Vixen*.

Most friends of Childers could see much of him in Davies: unsociable, self-conscious, unpretentious, painstaking and versatile. But, in fact, Davies and Carruthers each represent one half of Childers' complex personality: Davies, the perfectionist, who loves the wild islands, and Carruthers, the intelligent if impractical man of the world. *The Riddle of the Sands* appealed to a wide spectrum of British society: yachtsmen, detective story readers and politicians. John Buchan, newly arrived colleague of Basil Williams in Lord Milner's political and administrative 'kindergarten' – as his group of bright young men were known – read it and was impressed. Perhaps the book inspired him, for it was very much in the tradition of the patriotic 'shocker' that he himself was to write. He described Childers' book as 'the best story of adventure published in the last quarter of a century . . . as for the characters, I think they are the most fully realized of any adventure story that I have ever met, and the atmosphere of grey Northern skies and miles of yeasty water and wet sands is as masterfully reproduced as in any story of Conrad's.' The book was also universally acclaimed by the reviewers, despite its awkward plotting, the statutory girl and the rather bogus Royal Navy officer turned German spy. Politicians and military strategists were particularly interested, yet were puzzled as to who Childers was and how he had arrived at such a strangely precise knowledge of the German coastline.

And they began to wonder just how vulnerable Britain's unprotected seaboard was. *Could* it be successfully invaded by an army landed from a fleet of small ships, as Childers implied? Basil Williams wrote: 'Few realized that the unobtrusive little man with the glasses and the sciatic limp was leading a double life. He let none of us know – until the information tumbled out one day, quite by chance – that his weekends were spent in the Thames estuary, sailing single-handed a scrubby little yacht.' In the book, Davies warns: 'And we aren't ready for her [Germany]; we don't look her way. We have no naval base in the North Sea, and no North Sea fleet. Our best battleships are too deep in draught for North Sea work. And, to crown it all, we were asses enough to give her Heligoland, which commands the North Sea coast.'

Childers rejected the view that Germany felt strong enough to invade England immediately; he was sure that she realized that trying to take command of the North Sea would only result in a defeat by the British Navy. He felt certain she had seen the alternative possibility of mounting an invasion in and around the Frisian Islands, and from there dispatching infantry with the lightest type of field gun in large sea-going lighters, towed by powerful, shallow-draft tugs. These would be escorted by warships that would approach the British shores at high tide.

In his postscript to the first edition in March 1903, the First Sea Lord, Admiral Sir John Fisher, wrote: 'It so happens that, while this book was in the press, a number of measures have been taken by the Government to counteract some of the very weaknesses and dangers which are alluded to above.' In fact, Sir John Fisher was to some extent understating the government's reaction. As a result of the book's publication, a Committee of National Defence was hastily created – a move which received a reassuringly warm welcome from the Commons. A site on the Forth, in Scotland, was selected for a new North Sea naval base, and a North Sea Fleet was established. Unfortunately, its ships were old-fashioned and certainly not capable of standing up to the German squadrons. A manning committee also stressed the need for a volunteer reserve, but this was only a recommendation, and made Childers considerably frustrated, for he believed that the time had come to train every Englishman in the defence of the realm. Fisher blandly pointed out that there was no fear of an imminent invasion of the British Isles. He did not seem to consider the obvious problem of the long-term invasion threat, not because Britain had total control of the sea, but because there was a very strong chance that in an even battle the command of the sea would hang in the balance for an indefinite time. But, nevertheless, a vulnerable chink in Britain's armour had been discovered by Childers' imaginative powers – an attribute that the British Secret Services would look for in writers that they were to use in the future.

Childers' military intelligence became a subject of great interest, and among many distinguished political figures who contacted him to find out more was Lord Rosebery, who wanted to know exactly how much of *The Riddle of the Sands* was fact and how much was fiction. Rosebery also urged Childers to keep on writing, for, after an invasion scare of these proportions, he was interested in how much more information Childers' imagination might reveal. Childers himself was a little bemused, for he knew he had invented the whole concept, albeit building on his own careful observations of the German coastline. But Leopold Amery, a much travelled journalist on *The Times* who had worked in Germany, the Balkans and South Africa, agreed with his assessment of German military ambitions and intentions. And it was soon after Childers wrote the book that Churchill told him that this very method of invasion had already been worked out by the Germans.

In the autumn of 1903 Leopold Amery, who was undertaking the arduous general editorship of *The Times History of the War in South Africa*, asked Childers to write volume 5. Childers had carefully studied the first two, which had been written by the now exhausted Amery. Initially he was not keen to take up the offer, but partly because his friend Basil Williams had been commissioned to write volume 4, he eventually agreed. Childers stipulated one condition: his regimental history of the Honourable Artillery Company's role on the veldt must be completed first. Despite the generous fee he would collect for the new project, he was depressed, as he knew the vast amount of work involved would take up all his spare time for at least the next three years.

The publication of *The Riddle of the Sands* eventually pushed British Naval Intelligence into action, and in May 1910 two officers were sent on a tour of the German sea-coast defences and the Frisian Islands. They soon discovered that existing Admiralty charts as well as intelligence information was totally out of date, and that their only real knowledge of the mysterious Frisian Islands had been gathered from Childers' book. In fact, all Childers had done was to combine information from German and British maps and incorporate the result into the charts in his book.

The two officers, Lieutenant Brandon RN and Captain Trench RN, inspired as they were, in their espionage mission, by Childers' book, were unfortunately arrested by the Germans and given a prison sentence – a highly embarrassing situation for the British government. Pardoned by the Kaiser as a result of King George V's state visit to Germany, they were released in May 1913, seventeen months before the sentences expired. Naval Intelligence was completely reorganized as a result of this fumbling attempt at reconnaissance.

After the publication of his book Erskine Childers basked in patriotic praise; he was seen by public and politicians alike as one of the great English adventurers, despite his uncharismatic looks and personality – and the fact that he was Irish. But his passion for the Irish cause was to be his undoing; the widespread admiration for the author of what was fast becoming a classic work of espionage was to evaporate – in English eyes, at least. For some years he had been devoting more and more time to the burning issue of Irish independence, and in 1910 had become a dedicated convert to the campaign for Irish Home Rule. In July 1914 he and his wife, Mary, whom he had married in 1904, used their yacht *Asgard* to carry arms from the coast of Europe to Howth harbour, on the Irish coast, justifying this on the grounds of Asquith's Home Rule Bill, for he did not want to pursue his cause by being treacherous to a Britain now at war. Nevertheless, Childers was gradually becoming a fanatical supporter of the Irish cause, mixing more and more with extremists. In 1919 he and his family settled in Ireland, where he became principal secretary to the delegation negotiating an Irish treaty with the British government. He fiercely opposed both Michael Collins and Arthur Griffith, republicans who favoured accepting the treaty, on the grounds that it did not provide for complete independence. He believed that to separate Ulster from the rest of Ireland, which the treaty proposed, would only prolong the problem.

When the Irish Free State government was established in 1921, Childers joined the Republican Army which was created to oppose it, and became involved in the civil war between the pro-treaty and the anti-treaty forces. As a result, he found himself regarded as a traitor by both the British and the Irish Free State governments, and on 10 November 1922 Free State soldiers came and surrounded his mother's home where he was currently living. Childers was arrested but did not resist despite the fact that he was armed, as he feared for the lives of his mother and his wife. He was arrested and court-martialled in Dublin, although he refused to recognize the authority of the court. Condemned to death, he was executed at Beggars Bush barracks. Childers shook hands with each member of the firing squad before he was shot – a fate that many fought to save him from, including George Bernard Shaw.

Meanwhile, *The Riddle of the Sands* has remained in print, going into many editions, a living tribute to the vision of an intrepid explorer and a passionate individualist who not only had the imagination to pre-empt a possible enemy attack on his country but was also the first espionage writer to debate the question of the double agent and the moral validity of spying. At one point Carruthers describes the Englishman turned German agent as 'the vilest creature on God's earth'. But

13

Davies, conscious of their own vulnerable position and anxious to expose the double agent, points out: 'Mightn't we come to be spies ourselves? . . . If he's in with . . . Germany, he's a traitor to us. If we can't do it [that is, expose Dollman] without spying, we've a right to spy.'

CHAPTER TWO

JOHN BUCHAN:
THE ROMANTIC SPY

In 1905, the department of Military Intelligence was created as a result of the Army reforms carried out by Secretary of State R. B. Haldane at the War Office: here was the first recognition that military intelligence had to be efficiently organized. But the new organization resulted merely in a general staff who bickered about department control. The arguments were eventually resolved, however, by the establishment of MI5 (Military Intelligence, Department 5), with control being switched from the War Office to the Foreign Office. MI6 was later established in the same way.

'You think that a wall as solid as the earth separates civilization from barbarism. I tell you the division is a thread, a sheet of glass.'

John Buchan, *The Power House*

John Buchan was highly intelligent and a brilliant organizer, yet his recollections of his Secret Service experiences highlight the romantic appeal of Intelligence, which was to attract a number of writers to the Secret Services, both in Britain and America.

Buchan was born in Perth in 1875 into a Calvinist household. The eldest son of the Reverend John Buchan of Broughton Green in Peeblesshire, he was educated at Glasgow University and Brasenose College, Oxford, where he had a very distinguished academic career, winning the Stanhope Essay Prize in 1897 and the Newdigate Prize in 1898. In 1901 he was called to the bar, and in the same year became private secretary to Lord Milner, who was then High Commissioner for South Africa. This highly successful appointment lasted until 1903. Lord Milner, a great believer in Britain's imperial mission, had held various important posts abroad, such as Under-Secretary of Finance in Egypt between 1890 and 1892, followed by a period at home as chairman of the British Board of Inland Revenue between 1892 and 1897. In 1901, towards the end of the Boer War, while he was High Commissioner for South Africa, Milner was busy recruiting clever young men for his programme of reorganization of the Transvaal and the Orange Free State. He told his colleague Sir Percy Fitzpatrick:

I mean to have young men . . . There will be a regular rumpus and a lot of talk about boys and Oxford and jobs and all that . . . Well, I value brains and character more than experience. First-class men of experience are not to be got. Nothing one could offer would tempt them to give up what they have . . . No! I shall not be here for very long, but when I go I mean to leave behind me young men with plenty of work in them.

Buchan was officially recommended to Lord Milner by Leopold Amery of *The Times*, but Buchan's reputation had already reached him, for the young man was now moving in influential circles. He knew St Loe Strachey (Editor of *The Spectator*) and the Asquiths, who had nothing but praise for his intelligence and perception. Consequently, his job with Lord Milner's 'kindergarten' was assured.

Once in South Africa, Buchan soon became deeply immersed in Milner's work. In September 1902 he wrote in his journal:

My work is as multifarious as the Army and Navy stores. This week I have been sitting on a legal commission, drafting company prospectuses, organizing relief camps, founding two new settlements and auditing the accounts of an Irregular Corps. It is a splendid training, but a little too much responsibility is thrown on my shoulders, and I shall be glad when I can turn over a lot of it to departments.

Nonetheless, Buchan found the work extremely stimulating. For him it was the complete marriage between the physical and the intellectual life. He went on long treks out into the bush and was deeply regretful when the time came to sail home.

In July 1907 he married Susan Grosvenor. Her father, who had died when she was sixteen, was the son of Lord Ebury and a cousin of the Duke of Westminster, as well as being a great-nephew of the Duke of Wellington, so between them they had a large number of distinguished friends and relations. After his marriage, Buchan became editor and literary adviser to T. A. Nelson, the publishers, where he was expected to improve a largely unremarkable list. Nelson at this time had a religious and a children's list but its main output was reprints. Its staff had little knowledge of good contemporary writing – but Buchan did. He was also given the opportunity of editing the *Scottish Review*, a paper that he determined to turn into a Scottish *Spectator*. He began to recruit a number of distinguished contributors, amongst whom were R. B. Haldane, Hilaire Belloc and the scholar Andrew Lang. He also regularly contributed a leading article himself. During this time, the Buchans led a full social life in London. John flourished in his role as bright young man; Susan attended lectures at the London School of Economics, worked at the Personal Service League, and was an active member on the constitutional side of the women's suffrage movement. Despite all these calls on her time, she also managed to study Greek, causing Buchan to pen this rhyme:

> To patronize the poor, with votes to fuss,
> And leave Greek grammars in the casual bus.

In 1908 their daughter Alice was born, and in 1911, their first son. The next year Buchan became an elder of the Church of Scotland. The young family's Establishment credentials were prematurely won. They dined with the Stracheys and the Amerys, met Roosevelt and lunched at Downing Street with the Asquiths. Milner and Haldane often came to their dinner parties. They also met Hugh Walpole and Henry James, who persuaded Buchan to read Robert Louis Stevenson again, after having complained that his literary tastes – romances and thrillers – were too low.

Buchan had now been writing for some time. He was prolific, publishing essays, political works, and, in 1910, his first novel, *Prester John*. But he had little interest in becoming a full-time writer, and explained his refusal to accompany Walpole to a Royal Literary Fund dinner with the comment: 'I really cannot go to these beanfeasts. I love writers individually, but assembled in bulk they affect me with overpowering repugnance, like a gathering of clerics.' In 1912 he published a collection of short stories called *The Moon Endureth*, which began to reveal his imaginative qualities as a writer, but he still harboured no serious literary ambitions, and was far more interested, at this time, in a political career. In 1911 he had been adopted as Unionist candidate for Peebles and Selkirk, despite the fact that he came from a strong Liberal family; but his phenomenal energy was soon to burn itself out. In 1912 he was told to rest, alter his diet and cut out smoking; no one could diagnose exactly what was wrong with him, but he constantly suffered considerable stomach pain.

Condemned to bed, Buchan began to distract himself by planning one of his most interesting and atmospheric books, *The Power House*, which was published in 1916 by William Blackwood. The story concerns the strange disappearance of Charles Pitt-Heron, the Oxford chum of one Edward Leithen, considered to be the Buchan hero most like Buchan himself. Unlike later Buchan heroes, such as Richard Hannay and Sandy Arbuthnot, Leithen is not a man of action unless he is forced to be. He is a busy man with a seat in the House of Commons and a home in the Cotswolds. Like Buchan, he has a Calvinist upbringing and a Scottish background. Again, like Buchan, he is a great reader, with an enormous collection of books. There are some differences, however: Leithen is a barrister and remains one, while Buchan left the bar in 1907 to work as a publisher. Leithen was educated at Oxford, but remains single throughout his life, despite a tempestuous infatuation with Kore Arabin in *The Dancing Floor*, published in 1926.

The Power House was written on a convalescent cruise to the Azores. Before departing, Buchan wrote to Walpole: 'I plan to amuse myself, writing a real shocker – a tribute at the shrine of my master in fiction – E. Phillips Oppenheim – the greatest Jewish writer since Isaiah.' The book is both romantic and mysterious, with an overlay of brisk description, and is typical of Buchan's popular writing. He describes the missing man, Pitt-Heron: 'He knew the Indian frontier as few men knew it, and in the wild tangle of the Pamirs he hoped to baffle his enemy.' Leithen finds he has stumbled on the kind of world-wide conspiracy of which Buchan was so fond, where international villains gamble high stakes for enormous power gains, and an evil master-mind reigns temporarily supreme. Having, to his satisfaction, confronted the latter, Leithen takes his leave and confides to the reader:

> It was with profound relief that I found myself in Piccadilly in the wholesome company of my kind. I had carried myself boldly in the last hour, but I would not have gone through it again for a king's ransom. Do you know what it is to deal with a pure intelligence, a brain stripped of every shred of humanity? It is like being in the company of a snake.

In statements such as this, *The Power House* underlines the plight of a world where civilization was only a veneer under which a barbaric new threat was struggling to emerge.

Buchan's health broke down again in the summer of 1914, largely because of family problems. Alice was being operated on for a mastoid, and it had fallen to Buchan's lot to try and sort out the affairs of some of his wife's relations, who were in financial trouble as a result of the Canadian Grand Trunk fiasco.

In August the family took a house at Broadstairs in Kent, so that Alice could convalesce and Buchan could find tranquillity, but he was restless. There were, of course, significant reasons for his inability to relax. War on Germany had been declared, there were numerous spy scares, and Buchan was anxious to join the Army. Deeply frustrated, he began to write his second 'shocker' – as he himself called his thrillers – *The Thirty-Nine Steps*. (It is interesting to note that Buchan always preferred to be publicly dissociated from his 'shockers', which he regarded as schoolboy stuff.)

Buchan based his famous character Richard Hannay on Lieutenant Edmund Ironside, whom he had met in South Africa. Known to his friends as Tiny, he was in fact six foot four and exceptionally versatile, speaking fourteen languages. Ironside had seen much of the action in the Boer War, and in 1902 had personally escorted General Smuts to the peace conference at Vereeniging as well as undertaking Intelligence work, for which he was ideally suited. Disguised as a Boer transport driver, Ironside had spoken such good Cape Dutch that he went entirely unsuspected by even the genuine Boers who were subordinate to him. With them, he accompanied a German military expedition against the Herero tribe in south-west Africa. Admittedly, Ironside made several amateurish mistakes – although one can't help thinking that they were the kind that English gentlemen at war would somehow naturally make, and be all the better chaps for making them. For instance, he was careless about detail: at one point a German officer noticed Ironside's real name on the collar of his dog. He managed to bluff his way out of this unfortunate situation, and was eventually awarded a German military medal before beating a speedy retreat back to South Africa. (When introduced to Hitler in 1937, he was to proudly display this same campaign medal.) All this was the kind of stuff that stirred Buchan's soul, and in Hannay he was to create a sporting English secret agent capable of any kind of adventure.

In 1914 the intrepid Ironside was the first to land in France, and he spent the rest of the war on the Western Front. In 1918 he was dispatched to command the Allied expedition to Archangel, and then went on an Intelligence mission to Hungary where he was one of those responsible for drawing up the country's frontiers. He was also involved in commanding Allied troops on the Ismid peninsula against a would-be Turkish uprising, and in leading troops in Northern Persia against the possibility of an invasion by the Bolsheviks. At the conclusion of these adventures, Ironside was promoted to major-general – the youngest in the British Army to hold this rank.

The difference between Hannay and Ironside was that Hannay was drawn into adventure, while Ironside was committed to it in the course of duty. His character and exploits were so rich in material that characteristics of Ironside's appeared in many of Buchan's books – and not only to embellish the character of Richard Hannay. Ironside, like Hannay, gave scant regard to his own personal comfort. One of his idiosyncrasies – his habit of playing patience when thinking out a problem – was invested in Hannay's American ally Blenkiron.

During the Second World War, General Ironside was deeply concerned about the activity of fifth columnists in Britain: shortly before being replaced as Commander-in-Chief Home Forces in July 1940, he issued a warning to the effect that there were 'people quite definitely preparing aerodromes in this country' for the invader. This prompted the Ministry of Information to issue a pamphlet which read:

> There is a fifth column in Britain. Anyone who thinks that there isn't, that 'it can't happen here', has simply fallen into the trap laid by the fifth column itself. For the first job of the fifth column is to make people think that it does not exist. In other countries the more respectable and neighbourly citizens turned out to be fifth columnists when the time came.

Ironside and Hannay had much in common.

Lord Ironside was to remember Buchan as 'a very highly

educated product of Oxford. I was a Horse Artillery subaltern, who had been through the whole of the South African war. We were both Scotsmen.' They talked regularly in South Africa and Ironside was impressed by Buchan's ability to observe and record. No correspondence passed between the two men, but their friendship endured; they continued to meet and talk on a wide variety of subjects until Buchan's death in 1940. Buchan's son, Lord Tweedsmuir, remembers his father saying that Ironside was the main figure from which he drew Hannay. He added that most of Buchan's other characters were 'usually an amalgam of two or three real people, often going through the adventures of several other real-life figures'.

But the character of Hannay is not entirely attributable to Ironside and his exploits. Buchan was thirty-nine when he completed the book, and much of the background and attitudes belong to his fondly remembered golden youth. The walking tours in the Galloway hills, the waters of the Kennet where he had fished, the nights spent in shepherd's cottages and the political meetings are all drawn from Buchan's own experiences. This description from *The Thirty-Nine Steps* (1915) is particularly reminiscent of his youth:

It was a gorgeous spring evening with every hill showing as clear as a cut amethyst. The air had the queer rooty smell of bogs, but it was as fresh as mid-ocean, and it had the strangest effect on my spirits. I actually felt light-hearted. I might have been a boy out for a spring holiday tramp, instead of a man of thirty-seven very much wanted by the police.

The unmasking of the villains in the villa with the thirty-nine steps leading down to the beach was the only scene that belonged to Broadstairs, for the house in which he was resting in that summer of 1914 had a similar flight of steps.

Despite Ironside influences and the undertones of Buchan's youth, Hannay is a lightweight, emerging as a breezy, down-to-earth sort of chap, resourceful when it comes to sleeping rough and always ready for a scrap with the odd villain or six. His physique is far more like Ironside's than Buchan's, who was thin and bird-like, but he is every inch cast in the mould of Buchan's boyhood spirit. Hannay is intensely patriotic; his mission is to represent good against evil, and he must ensure that 'our side' wins. At the same time he has the qualities of a good loser, much as Buchan had been taught at school. But this, of course, does not mean that he prefers to lose rather than to win – particularly in a team game. Even in a solo sport like boxing, rackets or golf, he must play for a cause that is greater than himself – his house, school, club or, at best, England herself. Beating the foreigner is a particularly popular sport. Buchan based his 'shockers' not only on the morality of winning and losing as an Englishman should, but also on the greater battle between good and evil that he had been taught about in his Calvinist childhood.

In *The Thirty-Nine Steps*, Hannay prevents secret documents relating to the position of the British fleet from slipping into German hands, and as a result he is officially recognized and begins to move in the same high places as Buchan himself. In *Greenmantle* (1916) he prevents the fanatical spirit of Islam from harnessing itself to the German Army. In *Mr Standfast* (1919) he disguises himself as a pacifist and 'rumbles' a top-level German spy working in England under the guise of a liberal intellectual, and in *The Three Hostages* (1924) he and Sandy Arbuthnot, who had also appeared in *Greenmantle*, battle against international criminals. Finally, some eleven years later (in fictional terms), when Hannay has been knighted for what can only be described as extraordinary services to his country, he becomes involved in another adventure called *The Island of Sheep*, in which a figure emerges from his South African past and insists that he keeps a promise he made twenty-five years ago. Hannay, being a man of honour, does not fail to comply.

Hannay does, however, have some less appealing features: he has very little sense of humour, he shouts his head off in a scrap, is a bad sailor and as late as 1915 is still in the habit of wearing a nightgown. He is also often worried about his courage – or lack of it – fearing that he will funk it. Once he even calls himself a 'cunning coward'. Yet Hannay never really funks it in the end. He is not a dominator of men, but he triumphs against the odds in his Secret Service assignations because he possesses a 'tough knuckle of obstinacy'. He is good at ciphers, and particularly shines at being an amateur in a high-risk professional world. Like Ironside, Hannay is a master of disguise and variously appears as a milkman, a roadmender, a chauffeur, a traveller in religious books, a film producer and a private soldier, among others. He is a late starter with women, however, and apart from a couple of passing romances, is only interested in a Secret Service career girl, an entirely cardboard character named Mary Lamington, whom he eventually marries.

Hannay's heroism lies in the fact that he is the kind of chap who does as he is told, and worries at the problems he is plunged into until he solves them. 'There seemed only one thing to do – go forward as if I had no doubts, and if I was going to make a fool of myself to do it handsomely,' he says typically in *The Thirty-Nine Steps*. Hannay has the descriptive powers of a scholar and a poet, but he can only lead men on the battlefield – off it he is an amateur, often a naive one. He expresses the conventional upper-class attitude towards the lower classes:

A man of my sort, who has travelled about the world in rough places, gets on perfectly well with two classes, what you might call the upper and the lower. He understands them and they understand him . . . I can't explain why, but it is a fact. But what fellows like me don't understand is the great comfortable, satisfied middle-class world, the folk that live in villas and suburbs. He doesn't know how they look at things, he doesn't understand their conventions, and he is as shy of them as of a black mamba.

Still convalescing at Broadstairs, Buchan found that each day now brought news of the deaths of more and more of his friends, and he was deeply frustrated by his enforced inactivity. When, by the spring of 1915, he had recovered, he was asked by *The Times* to serve as correspondent at the Front. He accepted with alacrity; at thirty-nine, he was well over the age for official enlistment.

Buchan remained *The Times* correspondent until after the Battle of Loos, when he returned for a short time to work in the Foreign Office. In 1916 he was commissioned as an officer in the Intelligence Corps. During that year he was much in demand by both the War and the Foreign Offices. The Foreign Office asked him to look after the welfare of a Russian delegation, and eventually to take them to Scapa Flow. He also visited GHQ in France in his capacity of major in the Intelligence Corps, working directly under the aegis of General Charteris, and would sometimes be detailed to take some distinguished visitor up to the Front. One of his other duties was to write a propaganda version of the first phase of the Battle of the Somme. In the September, General Haig asked the Foreign Office to release him until the end of the year, so that he could rejoin the staff at GHQ and carry on summarizing the battle. By now, his initial enthusiasm for the war had evaporated, to be replaced by a distinct loathing. His old stomach problems recurred and he was in great pain from what was eventually to be diagnosed as a duodenal ulcer.

In *Greenmantle*, his second Hannay thriller, published in 1916, Buchan introduced his most eccentric hero, Sandy Arbuthnot. Arbuthnot emerges as one of the least probable of Buchan's heroes, but in fact he is the most accurate, based as he is on the bizarre personality of Aubrey Herbert. Buchan had known Herbert at Oxford; his improbable and eccentric personality attracted Buchan immediately. He also spent a holiday with Herbert at his home on Exmoor – a visit that he described in his journal:

> We climbed the hills, fished, slept out one night on the heather, and galloped horses over the downs. On Friday I rode to the last meet of the Dartmoor hunt – fifteen miles to hack, then a wild run on your hunter, then fifteen weary miles back. I did pretty well, save that I smashed my bowler going over a stone wall.

While Buchan had been recuperating and writing at Broad-stairs, Herbert had contrived to attach himself to the Irish Guards as an interpreter; he had been captured by the Germans, but escaped. His adventures had in fact begun many years before the war when he had travelled extensively in Albania, Greece, Turkey and Arabia, making a rich assortment of friends, both heroes and villains. Half-brother to Lord Carnarvon, who was to be one of the two explorers to excavate the tomb of Tutankhamun in 1922, Herbert had also been a Tory member of parliament. In addition, he had twice been offered the throne of Albania, as well as having been invited by the exiled Albanians in America in 1922 to command the regiment they had raised. L. E. Jones wrote in his book *Edwardian Youth* (published in 1956):

> Aubrey lived in high romance. Each girl was a poem to him and to most of them he wrote one. He simmered and bubbled and boiled over with enthusiasm, for whatever Aubrey had in his mind he had at least a phrase, sometimes an epigram, often some verses. He delighted in words as some women in jewels, but he did not keep them, as some jewels are kept, for great occasions. All his thoughts were open and at our service, he had no reserves with those he liked; and because his mind was singularly original and fertile, as well as romantic, there was no resisting the charm of his conversation. His activities were abreast of his knightly imagination.

With Herbert, Buchan had little need of invention. No one could have been more romantic, no real-life figure more groomed to become a character in one of his novels. He spoke as many languages as Ironside, and although he was an aristocrat, he frequently looked like a tramp and continually supported the underdog. At Gallipoli, he was successful in securing an armistice so that several thousand bodies could be removed and buried, but his popularity faded at the end of the war when he advocated a negotiated peace.

In *Greenmantle*, the first adventures of Sandy Arbuthnot closely resemble the pre-war adventures of Aubrey Herbert in Albania and the Levant. The climax of the book is the Russians' capture of Erzerum from the Turks, which is firmly based on the real capture of the city in 1916 after a charge by the Cossacks. Sandy Arbuthnot is a far more exotic creation than Richard Hannay, and his activities are often bizarre. In *Greenmantle*, Hannay, with understandable awe, describes Arbuthnot posing as the leader of some fanatical religious dancers:

A tall man dressed in skins, with bare legs and sandal-shod feet. A wisp of scarlet cloth clung to his shoulders, and, drawn down close to his eyes, was a skull cap of some kind of pelt with the tail waving behind it. He capered like a wild animal, keeping up a strange high monotone that fairly gave me the creeps.

In words that could equally well have applied to Aubrey Herbert, Arbuthnot is first described in *Greenmantle* by Sir Walter Bullivant of the Foreign Office:

He rode through Yemen, which no white man ever did before. The Arabs let him pass, for they thought him stark mad and argued that the hand of Allah was heavy enough on him without their efforts. He's blood brother to every Albanian bandit. Also he used to take a hand in Turkish politics and got a huge reputation.

When Herbert died in September 1923, Buchan was greatly saddened. He considered him to be a unique survivor from the days of chivalry, the possessor of the most powerful combination of tenderness and daring that he had ever known.

At the beginning of 1917 Buchan received much-needed surgery, which was successfully completed after a two-hour operation. Once again he was ordered to rest, yet once again he was writing within a matter of days. On 9 February 1917, with the backing of Milner, Lloyd George offered Buchan the post of Director of Propaganda – hardly the right kind of job for a sick man, but he relished the frenetic activity. His salary was £1,000 per annum and his responsibilities were arduous in the extreme. Under the general designation of Production Section, the War Propaganda Bureau, the Neutral Press Committee and the news department of the Foreign Office had been unhappily and unwillingly amalgamated. Unfortunately they were all still housed in separate buildings, and Buchan had to visit them regularly to keep his staff on their toes. At this time propaganda was an extremely dirty word to the British government; most ministers felt that the country should be judged by its deeds alone. In an attempt to reassure them, Buchan maintained the policy that facts should not be invented or even coloured, but communicated in the most direct way possible. He was also responsible for extending the department's range to America, and to the American Press, so that Britain's achievements in the war should be accurately reflected there.

Buchan came more directly into contact with the Secret Service when his department organized the smuggling of pamphlets and information through Holland and Switzerland, as well as the accident-prone operation of sending leaflets by balloon over the enemy lines. It was as if he had now moved into his own fictitious country, where good use could be made of his lively imagination – a factor that Milner had not failed to predict when he recommended Buchan to Lloyd George.

As a result of the smuggling of propaganda, Buchan met Sir Reginald Hall of Naval Intelligence. He was delighted to make the contact, as he had always admired the man and his department. Blenkiron, in *Greenmantle*, is in no doubt: 'If I had a big proposition to handle and could have my pick of helpers, I'd plump for the Intelligence Department of the British Admiralty.' Buchan himself was now using secret agents and his days were furiously busy. In the mornings he often went to Buckingham Palace, as the royal family were beginning to take a strong interest in his work and wanted to be regularly briefed on how Britain was regarded abroad. In the afternoons he would attend the War Cabinet and then have a long session with Lloyd George. This was followed by correspondence and talking to Secret Service agents until late into the night. On 3 July 1917 Buchan received a commendation from Leopold Amery, who was now an assistant secretary to the War Cabinet. He told him that although it was strictly against orders to divulge proceedings of the War Cabinet, he did not think it would matter if he privately let Buchan know that the weekly reports of his Intelligence bureau were very highly regarded.

Janet Adam Smith, Buchan's biographer, feels that a distinction should be drawn between Buchan's public Intelligence activities and any possible Intelligence activities on behalf of the Secret Services. She is sceptical of him being directly involved in the latter, but his son, John Tweedsmuir, apparently claimed he had been, although he could find no hard evidence. But she also states that as Buchan had regular contact with Sir Reginald Hall, then it is likely that he was kept in touch with many secret affairs, the most romantic of which was the secret mission to Kut undertaken by the fascinating duo of T. E. Lawrence and Aubrey Herbert.

With the capture of Nasiriya in July 1915, the British forces were in possession of the lower part of Mesopotamia. This meant that the original objectives of the campaign had been fulfilled and the Turks had been driven back from Ahwaz and soundly beaten on the Tigris. As a result, British oil fields in the Persian Gulf were safe, and prestige was fully restored in every way. Unfortunately, on the crest of this success, other problems loomed. The British forces were beset by a shortage of rations and a considerable degree of sickness. In addition, the humid summer and the lack of cooperation of the local population had substantially reduced the physical tolerance of the British Army. The Commander of the Indian Expeditionary Force, General Nixon, decided to advance on Baghdad when he should have fallen back and rested his men. Spurred on by a mixture of complacency and a lack of clear instruction from India, he decided to press on, particularly as India had promised – a promise that was not to be fulfilled – food, transport, medical supplies and reinforcements. In November 1915 British troops came to a shuddering halt at the Battle of Ctesiphon just outside Baghdad, and General Townshend, one of the commanders, had to fall back on Kut. Townshend then made the mistake of deciding to stay and hold the town against a Turkish siege.

The situation worsened when a relief ship failed to get through to them and was captured. A top secret mission was then mounted to negotiate the terms of a surrender. Aubrey Herbert was proposed by the War Office as a negotiator, and the services of Captain T. E. Lawrence – more often known as Lawrence of Arabia – from the Arab Bureau were also offered and accepted. Herbert himself was uneasy about negotiating through intermediaries, for he knew from personal experience that the Turks believed in honour, and on that basis General Townshend would be better advised to conduct the negotiations himself. Unfortunately, this was impossible as the general was cracking up under the strain of the siege, and on 29 April Aubrey Herbert, Lawrence of Arabia and Captain Beach, the head of Intelligence at force headquarters, began negotiations with the Turks. The adventure this plunged them into is worthy of anything Buchan later wrote, and indeed inspired him for future work such as *Greenmantle*.

Herbert, Lawrence and Beach were blindfolded and 'went into a string of hot hands to the trenches, banging against men and corners, and sweating something cruel'. They travelled beyond the trenches for about half an hour, while Herbert's handkerchief became a 'taut wet rag' across his eyes. When a halt was eventually made, they were met by Bekir Sami Bey, one of the military leaders. He was a very fine man and very jolly, something between an athlete and Old King Cole. He lavished hospitality on them, providing them with much-needed coffee and yoghurt, begging to be told if there was anything more he could do, as Herbert describes,

while we sat and steamed with perspiration. He told us how he had loved England and still did. Then as we went I said that he had opened our eyes, putting my taut wet rag ostentatiously into my pocket. He shouted with laughter and said: 'No, no; you have chosen soldiering, a very hard profession. You have got to wear that for miles and you will have to ride across ditches.'

Whereupon he slapped them all on the back and they proceeded on their arduous journey. Although Herbert negotiated some merciful terms for the prisoners of Kut, the bargain was soon broken, for the Turks robbed, beat and starved them. Seventy per cent died, although for some time official censorship prevented the truth from leaking out.

Buchan found that writing his thrillers was the best possible means of release from the pressures of his new job, but his problems were now becoming very bureaucratic – a far cry from Hannay's. There were no 'fair scraps' in the department, and much of the real intrigue tended to be of the knife-in-the-back variety; in addition, there was no question of the slightest whiff of good moorland air permeating the dreary corridors of power. Buchan was directly responsible to the Prime Minister, Lloyd George, but he had tremendous problems in getting to communicate with him. By September 1917 he could stand the petty arguments, senseless blockings and lack of access to the Prime Minister no longer. He asked Milner, in his capacity of member of the War Cabinet, to intervene by putting the department under someone to whom he could have access, thereby improving the poor communications. Milner acted immediately: Sir Edward Carson, another member of the War Cabinet, was appointed to supervise policy on behalf of the Cabinet, while Buchan remained the executive head. But this proved not to be a particularly good solution, and Buchan still felt very much on the outside. In the end, a Ministry of Information was formed to take over most of the work of the department, which had the advantage of ensuring that a minister could now support the department in the House of Commons. Propaganda in enemy countries was made a separate agency under the auspices of Northcliffe, Beaverbrook was appointed

Minister of Information, and Buchan further penetrated the world of Richard Hannay by becoming Director of Intelligence.

Delighted by the appearance of Beaverbrook, Buchan noted in his journal: 'I am very busy, but finding my work much more satisfying. Beaverbrook has an astonishingly candid mind and is so willing to learn. On the whole I am having a much easier time than last year, for I have far more assistance now.'

In his original role as Director of Propaganda, Buchan had not always been popular, particularly with the more reactionary Press. To many the word 'propaganda' still meant lies, and he spent a good deal of his time trying to establish what he saw the process as really meaning, and how it could be put to good, honest purpose during wartime. Buchan genuinely wanted to tell the truth about Britain and her wartime struggle – to America, to the dominions, to neutral countries and to his own people. He used every possible device, including filming on the battle-field as well as, for the first time, commissioning a number of war artists. His new role, with its intrigue, haunted him. Some years after the war, when having lunch with his son William at the Café Royal, Buchan suddenly paused, looked round the room and said: 'Something's just come back to me. I have some funny memories of this place. I used to interview people here, in an upstairs room, under the name of Captain Stewart.' His work before the end of the war as Director of Intelligence is shrouded in mystery. Nigel West claims that he also became Press liaison officer for MI5, a position engineered for him by the head of MI5, Vernon Kell. But his position as Director of Intelligence would probably have given him these powers anyway, and Janet Adam Smith feels that he was kept so stretched with his administrative work and with writing his *History of the Great War* for T. A. Nelson, that he would have had little time for individual clandestine affairs.

After the war, he became successful in politics. He was Conservative MP for the Scottish Universities from 1927 until 1935, and Lord Commissioner of the Church of Scotland between 1933 and 1934. In 1936 he was made a Companion of Honour, and in 1939 he was created the first Baron Tweedsmuir of Elsfield – the Buchans' country retreat. In the same year he was made Governor General of Canada – an inspired choice, for Buchan brought all his enlightened verve to the job, and on the eve of the Second World War he established a friendly and productive relationship with President Roosevelt.

William Buchan has his own particular view on Hannay and *The Thirty-Nine Steps*. He feels that it was probably the first book about 'the enemy within'. Buchan needed to visualize evil events in normal surroundings, but he had a genuine faith in human nature and its ability to rise above the most difficult circumstances. Nevertheless, William Buchan believes that his father's Calvinistic upbringing made him feel that it was necessary always to be on the alert, aware that evil is always just below the surface. Even Hannay is not above reproach. In *Greenmantle*, for instance, having convinced the German Intelligence officer, Stumm, that he is a pro-German South African, Hannay suddenly begins to see 'the queer other side of my host, that evil side which gossip had spoken of as not unknown in the German army'. When Stumm starts to bully him, Hannay loses his temper and, in what appears to be a hysterical rage, beats the German unconscious and then runs for it. This is hardly the most rational course of action, as Hannay has now blown his cover story completely, thrown away his chances of penetrating German Intelligence and made himself a fugitive.

In *The Dancing Floor*, as the ageing Leithen lies weak and in danger of dying in the Arctic, his mind returns to his fishing expeditions in Scotland, and to a filthy old tweed coat of which he was particularly fond and which had enormous pockets for sandwiches. His thoughts also return to the good friends that he has made in his lifetime:

> As he thought of them he felt a glow of affection warm his being. He pictured the places to which they specially belonged: Lamancha on the long slopes of Cheviot; Archie Roylance on the wind-blown thymy moors of the west; Sandy in his border fortress; and Dick Hannay by the clear

streams and gentle pastures of Cotswold. He pictured his meeting with them . . . restored from the grave. They had never been told about his illness, but they must have guessed. Sandy at least, after that last dinner in London. They must have been talking about him, lamenting his absence, making futile inquiries. He would suddenly appear among them, a little thinner and older perhaps, but the same man, and would be welcomed back to that great companionship.

Buchan, like Kipling, saw his fictitious spies as playing the Great Game, overcoming evil with good and routing power-crazed fanatics and international villains with a clean upper-cut to the rotten chap's chin. But despite the stereotyping, his heroes play the game with all the frantic freedom of schoolboys on the loose. His spies never question the morality of British Intelligence – to them it is a noble organization. In *Mr Standfast*, Blenkiron underlines this when he says to Hannay: 'I reverence the British Intelligence Service. Flies do not settle on it to any considerable extent. It's got a mighty fine mesh, but there's one hole in that mesh and it's our job to mend it.' Buchan's preoccupation with evil is reflected in a passage in his book on the Emperor Augustus, published in 1937, where Buchan compares the ancient Roman dictator with the rising Italian, Mussolini: 'Once again the crust of civilization has worn thin, and beneath can be heard the muttering of primeval fires. Once again many accepted principles of Government have been overthrown, and the world has become a laboratory where immature and feverish minds experiment with unknown forces.'

In reality, despite his high position, Buchan's own Intelligence work was dogged by bureaucracy, and by lack of cooperation and access to the decision-makers. No wonder he longed for the moorland fantasies of Richard Hannay.

CHAPTER THREE

SOMERSET MAUGHAM:
THE WORKADAY SPY

*MI6 (Military Intelligence, Department 6), otherwise known as
the Secret Intelligence Service, was established in 1909, with the
purpose of conducting espionage overseas. The organization's
first head was Captain Sir Mansfield Cumming, whose initial C
was to become the perpetual pseudonym for the head of MI6.
Somerset Maugham was one of its earlier and most interesting
recruits.*

'Fact . . . is a poor story-teller.'
Somerset Maugham, preface to the Ashenden Stories

Superficially, William Somerset Maugham was an unlikely
candidate for MI6. Born in 1874, he had a particularly traumatic
childhood which left him with permanent psychological as well
as physical disabilities. He lived in Paris until he was eight, when
his mother, Edith, died in childbirth – a blow from which he
was never to recover. Doctors had suggested childbirth as a
remedy for her consumption – a popular theory among the
medical profession at that time. Two years later, his father,
Robert, died of stomach cancer, leaving an estate heavily
depleted by expensive holidays and by the extravagance of his
late wife, who had been half his age. Maugham was now forced
to leave France for England, to spend the rest of his childhood
with his uncle, the vicar of Whitstable.

As a result of being orphaned in this way, Maugham
developed a stutter, which, together with a club foot and

shortness of stature, made him a prime target for bullying. Consequently he took refuge in books, sealing himself off from the narrow provincialism of the Victorian seaside town and the education he hated at the King's School, Canterbury. His three older brothers, all in their teens when their mother died, had left home for boarding school when Maugham was very young and were doing well at Dover College; it was only Maugham who had the problems. In *Of Human Bondage*, published in 1915, he gave a very precise account of his days at the King's School, writing of his central character, Philip: 'He had quite a collection of prizes, worthless books on bad paper, but in gorgeous bindings decorated with the arms of the school; his position had freed him from bullying and he was not unhappy. His fellows forgave him his success because of his deformity.'

Maugham excelled at Latin and Greek, but because of his club foot was no good at games. By the time he was in the senior school the bullying had stopped, but his defence – a caustic wit – had been implanted en route, and did not help him gain popularity. That he was familiar with the process of fantasizing is clear from another description of Philip: 'He took to a singular habit. He would imagine he was some boy whom he had a particular fancy for; he would throw his soul, as it were, into the other's body, talk with his voice and laugh with his laugh . . . In this way he enjoyed many intervals of fantastic happiness.' This 'habit' was to become a strength in his Intelligence work, enabling him to penetrate the personality of his agents and adversaries. Philip then moves from fantasies to heart-breaking reality when he begins a passionate but largely one-sided friendship with a boy named Rose, who is all that Philip is not – popular, extrovert and good at sport. When, one day, they walk into chapel arm-in-arm, Philip experiences a state of all too temporary euphoria, soon to be followed by his first pangs of unrequited love when Rose fails to honour a previously arranged assignation. Worse still, returning to school after an illness, Philip finds that Rose has made friends with another boy. A painfully well executed scene ensues, in which Philip accuses Rose:

'I say, why have you been so rotten to me since I came back?'

'Oh, don't be an ass,' said Rose.

'I don't know what you see in Hunter.'

'That's my business.'

Philip looked down. He could not bring himself to say what was in his heart. He was afraid of humiliating himself. Rose got up. 'I've got to go to the gym,' he said.

When he was at the door Philip forced himself to speak. 'I say, Rose, don't be a perfect beast.'

'Oh, go to hell.'

Later, when Rose attempts a reconciliation, Philip refuses to forgive him and, having masochistically forgone the opportunity, wallows in his own misery.

Ted Morgan, Somerset Maugham's biographer, combed the King's School records for traces of a boy called Rose. There was no Rose, but there were two Rosses. He also discovered the name of a classmate with whom Maugham had shared a prize – Ashenden. This was the name Maugham gave to his auto-biographical narrator in three books: *The Moon and Sixpence*, *Ashenden* (a collection of Secret Service stories) and *Cakes and Ale*. Since he had painfully fantasized himself into another boy's personality and had later borrowed the name of a classmate to portray himself, the conclusion could be drawn that Leonard Ashenden may have been someone he had formed a relationship with, either in imagination or in reality. It is also interesting that in the first draft of *Of Human Bondage*, which Maugham called 'The Artistic Temperament of Staple Cary', Staple has a passion for a woman called Rose Cameron, but when the name Rose appears in the final draft it is as the name of a boy. If homosexuality was to be implanted at an early age, no ground was more fruitful than the English public school.

In the spring of 1890, Maugham left England to spend a year and a half in Heidelberg, where he discovered new freedom, escaping from the emotional tensions of school and the narrowness of Whitstable. It was here that he first met the homosexual aesthete, John Ellingham Brooks, who not only influenced his literary tastes but also took his virginity. Maugham was sixteen.

It was on returning to England in early 1892 that Maugham made up his mind to write – information he withheld from his uncle, who had used family influence to place him in the business world. But Maugham, feeling a total outsider, hated the accountants' office in Chancery Lane as much as he hated London itself. The desperate loneliness he felt is mirrored in Philip's feeling of exclusion in *Of Human Bondage*: 'Late in the evening he wandered through the West End till he found some house at which there was a party. He stood among the little group of shabby people, behind the footman, watching the guests arrive, and he listened to the music that floated through the window.'

But the rigours of accountancy were not to last for long; after a month Maugham returned to Whitstable and an angry uncle, who in some desperation sought the advice of a local doctor who suggested his nephew could do nothing better than join the medical profession. At first Maugham was very much against the idea, yet still could not bring himself to confess to wanting to be a writer, and thereby give his uncle apoplexy. So he became a medical student, which was an improvement on the accountants' office, and although he still detested London, it meant at least an escape from Whitstable. He entered St Thomas's Hospital in London on 27 September 1892. He was now eighteen. Still obsessed with his mother's death, he lost no time in taking up the position of obstetric clerk in the midwifery department, and later had the opportunity to attend confinements in the surrounding district. During his third year as a medical student, the Oscar Wilde scandal occurred, terrifying him and determining him to keep his homosexuality a carefully guarded secret.

In 1897 Maugham published *Liza of Lambeth*, his first novel, which was based on the slum life he had seen as a student. It was a well observed if rather superficial book, and in the preface

Maugham commented: 'I was forced to stick to the truth by the miserable poverty of my imagination.' But it sold well, and the *Daily Mail* declared on 7 September: 'The whole book reeks of the pot-house and is uncompromisingly depressing; but it is powerfully and even cleverly written and must be recognized as a true and vivid picture of the life it depicts.'

After his finals, Maugham travelled in Europe, returning in 1899 to London, where he wrote the first draft of his next book, *Of Human Bondage*. At first disheartened when it was rejected by a series of publishers, he was later to come to see the rejections as distinctly useful to him. He wrote in the foreword to the New York edition of 1936: 'If one of them had taken my book . . . I should have lost a subject which I was too young to make proper use of. I was not far enough away from the events I described to use them properly and I had not had a number of experiences which later went to enrich the book I finally wrote.' Over the next eighteen years, he contrived to build a literary career for himself; he published a book or a play at least once every year, and continued to travel extensively. As his career blossomed, he repressed his homosexuality even more, but gradually found the right level of confidence by which to move in fashionable circles.

He first met Syrie Wellcome at a dinner party in the winter of 1911, and found her very attractive. Although she was separated from her husband, Henry Wellcome, founder of the pharmaceutical firm, she was still wealthy, as Henry had settled £2,400 a year on her. She was fashionable and had a number of lovers including the British store magnate, Gordon Selfridge, but had a mentally ill son who was largely cared for by Henry and who only visited her in the summer.

Two years later Maugham asked an actress, Sue Jones, to marry him. Now in his forties, he needed marriage, partly for respectability's sake and partly because he now felt capable of having a sexual relationship with a woman. But Sue was promiscuous and did not want marriage, offering to go to bed with him instead, which did not suit him at all. A few months later she married Angus McDonnell, the second son of the sixth

Earl of Antrim. Maugham was mortified and later depicted Sue as Rosie in *Cakes and Ale*. Rosie was the most credible of all his women characters.

Maugham then went to New York where his play, *The Land of Promise*, was received with mixed critical notices. In January 1914 he returned to London, where he again met Syrie Wellcome. Having lost the custody of her mentally ill son to Henry, Syrie was now anxious for another child, and Maugham reluctantly agreed to be the father. The union was consummated in Bordeaux. When, without warning, Syrie told him that she was thinking of divorcing Wellcome, Maugham instantly became alarmed. She had a miscarriage very soon after, but when she timorously asked Maugham if he wanted to end their relationship, he, compassionately, rejected the idea.

With the coming of the First World War, Maugham found that he was too old and too short to enlist. The minimum height was five foot eight. Deeply frustrated, he joined an ambulance unit, which had been sent to France to help cope with the casualties from Ypres. He had originally been commissioned as an interpreter, but it soon became clear that drivers were far more in demand and he returned to England for training. When this was completed he was sent to Flanders and then on to Steenvoorde and Poperinge, the latter being very close to the Front Line.

It was at the Front, in the ambulance unit for which they were both working, that Maugham first met the man he was to love for the remainder of his life – Gerald Haxton, who was then twenty-two years old. His father was American and his mother English; he was far from good-looking, but he had an adventurous spirit that Maugham found deeply attractive. Haxton was able to communicate in a relaxed manner, and Maugham, who had always lacked this particular quality, was immediately drawn to him. To Maugham, Haxton epitomized the kind of athletic, confident boy that had appealed to him at the King's School, Canterbury.

Gerald Haxton was to become an excellent secretary to

Maugham, and proved invaluable during his extensive travels, where his outgoing personality was a great asset in contrast to Maugham's more inhibited, stuttering approach. Maugham was to write in 1938 in *The Summing Up*, an autobiographical essay:

I am shy of making acquaintance with strangers but I was fortunate enough to have on my journey a companion who had an inestimable social gift. He had an amicability of disposition that enabled him in a very short time to make friends with people in ships, clubs, bar rooms and hotels, so that through him I was able to get into easy contact with an immense number of persons whom otherwise I should have known only from a distance.

But Haxton had another side to his nature: he was an alcoholic, highly promiscuous, violent and dishonest. Maugham was gradually discovering these problems when Syrie announced her pregnancy in England. The news considerably disquieted Maugham: his life was becoming too complex for comfort. He applied for leave and returned to London on 4 February 1915.

On 13 August 1915 William Heinemann published *Of Human Bondage* in London, with simultaneous publication by Doubleday in America. Maugham wrote the book as an autobiographical novel, inextricably fusing fact and fiction. The first run (on both sides of the Atlantic) was five thousand copies – his greatest sales achievement so far. *Of Human Bondage* did not have a good critical reception in London, but Maugham, distracted by being away in Rome and waiting for Syrie to give birth (which she eventually did by Caesarean section), was not as concerned as he might normally have been. Their daughter Liza was born on 1 September 1915, and, hopelessly enmeshed by divided loyalties, Maugham became even more anxious to rejoin the war effort. But there were no vacancies now in the ambulance unit, and he hovered around in London, frustratedly searching for an escape route. Ironically, it was Syrie who came to his rescue, by arranging some social occasions with a friend, Sir John Wallinger, who had been a member of the Indian police

41

force and was later to become head of the French and Swiss
Intelligence Service, a post he held throughout the First World
War. Wallinger suggested to Maugham that with his fluency in
French and German and his occupation as a professional writer,
he had all the qualities of a potentially first-class secret agent.
When Maugham had recovered from his astonishment at this
proposal, Wallinger offered him a job. His role would be to live
in a neutral country while making the pretence of being there to
write a book. Maugham was much intrigued by the idea, for it
would make for an interesting clandestine life and would at the
same time, he hoped, provide material for future books as well
as an escape route from current responsibilities. Wallinger told
him that he would be sent to Switzerland to replace an agent
who had had a nervous breakdown, and that his departure was
imminent.

While Maugham was waiting to depart, a distraught Syrie told
him that Henry Wellcome was preparing to divorce her and that
he was named as co-respondent. Maugham was appalled: all his
former fears of public scandal were realized. To underline her
own misery, Syrie took an overdose, and although this was not
serious the crisis now reached further heights of emotional
trauma. Maugham passed his mounting legal problems over to a
high-ranking divorce lawyer, Sir George Lewis, who told him
that he would be a fool to marry Syrie. Instead, he should settle
on her some twenty or thirty thousand pounds – round sums
that were just within Maugham's financial resources. But he
rejected Sir George's advice. It was certainly true that he did not
want to marry Syrie, but if he did not, what was to become of
Liza? All the miserable experiences of his own rejected
childhood stared him in the face, as did the emotional trap that
he knew he was being slowly and inexorably drawn into.

Shortly after Maugham's interview with Sir George, Wallinger
told him that his clandestine operation in Switzerland was ready
to begin, and that he was to go to Lucerne, where he was to
undertake an investigation into an Englishman who was living
there with a German wife. When this investigation was
satisfactorily completed he was to proceed to Geneva, there to

make his headquarters. Wallinger did not promise any accolades – indeed, he was quick to underline a fact that all Secret Service employees had to face. 'If you do well,' he told Maugham, 'you will get no thanks and if you get into trouble you'll get no help.'

Maugham carried out the Lucerne investigation successfully, reported back and continued on to Geneva. There he was advised to go to the Hotel Beau Rivage, which he later discovered to be something of a headquarters for spies. He took a room, hoping that this would be the springboard to some mysteriously romantic assignments. But they were not to materialize, and over the next few months he found that even espionage could be a routine. By the end of 1915 he had settled into it.

Once a week, Maugham crossed Lake Geneva to file his reports on the French side. His only real worry was the possibility that he might be arrested for violating Swiss neutrality. Meanwhile in his spare time he explored the city and wrote a play. In the foreword to *Ashenden*, published in 1928, Maugham wrote of his own routine experiences:

Since they are connected by this character of my invention I have thought it well, notwithstanding their great length, to put them all together. They are founded on experience of my own during the war, but I should like to impress upon the reader that they are not what the French call *reportage*, but works of fiction. Fact . . . is a poor story-teller. It starts a story at haphazard long before the beginning, rambles on incessantly and tails off, leaving loose ends hanging about, without a conclusion. The work of an agent in the Intelligence Department is on the whole monotonous. A lot of it is uncommonly useless. The material it offers for stories is scrappy and pointless; the author himself has to make it coherent, dramatic and probable.

Given enforced leisure, Maugham had plenty of time in which to worry about the personal problems that would be posed if he married Syrie. Then, on 13 November 1915, Gerald Haxton was charged with gross indecency, having been arrested in a Covent Garden hotel while apparently having homosexual relations with a John Lindsell. Eventually Haxton was acquitted, but the slur remained. Shortly after the case he left England for Copenhagen, but when he returned, in February 1919, hoping that the worst of the scandal had blown over, he was amazed to be deported and banned from further entry to England. This was the reason for Maugham's eventual decision to live in the South of France, where he was to employ Haxton as his secretary. The reason for the deportation seemed at first quite mysterious. Such a punishment did not in any way measure up to Haxton's offence, even if it had been proved against him – which it had not. Indeed, this seems not to have been central to the issue, for Maugham's biographer, Ted Morgan, discovered, as a result of research at the Home Office, the interesting fact that Haxton had been deported on 'security and other grounds'. This opens up the possibility that Haxton may have worked for Belgian Intelligence.

In 1916 Maugham returned to London for rehearsals of his new play *Caroline*, and on 13 February of that year Syrie's divorce was heard. The result was a decree nisi, which gave Henry Wellcome the custody of his son. Maugham immediately returned to Geneva, where he was rapidly joined by Syrie. But she soon became bored with Geneva and with Maugham's regular absences, and much to his relief she returned to England. Exhausted by the complexities of his relationsips with Syrie and Haxton, as well as the still nagging worry about the possibility of his own arrest, Maugham took a holiday at a French spa. By the July he found that his espionage work in Switzerland was becoming more and more sporadic, and, thoroughly disappointed with the experience, he decided to ask Wallinger if he could be released. Wallinger agreed, and the more routine phase of Maugham's spying was over. He had been an agent for a year.

Ever since the remarkable foresight of Erskine Childers, the Intelligence Services had been recruiting agents with imagination and initiative. The English writer Compton Mackenzie, the American playwright Edward Knoblock and the painter Gerald

Kelly were all working for Intelligence at the same time as Maugham. When the Ashenden stories were first published in 1928 they overshadowed the publication of Mackenzie's Intelligence novel, *Extremes Meet*. With considerable irritation, he was to write in his autobiography:

> Maugham's work of Intelligence during the war had consisted of acting as a kind of intermediary to gather the information of agents he met in Switzerland and communicating that information to Intelligence Headquarters in London. My experience and Maugham's were completely different. He handled his own material in the best Maugham manner; he could not possibly have handled mine.

Gerald Kelly had been an Intelligence agent in Spain. A friend of Maugham's, he had painted him in the famous portrait, 'The Jester', and at least two of the Ashenden stories, *The Hairless Mexican* and *The Dark Woman*, were based on events in Kelly's life. Most of the stories, however, stayed very close to Maugham's own experiences in 1915–16 – however tedious these may have been. Maugham was forced to burn other, unpublished, stories when Winston Churchill, having seen the manuscript, warned him that they contravened the Official Secrets Act. But the remaining pieces offer some very sharp pictures of Maugham's Intelligence activities.

For instance, when, at one point, Ashenden is interviewed by the Swiss police in his Geneva hotel room, they ask him to account for his activities in Switzerland. He tells them that he is writing a play, and when they ask why he is writing it in Geneva he tells them that England is in too much of a turmoil to provide a satisfactory writing base. Again, just as Maugham was to have problems with his fellow agents, so did Ashenden. One of them, stationed in Basle, is selling information to the Germans, while another threatens to expose Ashenden to the Swiss authorities unless he comes up with a rise. Ashenden's role is similar to Maugham's in that he visits his agents, passes on the information, then waits for instructions from England. He also writes reports which he is sure will never be read, until, having included a joke in one of them, he is chastised by his immediate boss for being facetious – just as Maugham once had been. And again like Maugham, Ashenden is sent to Lucerne to watch a British traitor and his German wife, only to realize that his sole function has been as a decoy to ensure the traitor's return to England.

These, and others, were incidents that Maugham had partially experienced but had considerably heightened in his portrayal of Ashenden. Despite the burning of some of the stories at Churchill's behest, even those remaining were uncomfortably close to the truth.

Speaking of his own work, John le Carré told Maugham's biographer: 'The Ashenden stories were certainly an influence . . : I suppose Maugham was the first person to write anything about espionage in a mood of disenchantment and almost prosaic reality.' And the *Times Literary Supplement* of 12 April 1928 commented: 'Never before or since has it been so categorically demonstrated that counter-Intelligence work consists often of morally indefensible jobs not to be undertaken by the squeamish or the conscience-stricken.' The similarity between Ashenden and Maugham was not limited to their experiences. Ashenden also had many of Maugham's personal characteristics: he played bridge, he was middle-aged, his hair was thinning and he had a horror of baldness. He was tolerant of human frailty and he could be objective, and though shy, he talked to people who bored him because they were his raw material. But Ashenden did not have Maugham's two main bugbears: the club foot and the stutter. That would have been too painful.

By the summer of 1916, Maugham had grimly accepted the idea of marrying Syrie. But fortunately her divorce was still not through, and, feeling like a man undergoing a temporary reprieve, he went to New York. Three weeks later, however, Syrie cabled, saying she was on her way to join him. The brief panic that now ensued forced Maugham into some quick thinking: when he met her on the dock-side he told her he was just about to leave for the South Seas, where he intended to research a novel based on the life of Gauguin. In fact Maugham did intend to go to Tahiti but Syrie was determined he would marry her first. He also told her he wanted to nurse his lungs, which had been adversely affected during his espionage work in Switzerland. But there was to be no permanent escape, and on 26 May 1917 Maugham married Syrie in Jersey City. He was forty-three and she was thirty-seven.

Shortly after the marriage, he received a call in New York from Sir William Wiseman, an old family friend. Wiseman had had a distinguished war record, but had been invalided out of the Army after being gassed. He went to America with the cover story of working as the chief of the British Purchasing Mission, but in reality became Chief of British Intelligence in America. In this capacity he built up such an excellent relationship with President Woodrow Wilson's foreign policy adviser, Edward M. Hurst, that it was largely due to his efforts that America was encouraged into the war. Wiseman's current preoccupation, however, was to put a stop to German pacifist propaganda in Russia, and to that end he wanted to send a mission there. In March the Tzar had been overthrown, and there was a danger that the provisional government would also be overthrown by the Bolsheviks, who would undoubtedly make peace with Germany. With this in mind, Wiseman was urgently seeking someone who could lead a mission to Petrograd to support the Mensheviks, the moderate Socialist party who were opposed to the Bolsheviks, and keep Russia in the war. After much consideration – and recommendation – he approached Maugham.

At first Maugham was uninterested. His lungs were still in poor shape, and he was concerned that a Russian winter would only damage them further. Neither did he speak the language, which he felt must be a substantial drawback to such an important mission. Yet he was fascinated by this vast and mysterious country and, once again, the thought of researching fresh material was tempting. Also, as Graham Greene and Malcolm Muggeridge were to find later, it would provide a useful means of escape from personal responsibilities.

On 20 June Maugham eventually agreed to Wiseman's proposal, despite the fact that he was going against his doctor's advice. Other members of the mission were Emmanuel V. Voska, a Czech refugee who was secretary of the Bohemian National Alliance and director of the Slav Press Bureau in New York; Ven Svarc, an attorney; A. B. Koukol, president of the Slavonic Emigration Institute in New York; and Joseph Martinek, editor of the Ohio-based Socialist newspaper, *De Inicke Listy*.

In a long letter written on 7 July from the Maidstone Inn in East Hampton, Long Island, Maugham described his preparations in some detail:

My dear Wiseman,

(i) I saw Dr Wise yesterday and he is arranging for me to meet two important Russian Jews when he next comes to New York. I suggested that I desired to make the acquaintance of the Jewish circles which are opposed to the Jewish socialists, and he is going to give me letters which will facilitate this. My idea is that there must be Jews of fortune and position whose views are diametrically opposed to their socialist co-religionaries; and it should be possible to get them to work against the latter. They would have more effective ways of dealing with them than we could possibly have.

(ii) Voska has arranged to find me a Bohemian servant and will communicate with you on the subject. I might interview the applicant next time I come up to New York. I suggest that Voska should go to Petrograd as soon as possible, since I do not see how the part of the work he is connected with can proceed in his absence.

(iii) I find the *Empress of Russia* sails from Vancouver on August 2. That apparently is the first boat that does, and subject to your approval, I propose to take it.

If I send my passport to you would you very kindly see that I get the necessary visas?

Concerned to know whether or not he would receive some kind of salary or fee for the work, Maugham raised the subject in this letter, stating delicately: 'I will not pretend that I actually need one.' He went on to add, however, that by refusing to accept a remuneration for his Swiss assignment, he had ended up as the only man in the organization working for nothing – a situation that was unfortunately not regarded as either patriotic or generous, but merely as foolish.

Voska's aim in the current mission was to liberate Czechoslovakia from the Austro-Hungarian Empire and to contact Thomas Masaryk, who was to be the future president of Czechoslavakia and who controlled an organization of some seventy thousand men. Voska was instructed to go to Petrograd, where he was to establish a branch of the Slav Press Bureau. From this base he was to organize the Czechs and Slovaks in the Russian Empire to do all they could to keep Russia out of the war. He could take three men with him, all reasonable expenses would be allowed and he would have complete freedom of action.

Maugham's code-name was Somerville, the name he had used in *Ashenden*, and his cover story was that he was in Russia to write for various American publications. Other code-names to be used were Marcus (Masaryk), Lane (Alexander Kerensky), David (Lenin) and Cole (Trotsky). Various well known publishing houses stood as code-names for key organizations involved in the mission: the British government was Eyre and Company; the Workmen's and Soldiers' Council, Kent and Company; the Maximalists were Burton and Company, and the Russian government were Waring and Company. Wiseman provided Maugham with Japanese and Russian visas and agreed to give him the sum of $21,000, which was to cover his own expenses as well as to finance the Mensheviks. Maugham was looking forward to the mission; his enthusiasm for the great Russian novelists – Tolstoy, Dostoevsky and Turgenev – made him regard the project with romantic fervour tinged with considerable trepidation. Now he was becoming involved in 'real' espionage.

Maugham sailed on 28 July 1917. But he was forced to cool

his heels for a day for a day in Vladivostok, waiting for the Trans-Siberian express on which Voska and the three other Czechs would be travelling. (Maugham, however, had instructions to pretend not to know them.) He passed an unpleasant twenty-four hours, making a miserable dinner of cabbage soup and vodka. He found the service poor, too; an English-speaking Russian who joined his table told him plaintively: 'Since the Revolution, the waiting in restaurants has become abominable.'

The clandestine party arrived separately in Petrograd, joining up later to create a headquarters in the Hotel Europa. The political situation was now on a knife edge. Tzar Nicholas II's Act of Abdication had brought the moderate left to power, and Kerensky, who represented the Labour Party in the Fourth Duma, had been made Minister of Justice and later Minister of War under the provisional government of Prince Lvov.

During the rule of this government, the Bolsheviks were becoming more powerful and were demanding instance peace with Germany. Meanwhile, the Germans had given Lenin permission to cross from Switzerland, where he had been during the early years of the war, into Russia, clearly hoping that he would be able to seize power and bring Russian involvement in the war to an end. In June 1917, however, at the first all-Russian Soviet Congress, Lenin's group had been outnumbered by the Mensheviks and the Socialist Revolutionaries, and their first attempt at seizing power by an armed uprising in Petrograd was put down. Prince Lvov had resigned, and the fundamentally Socialist Kerensky government had been formed. Kerensky, however, was not strong enough to control the Bolsheviks; nor did he attempt to appease them in any way. Such was the situation when Maugham and his companions arrived, only two months ahead of the November Revolution.

For his part, Wiseman continued to provide Maugham with as many facilities in Petrograd as he could. He cabled to Sir Eric Drummond of the British consulate that 'Mr W. Somerset Maugham is in Russia on a confidential mission with a view to putting certain phases of the Russian situation before the public in the United States. Please give him facilities for cabling his principals through British Consul-General, New York. Please cable if he has presented himself at the Embassy yet.' This last was meant as a request for a private code for Maugham, and the British ambassador in Russia, Sir George Buchanan, was put in the infuriating position of having to forward Maugham's cables without the slightest idea of their contents. Predictably, Sir George refused to cooperate personally, passing Maugham on to be dealt with by H. J. Bruce, the First Secretary. Maugham's stammer and reticence did not make a good impression, either, merely confirming Sir George's prejudice that he was no more than a meddling, amateur intruder. Maugham himself swiftly came to the grim realization that the embassy was barren ground and would be of little help to him.

Fortunately, he had another much more important contact in Sasha Kropotkin, the daughter of the Russian anarchist, Prince Kropotkin. Maugham already knew her; they had had a short love affair while her father was living in London in exile. Sasha had been painted by Gerald Kelly and is vividly described in *Mr Harrington's Washing*, one of Maugham's Ashenden stories, in the guise of a revolutionary's daughter, Anastasia Alexandrovna Leonidor:

> [She had] fine eyes, and a good, though for those days too voluptuous figure, high cheekbones and a snub nose (this was very Tartar), and a wide mouth full of large square teeth, and a pale skin . . . In her dark, melancholy eyes, Ashenden saw the boundless steppes of Russia, and the Kremlin with its pealing bells, and the solemn ceremonies of Easter at St. Isaacs.

In memory of their past association, Sasha volunteered to help Maugham, even agreeing to act as his interpreter. She was close to the Kerensky government and, most important, to Kerensky himself. Meanwhile, Maugham's Czech colleagues were bringing in some highly charged information: famine was spreading, the Army were mutinous and Kerensky and his government were in considerable jeopardy. Lenin was concealed in Petrograd, awaiting his second opportunity to seize power, and the Bolsheviks continued to sow unrest. As the storm gathered, Sasha was eventually able to introduce Maugham to Kerensky. They got on well. Maugham invited him, and a member of his cabinet, to dine regularly with him each week (on his British government expenses) at the Medvied – the best restaurant in Petrograd. He also sometimes saw Kerensky in Sasha's apartment and at his own office. He swiftly formed the reluctant opinion that Kerensky was no more than a broken man, afraid of moving in any direction, and therefore remaining inert.

Maugham learned from Masaryk, who knew Russian politics very intimately, that conditions were even more serious than they appeared on the surface; and it was to the Allies' advantage, he said, to give Russia as much help as they could, although financial help was needed only in moderation and on explicit conditions. He told Maugham: 'If you give them all they ask without conditions, they will spend it like children, and you will get nothing in return.' However, if it were possible to send a Japanese army of at least 300,000 men, this would serve to restore the morale of the Russian troops. Masaryk suggested that Japanese intervention might be paid for, if money were not accepted, by the cession of a part of Manchuria, which, in fact, was already under Japanese influence; he also thought that Russia would be willing to hand over to China some part of Central Asia. Indeed, faced with the alternatives of losing a part of Asia or falling into complete political and economic dependence upon Germany, Russia might be induced to choose the former. But no such strategy could save the situation, unless it happened very quickly indeed.

Masaryk repeatedly insisted that the war could only be won by victories on the Western Front, and he urged that a substantial American army be placed in the field without delay. According to him, the internal and external weakening of Russia meant the strengthening of the Central Powers, which made it essential to form independent Bohemian, Polish and Southern Slav states as a neutral barrier against Pan-Germanism. Germany must be prevented from using Austria-Hungary – the dismemberment of which was the real object of the war – with its population of fifty-one millions, for her imperialistic aims.

Maugham was already aware that the situation in Finland was disquieting. A secret understanding had been arrived at between certain leaders in Sweden and Finland to encourage Finland to join the Central Powers if the Germans were to take Petrograd. Maugham knew that the Allies were paying little attention to this situation. It was therefore of paticular interest that Masaryk should make the suggestion that further propaganda should be conducted in Sweden. German agents had spent considerable sums influencing public opinion there through the Press. The dispatches of Russian correspondents in Sweden, which were given much space in the Russian papers, were very largely coloured by this opinion, whereas Allied opinion was very little represented, he insisted.

On 24 September Wiseman summarized Maugham's conclusions in a cable to England from America:

> Following for Sir Eric Drummond in private cipher:
> I am receiving interesting cables from Maugham, Petrograd:
> (A) He is sending agents to Stockholm for promised information and also to Finland. He has reports of secret understanding for Sweden and Finland to join Germany on capture of Petrograd.
> (B) Government change their mind daily about moving to Moscow to avoid Maximalists. He hopes to get agent into Maximalist meetings.
> (C) KERENSKY is losing popularity, and it is doubtful if he can last.
> (D) Murder of officers continues freely. Cossacks are planning a revolt.
> (E) There will be no separate peace, but chaos and passive resistance on Russian front.
> (F) Maugham asks if he can work with British Intelligence officer at Petrograd, thereby benefiting both and avoiding

confusion. I see no objection, providing he does not disclose his connection with officials at Washington. If D.M.I. [the Director of Military Intelligence] agrees, I suggest he be put in touch with KNOX, but positively not under him.

(G) I think Maugham ought to keep his ciphers and papers at the Embassy for security. He is very discreet and would not compromise them, and may be useful as I believe he will soon have good organization there. Anyway I will cable you anything interesting he sends me.

Maugham had now slipped into something of a routine, just as he had in Switzerland, although this one was not nearly so dull. His mornings were spent on the arduous task of learning Russian, and he passed long evenings coding messages for Wiseman, while still finding time to pay regular visits to the ballet and to the theatre. When not attending political rallies or lunching politicians, he did a certain amount of sightseeing, paying a visit to Dostoevsky's grave, and wrote to his friends in Europe and America.

On 16 October Maugham cabled Wiseman, stating that Kerensky was becoming more and more unpopular and that his regime was running out of time. He also outlined how the new branch of the Slav Press Bureau would be created, stressing the importance of supporting the Mensheviks. In the present unsettled state, Maugham added, the greatest menace was the unseen German influence which was at work in all aspects of Russian political life. However, he and his Czech colleagues were now determined to make use of all anti-German societies and organizations in Russia. Wiseman cabled back: 'These will be dealt with separately and used for their own particular purpose. No one but the Chief Agent will know that they are working under one direction; and even the Chief Agent himself does not know the people who are providing the necessary funds.'

The proposed Slav Press Bureau would do legitimate propaganda business and serve as a cover for less legitimate activities.

Part of the cost of the bureau would be met by existing societies in Russia, and the rest by the British Secret Service. Three departments would be formed. The first would distribute well illustrated popular literature in Russia, together with chosen news items received from the United States or Allied countries. The second would send speakers to political meetings, to church services, and to the Army; it would also organize its own meetings wherever possible. The third would support the Mensheviks, who favoured the reorganization of the Army and the continuation of the war. This department would start a newspaper at the Front for distribution amongst the soldiers, to counteract the Bolshevik newspaper currently being distributed. Other sympathetic newspapers were prepared to help, and an anti-German Press agency would be organized.

Another branch of the organization, which was to be dedicated to anti-German propaganda, would be administered under Maugham's supervision by Poles already living in Russia. This branch, too, would be financed by the British Secret Service. In addition, other secret organizations, working quite independently, would be used. These would be predominantly Polish, Czech and Cossack, and their main objective would be the unmasking of German plots and propaganda in Russia. Their agents were to be deployed in the pro-German pacifist societies, with two main aims: discovering information exposed by the patriotic party, and instilling fear and distrust among the German workers in Russia.

Maugham estimated that the total cost of all these activities would be approximately $500,000 per annum, whereupon Wiseman suggested that the British Secret Service should be prepared to put up that sum annually. They would wait to assess Maugham's results before deciding whether to increase the subsidy or to close down the organization.

The time would come, Maugham realized, when the Secret Service would want to initiate a movement among the Bohemian and Czech troops in Austria and the Polish troops in Germany – a movement that would be his own responsibility. He also considered that if the Polish army which was being raised in the

United States could conveniently appear on the Western Front displaying the Polish national flag, a mutiny might equally conveniently break out among the Polish soldiers serving in the German Army. The result could be disastrous as far as the German forces were concerned, and if this could be made to synchronize with a rising of the Bohemians and Czechs in Austria, the effect would be overwhelming. Maugham told Wiseman that communication with the enemy was comparatively easy through the Rumanian frontier, a line of communication which would also reach both the Poles and the Czechs.

From Russia, Maugham was able to take a more objective view of mankind's future than he might otherwise have been able to. He wrote to the American playwright Edward Knoblock, who was working with Compton Mackenzie in Intelligence in Greece:

> It seems incredible that one of these days we shall all settle down again to normal existence and read the fat, peaceful *Times* every morning and eat porridge for breakfast, and marmalade. But, my dear, we shall be broken relics of a dead era, on the shelf all dusty and musty. The younger generation will give us a careless glance as it passes us. We will hobnob over our port and talk of the dear old days of 1913, and you will agree with me that these young fellows of nowadays are dreary dogs.

On 18 October Maugham received an urgent summons from Kerensky, who gave him a message for Lloyd George. So secret was the content that Maugham was asked not to put it in writing, but to take it to London immediately in person. The message was desperate: Kerensky could no longer hold out, he urgently needed Allied guns and ammunition, and he was most anxious that the British ambassador should be replaced as quickly as possible, since he found him totally uncooperative. He, Kerensky, had to make the Russian soldiers understand what they were fighting for, he told Maugham. They had neither boots nor warm clothes nor food, and they had been fighting for a year longer than England. They were exhausted, needing new heart and courage to continue. He went on:

> The Germans have made three offers of peace and we have refused them all. We ought to make our offer now. If we offer peace without annexations or compensations the Germans will refuse. The mass of the population in Germany think they are winning. They will never give up the three islands in the Baltic. Our diplomacy is bad. We must be better diplomats. When the Germans refuse then I can go to my soldiers and say: 'You see, they don't want peace.' Then they will fight. They will fight to defend their country, but they won't fight to give Alsace-Lorraine to France.

Kerensky told Maugham that the Allies could help him raise a small but adequately equipped army. However, if assistance did not come before the cold weather set in, he was certain he would not be able to keep the present army in the trenches, and if he could not do that, there was no chance of Russia remaining in the war.

The March advance had been halted because the Allies had sent only a fraction of the guns and ammunition that were required – and these had arrived erratically. Naturally, Kerensky wanted a consistent supply. He also told Maugham that it was essential the world Press should view Russia's affairs more sympathetically. In his view, they were unfairly critical – which only helped to support the Bolsheviks. All Russia required from the Allies was sympathy, confidence and a little more money.

Maugham's return to England involved another circuitous and uncomfortable voyage. He travelled to Norway, boarded a British destroyer at Oslo and eventually landed in the north of Scotland.

He arrived at No. 10 exhausted. As intensely conscious as ever of his stutter, he had written down Kerensky's demands – when he thought it safe to do so – so that he would not humiliate himself when he faced Lloyd George. Having scanned

Maugham's note, the Prime Minister bleakly declared that there was absolutely nothing he could do; he was not prepared to meet any of Kerensky's desperate pleas, even half-way. Maugham walked disconsolately back to his hotel, consumed by a growing sense of failure and indecision. But while he was trying to think of further pressure to put on Lloyd George, the situation was taken out of his hands. On 7 November Kerensky was overthrown and the Bolsheviks took power. Maugham now realized that he had been sent to Russia far too late, and that if only he had been there even six months earlier he would have had a reasonable chance of persuading the British government to take positive action. In those circumstances, he thought later, he might have had the historic privilege of forestalling the Russian Revolution. But, in reality, the failure of his mission was due very largely to the ingenuous belief held by British Intelligence that sending one agent to Russia with a fistful of expenses could have achieved anything at all.

Although Maugham felt a deep sense of personal failure because his mission had been so unsuccessful, he was very well aware that his Russian experiences had given him marvellous writing material. One particular illustration of this is *Mr Harrington's Washing*, one of the stories in the Ashenden series, which Maugham based on Voska's reminiscences of a real-life event in 1917 (it is recorded amongst the Wiseman papers). Voska remembered: 'We foreigners at the Hotel Europa caught the Russian mood – "Nitchevo" ["no panic"] – and went about our business as calmly as the natives. We had only one casualty, and that towards the end. An American banker, whose name escapes me, arrived to conclude a loan to the Kerensky government.' The banker spoke no Russian, so he was found a Russian lady in reduced circumstances to act as his interpreter. The banker put his loan through, and returned to his hotel well pleased. Voska thought it 'a pity to pour cold water on his enthusiasm, but I felt it was my duty', and so he told him that the Kerensky government was likely to fall at any moment. If it survived, though, the deal was still on. 'If it doesn't, you've come to Petrograd for nothing. Staying here will do you no good. I advise you to get out while the going's good, for real hell may pop at any time. The weekly Trans-Siberian leaves tomorrow for Vladivostok. You'd better hop it.' After some prevaricating, the banker decided to take Voska's advice, and so, determined not to leave Petrograd before collecting his washing, he and his interpreter went off to the laundry. Half an hour later Voska heard firing down the street but paid little attention to it, and eventually it ceased. Soon afterwards the interpreter arrived in considerable agitation, and told Voska that, as a result of running into a street skirmish on the way back from the laundry, they had become separated. Now she could not find the banker anywhere.

Voska hurried to the scene of the trouble – and found him dead in the gutter. Underneath him was his pathetic bundle of washing.

The importance of Maugham's Russian mission far outweighed that of his activities in Switzerland, and *Mr Harrington's Washing* exactly describes Maugham's own mental attitude as Ashenden began his journey:

It was the most important mission that he had ever had and he was pleased with the sense of responsibility it gave him. He had no-one to give him orders, unlimited funds (he carried in a belt next to his skin bills of exchange for a sum so enormous that he was staggered when he thought of them), and though he had been set to do something that was beyond human possibility, he did not know this and was prepared to set about his task with confidence.

Predictably, the Russian winter had aggravated Maugham's lung condition and he returned home feverish, with his doctor recommending that he enter a sanatorium as soon as possible. But Downing Street was more pressing, summoning him to an urgent conference, where, amongst other high-ranking officials, sat Wiseman himself. Maugham presented them with another written report. When, at his request, Wiseman had read it out to the assembled company, Maugham was stunned to be asked to

undertake a new mission – this time to Rumania. Now that
Russia had withdrawn from the war, British Intelligence wanted
to send an agent there to put a stop to any possible peace moves.
Having recovered from his amazement at their sustained
confidence in him, Maugham felt flattered, for he still regarded
his Russian mission as a spectacular personal failure. But
directly he mentioned the state of his health and his doctor's
advice, the committee dropped the proposition, telling him
instead to go and recuperate. Maugham left them, deeply
touched by such unexpected solicitude.

In his autobiographical essay, *The Summing Up*, Maugham
looked back on his Secret Service activities with cautious pride.
He related how he had been taught to conduct secret interviews,
throw tails off his track, and smuggle reports over a frontier. In
retrospect he felt that it was possible to get used to anything –
even treachery. The war, however, had seemed unreal to him, as
did most of the risks he had been running. His legacy to the
reading public was the Ashenden stories.

In the Second World War, Maugham seems to have revived
his espionage activities under Sir William Stevenson, the new
head (code-name Intrepid) of the British Secret Service in
America. Stevenson has indicated in a letter to Ted Morgan
that Maugham was under his orders, but he made it clear that he
did not regard him as particularly useful:

> With regard to Somerset Maugham, he is typical of a
> problem we had in working with material from BSC
> [British Security Coordination] files. Quite a large number
> of volunteers in warfare against Nazism were loath to be
> known as part of any intelligence agency, arguing that their
> services were given in a period of desperate emergency.
> Few had much taste for the business and became involved
> because they saw no alternatives. Their wishes had to be
> respected.

Stevenson had a variety of friends and contacts working for
him; those he identified in his autobiography, *A Man Called*

Intrepid, later indicated that they did not mind public acknowledgement. Maugham, however, was more reticent.

Ashenden was the first of the anti-hero secret agents, to be followed by Len Deighton's Harry Palmer and John le Carré's Smiley. Like Maugham, Ashenden is bothered by discomfort. He is nervous, world-weary, well travelled and inclined to be hedonistic: he loves good food, reading, travelling by train and lingering in hot baths. In Geneva, Ashenden, like Maugham, though concerned about his own possible imprisonment, finds relief in his bath. As he lies back in this hotel luxury in the short story, *Miss King*, he gives a sigh of satisfaction: 'Really, there are moments in life when all this to-do that has led from the primeval slime to myself seems almost worthwhile.' Ashenden is neither brave nor successful, nor even a particularly important member of the Secret Services. In fact, much of his life is as routine as Maugham's. In the story entitled *Giulia Lazzari*, he muses:

> It might be that the great chiefs of the Secret Service in their London offices, their hands on the throttle of this great machine, led a life full of excitement; they moved the pieces here and there, they saw the pattern woven by their multitudinous threads [Ashenden was lavish with his metaphors], they made a picture out of the various pieces of the jig-saw puzzle; but it must be confessed that for small fry like himself to be a member of the Secret Service was not as adventurous an affair as the public thought.

Ashenden's official existence is very dull. He meets his agents at regular intervals, as Maugham did, to give them their salaries, and occasionally he employs a new one. He collects, collates and returns information to London. He travels over the French border once a week to meet colleagues and to receive orders. On market days, he visits the butter-woman to see if she has brought him any messages from the other side of Lake Geneva; and generally speaking, he keeps his eyes and ears open.

Ashenden is a cultured man, more interested in art galleries
and the theatre than in espionage activities, at which he is not
particularly adept. We learn in *Miss King* that he was recruited
by his chilling boss, 'R', in much the same way as Maugham
himself had been:

> He asked Ashenden a good many questions and then,
> without further to-do, suggested that he had particular
> qualifications for the Secret Service. Ashenden was ac-
> quainted with several European languages and his profession
> was excellent cover; on the pretext that he was writing a
> book he could, without attracting attention, visit any
> neutral country. It was while they were discussing this
> point that R said:
> 'You know, you ought to get material that would be
> very useful to you in your work.'
> 'I shouldn't mind that,' said Ashenden.

Ashenden enjoys playing bridge and, in particular, he delights
in gourmandizing. A food snob at heart, he thoroughly enjoys
humiliating those less knowledgeable – especially when R is
included in this category. In *The Hairless Mexican*, Ashenden
goads the unwary R, who has had the temerity to ask him if he
likes macaroni. Ashenden patronizingly replies:

> 'What do you mean by macaroni? It is like asking me if I
> like poetry. I like Keats and Wordsworth and Verlaine and
> Goethe. When you say macaroni, do you mean *spaghetti*,
> *tagliatelli*, *vermicelli*, *fettuccini*, *tufali*, *farfalli*, or just
> macaroni?'
> 'Macaroni,' replied R, a man of few words.
> 'I like all simple things, boiled eggs, oysters and caviare,
> *truite au bleu*, grilled salmon, roast lamb (the saddle by
> preference), cold grouse, treacle tart and rice pudding. But
> of all simple things the only one I can eat day in and day
> out, not only without disgust but with the eagerness of an
> appetite unimpaired by excess, is macaroni.'

'I'm glad to hear that because I want you to go down to Italy,' replied R suavely.

In the first part of the book, Maugham emphasizes that Ashenden is only one cog in a very small wheel and that he rarely knows even part of the full picture. This, of course, is Ashenden in Switzerland; the latter part of the book covers Ashenden in Petrograd during the Revolution, where the routine is less predictable.

Maugham's clash with the British ambassador in Moscow is paralleled in the short story, *His Excellency*, when Sir Herbert Witherspoon receives Ashenden with a 'politeness to which no exception could have been taken, but with a frigidity that would have sent a little shiver down the spine of a polar bear.' Later, the ambassador tells Ashenden:

'I have received a somewhat singular request to despatch telegrams for you in a private code which I understand has been given to you and to hand over telegrams in code as they arrive.'

'I hope they will be few and far between, sir,' answered Ashenden. 'I know nothing so tedious as coding and decoding.'

Sir Herbert paused for an instant. Perhaps that was not quite the answer he expected.

In *Mr Harrington's Washing*, Maugham's relationship with his four travelling companions on the Russian mission is also mirrored by Ashenden:

He felt lost in the immensity of Russia and very solitary . . . There was a knock at the door and Ashenden, pleased to make use of the few words of the language he knew, called out in Russian. The door was opened. He sprang to his feet.

'Come in, come in,' he cried. 'I'm awfully glad to see you.'

Three men entered. He knew them by sight, since they had travelled in the same ship with him from San Francisco to Yokohama, but following their instructions no communication had passed between them and Ashenden. They were Czechs, exiled from their country for their revolutionary activity and long settled in America, who had been sent over to Russia to help Ashenden in his mission and put him in touch with Professor Z, whose authority over the Czechs in Russia was absolute.

Maugham even brings Kerensky into the book:

Things in Russia were going from bad to worse. Kerensky, the head of the Provisional Government, was devoured by vanity and dismissed any minister who gave evidence of a capacity that might endanger his own position. He made speeches. He made endless speeches. The food shortage grew more serious, the winter was approaching and there was no fuel. Kerensky made speeches. In the background the Bolsheviks were active, Lenin was hiding in Petrograd; it was said that Kerensky knew where he was but dared not arrest him. He made speeches.

Later, after the November Revolution when Lenin and Trotsky come into power, Mr Harrington asks Ashenden what he thinks now of Russia and the Russians. He replies:

'I'm fed up with them. I'm fed up with Tolstoi. I'm fed up with Turgenev and Dostoevsky. I'm fed up with Chekhov. I'm fed up with the Intelligentsia. I hanker after people who know their own mind from one minute to another, who mean what they say an hour after they've said it, whose word you can rely on; I'm sick of fine phrases, and oratory and attitudinizing.'

Maugham and Ashenden were each all too aware of the callous hypocrisy of their superiors. When Ashenden is asked to order the sabotage of an Austrian munitions factory, with the resultant carnage of innocent people, he reflects:

> It was not, of course, a thing that the big-wigs cared to have anything to do with. Though ready enough to profit by the activities of obscure agents of whom they had never heard, they shut their eyes to dirty work so that they could put their clean hands on their hearts and congratulate themselves that they had never done anything that was unbecoming to men of honour.

In his introduction to the 1941 edition of *Ashenden*, Maugham relates that Goebbels, in a radio broadcast during the war, predictably described the Ashenden stories as a good example of the brutality and cynicism of the British Secret Service. In fact, Maugham successfully dramatizes the upper-class values that permeated these still very early days of British Intelligence. *Ashenden* had a lasting influence on post-war espionage writing – far more than *The Riddle of the Sands* or Richard Hannay's patriotic adventures. Eric Ambler, Graham Greene, John le Carré and Len Deighton all created middle-aged and often cynical heroes who were locked into a particular series of Intelligence rituals. But of all fictitious spy stories, Ashenden's adventures come nearest to the real-life experiences of his creator.

CHAPTER FOUR

COMPTON MACKENZIE:
THE INDISCREET SPY

Compton Mackenzie published the pseudonym, C, of Captain Sir Mansfield Cumming, first head of MI6, in his Greek Memories in 1932. This involved MI6 in an in camera trial during 1933, with Mackenzie as defendant. It was probably the most delightfully farcical situation ever encountered in the annals of British Intelligence.

> 'From the first moment I saw the little man with his mousy hair and pale, ragged moustache, his very pale blue eyes filmed by suspicion and furtiveness almost as if by a visible cataract, I recognized in him the authentic spy, the spy by nature.'
>
> Compton Mackenzie, describing Davy Jones,
> his contact in Athens

Compton Mackenzie was the only novelist in his time employed by British Intelligence who quite naïvely disclosed secret information in his fictitious writings. As a consequence of the trial resulting from the Mansfield Cumming case, which found him guilty and fined him £100 plus costs, Mackenzie nearly went bankrupt and was forced to sell precious manuscripts and books. So angry was he that he decided, in order to recoup his finances, to take a sweet revenge on the Secret Service by satirizing them in a novel.

Edward Morgan Compton Mackenzie was born in Hartlepool, County Durham, in north-east England, on 17 January 1883, the eldest son of Edward Compton, a successful actor-manager, and of Virginia Bateman, an American actress. He was educated at St Paul's School and Magdalen College, Oxford. Having

66

originally studied law, Mackenzie also considered acting as a profession before becoming, between 1900 and 1901, a second lieutenant in the 1st Herts Regiment. He published a book of poems in 1907, which was followed in 1911 by a successful novel, *The Passionate Elopement*. Then came *Carnival* in 1912, and his most critically successful novel, *Sinister Street*, in 1914. At the beginning of the First World War he joined the Royal Marines, rapidly achieving the rank of captain. He served with the Royal Naval Detachment in the Dardanelles expedition in 1915, was invalided out during the same year and was appointed military control officer in Athens in 1916. He later became director of the Aegean Intelligence Service in Syria.

At the beginning of 1916, when most of Western Europe was at war, Greece was in a state of armed neutrality. Domestically the country was divided by two factions, whose increasing enmity was threatening to cause a major crisis at any moment: on one side, the Royalists, followers of King Constantine, the Army and a group of right-wing politicians; on the other, the adherents of Venizelos, the Liberal ex-premier. He and his followers considered the dissolution of parliament in the previous June to have been totally unjustified, and despite having a considerable majority Venizelos had refused to stand in the elections of the previous December.

The king believed that a German victory was certain, but Venizelos was convinced that the Allies would win. Directly a German victory seemed more doubtful, the king's attitude to his rival hardened and he saw in his policy a direct threat to the throne. This hostility eventually led to the revolution of 1916. Throughout this period it was the unfortunate task of Sir Francis Elliot, the British Minister in Athens, to try to keep the balance of power and prevent hostilities breaking out amongst the rivals. To complicate matters even further, he was forced to act in concert with the French, Russian and Italian ministers, all of whom had their own patriotic axes to grind.

The Athens Intelligence organization was divided into two parts: the A branch, which was devoted to collecting information about the enemy, and the B branch, which was responsible for counter-espionage. Their joint chief object of scrutiny was the German legation in Athens. Mackenzie was also made head of the Anglo-French police in Athens. He was delighted with the post, for he had very particular ideas about how British policy should be conducted in the Balkans. He was also determined to encourage a Greek crusade against both the Turks and the Germans. He was thirty-two years old and burning with the excitement of intrigue – all of which he was to recount in *Greek Memories*, the third volume of his war memories published in 1933, the book that brought him into so much trouble.

British Intelligence in Athens was led by a Major Samson, who since February 1915 had been obtaining military intelligence about the Turks under the pretence of administering a fund for the relief of refugees from Turkey and Asia Minor. Samson, who had been military consul in Erzerum before the war, worked under 'C' – Captain Sir Mansfield Cumming RN, the head of the Secret Service. Funded by the Foreign Office, C was responsible for both espionage and counter-espionage in neutral countries.

When Mackenzie first arrived in Athens he had no idea who C was, and all he could gather from Major Samson was that this mysterious cipher grudged money for counter-espionage and was locked in deadly rivalry with Vernon Kell, who had just been appointed head of MI5. As a result, counter-espionage in Athens was in great disorder. The operation was at present being inadequately run by Major Monreal, a Regular Army officer of Maltese extraction, under Samson's supervision.

Mackenzie was determined to turn chaos into efficiency. Fortunately for him, Samson found an excuse to remove Major Monreal by spinning him the fantasy that he had arranged an assassination. Unwilling to be dragged into the murkier side of Secret Service life, Monreal hurriedly rejoined his regiment, whereupon Mackenzie took his place. For a number two he was given Charles Tucker, to whom he took an immediate liking. Mackenzie then set about acquiring contacts. A Greek porter at the German legation, whom he code-named Davy Jones, seemed promising, and at his first interview it became clear that he was indeed something of a catch. His character sketches of the German legation staff were far more perceptive than any Mackenzie had come across before, and his physical descriptions were totally accurate. Indeed, Jones seemed to take an artist's delight in his work. Nothing escaped him, from the military attaché's reaction to a visitor to the manner in which that visitor had rung the bell and made an inquiry. He would notice the smallest shred of paper in the minister's waste-paper basket, and would pick up such minutiae as the nail-print of the marine attaché's forefinger upon a map. Truly the *crème de la crème* of agents.

For over six months Mackenzie interviewed Davy Jones at least three evenings a week, never in the same location, and through him kept himself informed of the most intimate details of life at the German legation. Preventing Jones from being discovered was enormously difficult in the heavily populated city of Athens, but nevertheless, Mackenzie managed to keep him a secret from everybody except his assistant, Tucker. In this endeavour to make a good spy out of him, Mackenzie was helped by the acting abilities of Jones himself, who always had some subtle excuse to explain his frequent visits to key rooms in the legation. He spoke English sufficiently fluently, aided by a little French, to give Mackenzie regular information. His German was perfect, and he understood Italian. Consequently, he was always able to pick up what was being said when he passed through any room, and he had such an accurate memory that Mackenzie invariably received a word-for-word account of what he had overheard – but without the slightest embroidery, for he knew that Mackenzie would welcome the dull truth far more eagerly than the exciting lie. 'He had, indeed, for me the cordial devotion of an artist for a critic who, he feels, appreciates his work and understands the fatigue and patience and care which have gone to the production of it.' Mackenzie claimed, thanks to Jones, to have learned more about the German organization of espionage in Athens in the last week of December 1916 than anyone had learned during the previous nine months. And because of the many interesting facts he furnished for Mackenzie, the status of the British Intelligence Bureau in Athens was considerably improved. The bureau was also to become indispensable to the new French Bureau des Renseignements which was shortly to be set up in Athens.

Many wild and exaggerated stories circulated about Mackenzie's activities. He was reputed, for instance, to have made an attempt on the life of King Constantine, and to have strafed his palace with gunfire so that no one could escape. It was interorganizational rivalry that induced the British Foreign Office to circulate such rumours, in an attempt to discredit Mackenzie and other Secret Service agents. At one point, Captain Sir Mansfield Cumming accused Mackenzie of talking indiscreetly about diplomatic secrets at Maxims in Paris. In fact, Mackenzie had never been to Maxims, and the indiscretion could only have occurred at a dinner party held within the not so discreet walls of the British embassy. But there was no doubt that, rumour apart, Mackenzie was amateurishly unguarded to an astonishing degree. His *Greek Memories*, published on 27 October 1933, made this particularly apparent. The book contained affectionate but satirical accounts of Cumming and First World War Intelligence work. For instance, he gave details of a colleague in British Intelligence who had devised a plan for blowing up a bridge near Constantinople; so conscientious was this Intelligence officer that he had obtained samples of various different types of coal used in that particular part of Turkey and sent some pieces back to England as models for the casings of the bomb.

Mackenzie also revealed in his book the contents of wartime telegrams, which infuriated Admiral Hugh Sinclair, then head of the Secret Intelligence Service, particularly as he had also mentioned the names of fourteen wartime Intelligence officers, some of whom still had SIS connections. In addition, he had disclosed the secret acronym, 'Mile', which was still being used by Sir Stewart Menzies and the military section of SIS. Finally, he had exposed the fact that passport control was used as a cover for Secret Service work. But only SIS seemed really upset by the revelations; during Mackenzie's committal proceedings, MI5 and Special Branch demonstrated their lack of concern by buying him rounds of drinks.

Both the committal proceedings and the trial, each held partly in camera, had overtones of farce. And there were a number of embarrassing mistakes made by the prosecution. One of the wartime agents apparently dangerously compromised by Mackenzie (a Captain Christmas) was found to have died ten years previously. Another, Sir C. E. Heathcote-Smith, had brazenly included a reference to his Intelligence work in his *Who's Who* entry, while a third, Pirie Gordon, had already reviewed *Greek Memories* in *The Times*. Cumming himself had died in 1923, a fact of which neither the attorney-general, the prosecution nor the defence seemed aware. Eventually, Mackenzie had to furnish the information himself.

The prosecutor, Sir Thomas Inskip, condemned him for revealing the letter of the alphabet by which the head of the Secret Services was known. But the judge was moved to inquire why, if C was such a dangerous code-name, it was still in use nearly fifteen years after the war. Inskip replied: 'That I couldn't say, m'lud.' 'No, I shouldn't think you could,' said the judge wearily. 'The consonant should have been changed by now.'

The case should have been written off as unproved, but for some strange reason it dragged on. As a result, Mackenzie was plunged into immediate financial problems. He certainly had no wish to prolong the case, for if the judge were to decide that the court's time had been wasted, he might feel it necessary to impose a high fine or even a prison sentence. This in turn might persuade the public that he had committed a far more serious offence than was actually the case, and because the hearing had been held in camera, Mackenzie would have no way of convincing them otherwise. The case had already cost him in hard cash £2,533, and in wasted time another £2,240: he knew that he certainly could not afford to spend nine months in Wormwood Scrubs – interesting though the experience might have been for him in terms of source material for his writing. His counsel had persuaded him to plead guilty, which he had unwillingly done. In comparison with the sum that the case had already cost him, the judge's eventual fine of £100 plus £100 costs might have seemed light. But Mackenzie had been told at the beginning of the case that he would have to find an additional £500 'against eventualities', so by now he was in extreme financial difficulties. The *Daily Mail*, for which he had been working, contributed £500 in cash to help pay the fine and to obviate the necessity of his spending a night in Brixton Prison. To find the rest, he had to sell nearly all the manuscripts of his books, as well as some particular treasures from his library.

Mackenzie was to execute a highly satisfying revenge. To pay for his trial costs, he produced a satirical novel about the British Secret Service called *Water on the Brain*, which was published in 1933 shortly after the trial. In it he satirizes Admiral Sinclair and Vernon Kell, C and K, as the deadly fictitious rivals, N (Nutting) and P. He goes on to demonstrate his inside knowledge by revealing that N is also known as 'the Chief', uses green ink and shares his headquarters with code-breakers, who daily eavesdrop on the Russians. The code-breakers are very thinly disguised in the novel as 'a staff of Russian confidential scholars who sat in two-hour watches listening to the propaganda from Moscow, which they dictated to stenographers in England'. The SIS head of counter-espionage, Valentine 'Vee-Vee' Vivian (whom Mackenzie blamed for his prosecution), is satirized in the book as 'HH' – Hunter Hunt, slow but 'devilish sure' and 'equally polite'. The SIS headquarters, Broadway Buildings, he calls 'Pomona Lodge'. In a new preface written in 1954, Mackenzie wrote:

> *Water on the Brain* was written immediately after my trial at the Old Bailey under the Official Secrets Act. At the time, the book must have seemed to the average reader a fantastic Marx Brothers affair but during the Second World War many people discovered that those responsible for Secret Intelligence do, in very fact, as often as not, behave like characters created by the Marx Brothers. *Duck Soup*, for instance, appealed to me as a film of stark realism.
>
> *Water on the Brain* at one time looked like becoming a

serious textbook for neophytes of the Secret Service, and indeed if it had not for a time been so difficult to get hold of, it probably would have become a standard work. People who knew the book were convinced that the Edinburgh police had been studying it before the 'conspiracy' trial of four young Scots was embarked upon in November 1953. It has indeed become impossible for me to devise any ludicrous situation the absurdity of which will not soon be surpassed by officialdom.

In a letter to the late principal of Glasgow University, to whom *Water on the Brain* is dedicated, Mackenzie insisted that his book was only a grotesque fairy-tale. He had little hope that the public's experience of the absurdities of Secret Intelligence would persuade them to accept this disclaimer, he said, but he did insist that the book was intended to be a comedy: 'and if it does not succeed in being as comic as Intelligence I must plead the impossibility of painting the lily.'

The theme of the book concerns one Blenkinsop who, having been manager of the Hotel Multum in Parvo, therefore knows the country and people of Mendacia. This farcial and fictitious country was created by Mackenzie as a backdrop to his Secret Service satire. When summoned to meet the Director of Extraordinary Intelligence at the War Office and charged with a secret and dangerous mission, Blenkinsop discovers that, as a member of MQ99(E), (a department of the British Secret Service) he will have to frequent Pomona Lodge under conditions of the most ludicrous secrecy. And his mission, that of restoring King Johannis to the throne of Mendacia, will be constantly threatened by a rival security organization, the Safety of the Realm Department. En route, Blenkinsop encounters American agent Katzenschlosser, becomes involved with the alluring Señora Miranda, and finds his matrimonial stability severely undermined when he is forced to pose as an importer of bananas who writes secret novels under a *nom de plume*.

It gave Mackenzie considerable pleasure to write such passages as this:

'First and foremost,' [Colonel Nutting] began at last, 'let me say I believe you are going to be the ideal man to succeed Hubert Chancellor. I believe the D.E.I. told you about that unfortunate business?'

'About his writing a novel?'

'Exactly. He wrote a novel called *The Foreign Agent* which might have smashed up the whole of the Secret Service.'

'Surely he didn't give away any secrets?' Blenkinsop exclaimed in horror.

'He did what was almost as bad,' said Colonel Nutting. 'He wrote what he honestly thought was a completely misleading picture of the Secret Service as it really is. The consequence is that any foreign agent who reads Chancellor's novel knows perfectly well now what the British Secret Service is not, and to know what it is not is half-way to knowing what it is.'

'Quite,' Blenkinsop agreed. 'But then don't lots of novelists write stories about the Secret Service? I was reading one coming over. It was called *The Green-Eyed Spy*.'

'But the author of that isn't in the Secret Service himself,' Colonel Nutting pointed out.

'Quite, quite,' said Blenkinsop. 'But would a foreign agent know that?'

'Ah, but Hubert Chancellor's name is printed in the *War Office Guide* under M.Q.99(E).'

'Isn't that a bit risky?'

'Not at all. Nobody knows what M.Q.99(E) means. You see, if Chancellor was still on the active list and if he told people he was working in the War Office they would ask him what he was doing, and he would be able to say that he was working in M.Q.99(E). It offers what we call a convenient cover.'

'But suppose people tried to find out what working in M.Q.99(E) meant?'

'That's where the Safety of the Realm Division comes in.

Olf P who is the D. [Director of the] S.R.D. has a special set of sleuths who devote the whole of their time to preventing people from finding out what M.Q.99(E) means. Of course, now that Chancellor has published this novel we shan't be able to use M.Q.99(E) any longer, and in the next *War Office Guide* we shall have to find another convenient method of reference.'

As to his unfortunate revelations about C, Mackenzie was particularly sarcastic:

Now that Blenkinsop felt sure of his engagement in the Secret Service he called his superior officer 'Sir' by reflex action. His tongue formed the word automatically as the salivary glands of a dog respond to the sight of a bone.

Colonel Nutting held up a warning hand.

'No, not sir, Blenkinsop. We avoid any suggestion of rank in our work. One of the important things about it is not to let any foreign agent guess who is the head of the Secret Service. After all, war may break out any moment, and if the head of the Secret Service is known what chance do we stand against the enemy?'

'All right, N, I won't forget,' Blenkinsop promised, with a hint of self-consciousness in his tone.

'That's it,' N encouraged, 'you'll soon get used to calling people by their initials.'

The interior of Pomona Lodge, the headquarters of Mackenzie's fictitious Secret Service, is described with somewhat heavy-handed humour, and would certainly have offended no one in Intelligence circles. A frigidarium has been converted into a dark-room, where four expert developers work continuously at photographs – showing foreign weapons and fortifications – taken by British agents all over the world. A swimming-bath has been emptied and converted into a laboratory, where a staff of chemists crack secret codes and analyse specimens of poison gas which other countries intend to use in the next war. One of the most harmful of these, according to an agent's report, is to be dropped on gasometers in two-ounce packets by hostile aeroplanes, and will turn every living creature within a radius of two hundred miles a vivid pea-green as well as inflicting many with *dementia praecox*. Later, Pomona Lodge becomes an asylum, but this does not necessarily mean a change of clientele. The inmates are bureaucrats who have been driven crazy in the service of their country. Mad typists type away feverishly at reports which no one will read, worn-out servants of the Inland Revenue assess their own nurses' incomes at incredible amounts, and maniacal clerks write cheques for trillions of pounds, while collecting red tape with which to hang themselves.

Mackenzie had written earlier novels based on his Intelligence activities: *Extremes Meet*, published in 1928, was a light-hearted comedy, upstaged by the publication of Maugham's *Ashenden*, which came out the same year. As mentioned in chapter 3, Mackenzie was considerably annoyed at being overshadowed in this way. In 1929 *The Three Couriers*, another story based on his espionage activities, had been published. A comedy without indiscretions, it received little attention, and it too was overshadowed by the next volume of his own autobiography, *Gallipoli Memories*. *Greek Memories* had been withdrawn, because of Mackenzie's prosecution under the Official Secrets Act.

Unlike Maugham, Mackenzie took his Secret Service experiences lightly, and drew comic, rather than dramatic, inspiration from them. Nowadays their humour is dated and wearisome. It was Mackenzie's indiscretions that were interesting: they proved how vulnerable the security services were, how easily they could be exposed and how inept the courts were in dealing with leaks. British Intelligence was caught well and truly on the hop – but only by a court jester.

CHAPTER FIVE

MALCOLM MUGGERIDGE: THE INDIGNANT SPY

At the beginning of the Second World War, the British Secret Service still retained the atmosphere of the world of John Buchan's Richard Hannay. Senior management consisted largely of high-ranking officers from the services, who bustled with self-importance and were consumed with a boyish glee at being able to break the normal rules of social conduct in the cause of secret action. One raw recruit to the Secret Service, Bickham Sweet-Escott, remembered being taken to a bare room in the War Office where an officer awaited him, dressed to closely resemble Sherlock Holmes. 'I can't tell you what sort of job it would be,' the officer said. 'All I can say is that if you join us, you mustn't be afraid of forgery, and you mustn't be afraid of murder.'

MI5 was responsible for counter-espionage, and the Secret Intelligence Service (MI6) for offensive espionage. In 1940 these organizations were locked in deadly rivalry.

> 'Malcolm Muggeridge swam into our ken, wearing his usual air of indignant bewilderment.'
>
> Kim Philby, *My Silent War*

Malcolm Muggeridge is in his eighties and lives contentedly with his wife Kitty in a modest, isolated cottage in East Sussex, surrounded by farmland and rolling hillsides. Over the years he has absorbed a number of different political and spiritual philosophies, and has been a highly contentious and influential media figure, as well as an urbane writer. Above all, Muggeridge is a man of instinct, sometimes of whim, and very definitely of intuition. For most of his life he has possessed a restive, questioning spirit that has led him to explore many avenues of journalism, both at home and abroad. It was his restless spirit that drew him into the Secret Services. Much of his work as an agent alternately elated and depressed him; at one point it brought him close to suicide.

Today, vintage Muggeridge is as witty and astute as ever. His rubicund, kindly features have a drollery that is very distinctive; he is a weathered Mr Punch who now delights in the contemplative life. His inner resources are immense, yet he does not simply chew over the fat of his legendary career. Acutely self-critical, he is able to re-analyse his every move, demonstrating a profound humility.

Muggeridge's friend, Elizabeth Longford, wrote in an introduction to a recent collection of his essays and broadcasts: 'He uses his great gifts of irony, wit and style in the cause of humanity itself. In that sense he is indeed a guru, a "Saint Mugg" jeered at by unbelievers, many of whom stay to praise.' But perhaps Kitty would focus on a more caustic Saint Mugg, a roguish scribe with style and barbed wit, a restless roamer who has lived life to its extremes and who has nourished himself on rich conversation. 'Malcolm and Hugh [Kingsmill] used to talk for hours each evening. In fact they talked so much that I longed to throw a book at both of them,' Kitty Muggeridge told me.

Muggeridge was born in 1903. The semi-detached family house was typical of the Edwardian suburbs of Croydon – a vast sprawl which he and his brothers were taught to regard as *petit-bourgeois*. His grandfather, who had an undertaker's business in Penge, had abandoned the family when Muggeridge's father was twelve. As a result, his grandmother had been forced to run a second-hand furniture shop which barely supported them.

Muggeridge's father left school at thirteen and became an office boy at a firm of shirt manufacturers, where he remained an employee for the rest of his life. He fought his way up to company secretary – a long, hard battle to the top which, however, did nothing to detract from his determined Socialism.

He often spoke from a small platform in the Surrey Street market area of Croydon, competing with street vendors and traders, summarily dismissing the old order and advocating the new Socialist principles. His audience may have been small and lacking in concentration, but he did have a few loyal followers, amongst whom was his son, Malcolm. In *The Green Stick* (published in 1972), the first volume of his autobiography, *Chronicles of Wasted Time*, Muggeridge comments: 'Defiantly, my father, the two stalwarts and I sang "The Red Flag" together, my tuneless voice mixing with their deep ones.' Muggeridge's father duly became a Labour councillor, and for some years he was the *only* Labour councillor in the borough of Croydon. The Muggeridge family electioneered for him, enthusiastically wore their red rosettes, and even appeared, in presidential style, standing together as a family at his election address. There was a fundamental reason for these family appearances – there were rumours that the Bolsheviks intended to nationalize Russian women, and a strong family unit was considered necessary British Socialist propaganda.

At home, the young Muggeridge's first understanding of Russia came from reading Kropotkin's *Reminiscences*, for although the family library contained the Everyman edition of *Das Kapital* neither he nor his father had ever managed to face reading it. With his brothers Malcolm attended the local elementary school, before going on to Selhurst Grammar School from which he emerged without especial academic distinction. But he did well enough to get into Cambridge, and at seventeen entered Selwyn College to read for a natural science tripos. Four years later he scraped through his exams, but his subjects – chemistry, physics and zoology – had made little impact on him, and he never again took any interest in them. Muggeridge was one of the very few grammar school boys in his year, and this was the first time he had met the upper classes *en masse*. He soon discovered that their culture was very alien to his own and that, to him, Cambridge life was excessively tedious. He spent long, idle days, taking walks in the misty countryside. Looking back on this period, all Muggeridge has been able to remember is superficial enthusiasm and 'foolish vanity'; but in his last year a sudden change took place, when he met Alec Vidler, later to become a distinguished priest, scholar and theologian. Their deep friendship continues to this day. Because of Vidler, Muggeridge moved into the Oratory House (a residence for priests) in Cambridge, and for the first time in his university career began to enjoy himself and to discover the fruits of long and lasting companionship.

After leaving Cambridge, Muggeridge travelled in India, a continent from which he carried away sharp images of the spiritual calm of the Indian peoples – tyrannized as they were by poverty and the British Raj. Returning to Britain, he began supply-teaching English in overcrowded schools in Birmingham – an episode which led him to compare this urban, asphalt-dominated environment with a sojourn in a dilapidated jail. Then, in 1927, he married Kitty, the sister of Leonard Dobbs, with whom he had shared rooms at Cambridge after he left the Oratory House. Kitty was to be his companion for life. Her aunt was Beatrice Webb, the Fabian Socialist, and her mother, a bohemian artist whose family, the Potters, had drifted towards Socialism, despite the fact that many of them had accepted peerages and knighthoods. Mrs Dobbs was delighted with the match but her husband, a Protestant Irishman employed by Sir Henry Lunn of Lunn's Tours, was more dubious. Muggeridge lacked both financial stability and a positive future, and there was no evidence that the situation might improve.

Through his marriage Muggeridge met Hugh Kingsmill-Lunn, one of Sir Henry's son, who later dropped the name Lunn because of his antipathy towards his father, and was to become a distinguished writer and essayist. He and Muggeridge formed a strong friendship that lasted until Kingsmill's death.

Muggeridge had not been married long when his anxious father-in-law drew his attention to an advertisement for teachers at a British school in Egypt. The pay was higher than his current salary in Birmingham, and with a sense of mounting excitement he applied for the post. He was accepted, and shortly afterwards he and Kitty set out for Minia in Upper Egypt.

Muggeridge immediately noted certain similarities to the social conditions that he had criticized in India, but in Egypt the British administration was far more run-down. The job itself proved a disappointment, for he found himself standing in front of a class just as he had done in Birmingham – the only difference being the colour and culture of his pupils. In the evenings he sat at his typewriter, hoping to become a writer rather than stay a schoolmaster. This seemed a remote possibility until, by a lucky chance, he met the writer Arthur Ransome, who had come to Cairo as the *Guardian*'s special correspondent. Ransome had been in Russia during the Revolution, and he enthralled Muggeridge with his eye-witness account of this great blow for freedom. He had an inexhaustible supply of anecdotes, including one of the occasion when he had played chess with Lenin. Ransome recommended Muggeridge to the editor of the *Guardian*, C. P. Scott, and a few weeks later Scott responded by suggesting that he should join the editorial staff for a three-month probationary period. Muggeridge was overjoyed. At last the sterility of his schoolmastering days might be over.

The Muggeridges' first child was born in Egypt, and was still a baby when they returned to England in August 1932. During his work as a leader-writer for the *Guardian*, Muggeridge met such Socialist literati as Kingsley Martin, in whose Manchester house the Muggeridges temporarily boarded. Later they moved into a flat in Didsbury, and C. P. Scott himself would sometimes bicycle over for tea. In addition to leader-writing, Muggeridge began to write for the *Manchester Guardian Weekly* and to review books, a task he undertook for a variety of newspapers throughout his working life. His play *Three Flats* was produced by the Stage Society and performed at the Prince of Wales Theatre, to considerable acclaim. Constant Huntington, the managing director of Putnam, who published *Three Flats* in America, suggested to Muggeridge that he write a novel. The result was *Autumnal Face* (1931), based on his childhood memories of Croydon. This book was equally well received, and Muggeridge felt he had arrived. Nevertheless, he rejected the idea of becoming a freelance writer as too risky and too isolated from the vibrant newspaper world and its gossip that he was currently enjoying, and where he was laying the foundations for his waspish sense of humour.

With the return of the Tory government in 1932, Muggeridge's father, who had been elected Socialist MP for Romford, lost his seat. The young Muggeridge was feeling gloomy about the future. He saw Britain as a falling citadel with a greedy past, now at the mercy of any marauder. His interest in the new age in Russia had increased through listening to Arthur Ransome, and he was certain that this little known, revolutionary, albeit much romanticized, continent held the future of mankind. But how to get there? Conveniently, the *Guardian* came to the rescue. Muggeridge's news editor, normally an office enemy, suggested that he should replace the *Guardian*'s Moscow correspondent, William Henry Chamberlain, who was returning to America.

Overjoyed, the Muggeridges set out for Russia in late 1932 with the highest of hopes. Confident of the idyllic quality of post-revolutionary Russia, they planned to make their home there. Symbolically, Muggeridge burned his dinner-jacket and Kitty her formal dresses. They disposed of jewellery and even books that they did not feel would be welcome in the workers' state. They wound up their bank account and checked there were no further traces of their former bourgeois existence. The *Guardian* had arranged that Muggeridge would become a freelance journalist in Russia – a project which might well have deterred him – but in his present mood of heady optimism, he was sure that, once there, he would soon be able to give up his job on the *Guardian* and live a fully integrated Soviet life. Kitty was now pregnant again, and he was determined to bring up their second child as a Soviet citizen.

The Muggeridges' arrival in Moscow was dogged by ill luck. It was difficult to find accommodation, and when they did – a dacha in the country at Kliasma – Kitty became seriously ill. At one point Muggeridge felt sure that she was going to die, and this sombre fear entirely eclipsed his theoretical love affair with Russia. Kitty recovered, but returned to England to have their child, while Muggeridge remained to revive his Russian dream.

But this was not to be. As he researched three articles for the *Guardian* on the subject of the Russian famine, total disenchantment set in. He knew that by publishing the articles, which appeared on 25, 27 and 28 March 1933, he would undoubtedly lose his visa. This in no way deterred him, for he had been sickened by the man-made famine he had seen in some of the most fertile areas of Russia. More than that, he had been totally disillusioned by witnessing a military occupation that was causing acute misery. His Russian utopia was shattered, and when Kitty telephoned with the news that their second child had been safely born and that they had been offered the opportunity of living in a Swiss chalet, Muggeridge was all too pleased to give up his new life. Even the proviso that the chalet had to be run as a guest house for the World Travel Association – a tourist agency which was linked with the Labour Party, and in which his father had an interest – did not put him off. But despite the pleasure of his reunion with Kitty and the new baby – as well as the welcome comforts of the West – Muggeridge felt cheated, pouring out his indignation and nursing his bruised ego in a number of bitterly satirical articles. They spent three months in the chalet at Rossinière, during which, in a mood of considerable anger, Muggeridge wrote about his Russian experiences in a book which was published in 1934 as *Winter in Moscow*.

In the autumn of 1933, Muggeridge left Rossinière for Geneva, where he took a temporary post at the International Labour Office, then a division of the League of Nations. He returned to London, and received predictable castigation from Socialist journals in response to *Winter in Moscow*. His fortunes had now sunk to a dangerously low level: he was without a job, and feeling damaged by his experiences in the Soviet Union. But with the unpredictability that a professional writer's fortunes can bring, *Picture Palaces*, a novel that he had been writing about his experiences on the *Guardian*, was bought by Eyre & Spottiswoode, and Jonathan Cape commissioned him to write a book about Samuel Butler, designed to appear on the centenary of Butler's birth. Now the Muggeridge fortunes seemed to be looking up. In *The Green Stick*, Muggeridge reflects on the Etoile, where Jonathan Cape had lunched him at the beginning of the Butler project: 'an excellent restaurant that I never enter nowadays, if I can possibly avoid it, because, for me, it is haunted by the ghosts of the books I haven't written and the contracts I haven't fulfilled. Between the hors-d'oeuvres and the cheese, I hear them incessantly groaning and rattling their (or maybe my) chains.' *Samuel Butler* was a case in point. Jonathan Cape did not like the finished manuscript, and the book eventually appeared under another imprint.

Unfortunately, *Picture Palaces* also fell into trouble, and was withdrawn when the *Guardian* threatened a libel action because the personality of one of the central characters was too close to that of *Guardian* editor C. P. Scott. With money once again running out, it looked as if Muggeridge's finances were about to flounder in the rocky shoals of freelance life. Then, as had happened before, an interesting proposition came up: he was offered the assistant editorship of the *Calcutta Statesman*. He accepted with alacrity, but Kitty, who had just borne a daughter, Valentine, decided to remain in London with the children while the breadwinner sailed for India.

Muggeridge spent a miserable year in Calcutta, missing his family desperately. Fortunately, his exile was broken by an offer from the *Evening Standard* to become part of the 'Londoner's Diary' team at a fee of twenty pounds per week. He jumped at the chance, and returned to England. On 'Londoner's Diary' he met Bruce Lockhart, who had been the first British secret agent inside Soviet Russia, recounting his adventures in *Memoirs of a British Agent*, published in 1932. Muggeridge was fascinated by Lockhart's experiences, relishing the subterfuge and artful manoeuvres of that early Secret Service world.

Moving to Whatlington, near Battle in East Sussex, the Muggeridges soon found life to be all the richer for their recent separation. Their marriage prospered, and 'Londoner's Diary' was not a hard taskmaster. Now they had four children – three sons and a daughter – and were very contented. Soon, however,

Muggeridge once again became restless and, leaving 'Londoner's Diary', began another risky freelance phase, reviewing novels for the *Daily Telegraph*, ghosting work for Lady Rhondda's *Time and Tide* – and becoming poor again. He seemed to have a propensity for being unable to settle to any job – except writing – for very long. Life at Whatlington was austere: they had to draw the household water from a well and go, bucket in hand, to a spring some distance away to collect drinking water. But despite the hardships, the three years they spent at Whatlington were the happiest either had known. Hugh Kingsmill lived nearby, and their friendship matured. Muggeridge and Kingsmill began writing together for *Night and Day*, a short-lived magazine whose literary editor was Graham Greene. Contributors numbered a fascinating cross-section of the literary figures of the day, including Evelyn Waugh, Osbert Lancaster, Elizabeth Bowen, John Betjeman, Antonia White and Anthony Powell.

On the Monday after war had been declared, Muggeridge tried to enlist, but he was forced to return home later that day because only specialists were currently required. He was also informed, rather pointedly, that journalism was a reserved occupation. Frustrated and angry, he continued with his reviewing. Then, just as he had been told that his weekly review column in the *Daily Telegraph* was no longer required, he was offered a post in the Ministry of Information.

Muggeridge was delighted to be caught up in the war effort; he loved the unpredictability of it all. For the first time since his brief love affair with Soviet Russia, he felt excited and ready to be absorbed in the changing fortunes that warfare brings. His chronic restlessness was temporarily appeased, and he no longer felt that he was an onlooker, as he often did with journalism and even with his more serious writing. For the first time, he intended to use his talents for the common cause. But this would inevitably separate him from Kitty and the children – which presented him with a problem. With exceptional candour, he writes: 'I did this, not under compulsion, not from any genuine sense of duty, but just out of vanity and foolish bravado;

ultimately, I suppose, because I wanted to get away on my own, and behave as I liked. Something that wars make permissible, practicable and even praiseworthy.' Later, however, he was to miss the family so much that he became deeply depressed.

The Ministry of Information had been hurriedly assembled in the new London University building in Bloomsbury. There seemed to be two main classes of personnel: a vast mêlée of dispatch riders, and bustling, brief-case-carrying, uniformed types. Muggeridge found himself attached to a section producing propaganda feature articles designed to gain sympathy for the Allied cause. He was well received and respected for his journalistic experience and imaginative drive. Other writers had also gravitated to this kind of work: George Orwell was at the BBC in an Oxford Street studio, addressing himself to India and South-east Asia, while Graham Greene, also on the staff of the MOI, concentrated on Latin America.

Because of their proximity, a loose friendship sprang up between Greene and Muggeridge. Greene was living near the ministry in a cramped mews flat, where Muggeridge would visit him. If he stayed for a meal, he found the menu was usually limited, with sausages featuring as the main dish. He noted that whatever situation Greene found himself in, he always seemed to be living in lodgings and leading the most frugal life, rather like a displaced person. He came across Greene later in the war, after his Clapham Common house had been destroyed in the blitz. His family had moved into the country, and Muggeridge had the impression that he was glad to be alone.

A few months later, Muggeridge joined the Field Security Police at Ash Vale in Hampshire. Now in uniform and under military discipline, and finding the routine uncomfortable, he yearned for the cosy, desk-bound, tea-drinking days of the MOI. He undertook a course in security Intelligence, based on the British Army's only practical yardstick – the 1914–18 war. He encountered some ludicrous aspects to the training, such as the use of the Dames Blanches organization, which had originally been set up in Brussels. These were a collection of Belgian ladies who would sit knitting at their window, while counting the carriages of troop trains so as to assess the German troop build-up. Another part of the antiquated course involved the creation of an informers' network, which tapped the verbosity of civilians such as taxi-drivers and barbers. Scripts were provided, and there was a strong reek of amateur dramatics. Most members of the course considered the network quite irrelevant. Muggeridge was eventually transferred from Ash Vale to the Isle of Sheppey, where he gained rather more practical experience of security operations, by checking French troops fleeing from the German invasion of France for security risks.

His next post was at GHQ Home Forces in the Knellar Hall, London, where, as the prospects of a German attack diminished, he slipped into the dull tranquillity of being on the roster of duty officers manning the telephone that would give warning of an invasion. Should this occur, they would alert headquarters, who would then mount a massive security operation on key communication points such as Broadcasting House and the London telephone exchange. Essential personnel would be transferred to a specially constructed underground headquarters at Virginia Water, which would become an emergency operations centre. Muggeridge's other duties included helping to ensure that headquarters was safe from infiltration by enemy agents.

Muggeridge did not enjoy his army career. 'I wasn't popular,' he remembers. 'I got turned out of the mess because of the way I spoke.' But he was always resourceful, and his most notable operation during his Knellar Hall period was an investigation into his own commander-in-chief, General Ironside – Buchan's original model for Richard Hannay – who had mysterious, rather dubious connections with certain Fascist organizations, and who was later sacked.

During the blitz, Muggeridge would walk the dark and empty pavements of London, crossing streets that were often torn by explosions and ack-ack fire. Sometimes his companion would be Graham Greene, who also accompanied him to the Windmill Theatre with its drab audience and naughty, tatty girlie shows. Muggeridge felt that Greene liked the seediness, that this was the guise in which he preferred the devil's offerings to be presented. Certainly, this desolation has featured in much of his writing. The initiated knew just where to sit in the Windmill so as to ensure the best view, Greene told Muggeridge.

He noticed that Greene would make a special act of penitence before venturing out into the blitz – which made Muggeridge uneasy. He felt as if he were travelling in a first-class railway carriage with a first-class passenger, while he himself had only a third-class ticket. He imagined Greene being carried away to paradise, while he himself was left behind in purgatory. Ever since he had known Greene, Muggeridge noticed that he seemed to possess a special quality of detachment from the passions he wrote about in his novels. In his opinion, Greene's attitude to his everyday life was rather similar. When he came across Greene unawares, he seemed to see an expression on his face that indicated complete isolation from those around him. Rather glibly, he once said publicly that Greene was a saint trying unsuccessfully to be a sinner, while he, Muggeridge, was a sinner trying unsuccessfully to be a saint. The comment, widely quoted, annoyed Greene. He seemed to think that Muggeridge should not have claimed the status of sinner. Muggeridge told me: 'Greene's view is that it doesn't matter if you betray your country – but it does matter if you betray your friends. In my view he's cracked, forever saying he would rather live in the USSR than anywhere else. This just isn't true.' As to Greene's writing about the Secret Service, Muggeridge has very pronounced views on that too: 'I think *The Human Factor* is a tenth-rate novel whose central character was based on Trevor Wilson [an MI6 case officer]. His best and most accurate spy novel was *Our Man in Havana*.'

One of the first members of MI5 that Muggeridge met was Guy Burgess, who was inhabiting a basement flat in Bentinck Street belonging to Lord Rothschild, who was in MI6. Present on the same occasion were J. D. Bernal, John Strachey and Anthony Blunt. Burgess and Muggeridge met only once, but a lasting impression was made. Today Muggeridge describes Burgess as 'morally afflicted, the personification of evil', and he told me that Burgess 'lived in a sex market in Bentinck Street in a house once inhabited, with ironic appropriateness, by Edward Gibbon'. Burgess, apparently, used to have rubber bones to bite on during air-raids – so alarming did he find them. Muggeridge thought him exceptionally careless. He knew, for instance, that Burgess took plans of D-Day to America with him, and that he and Kim Philby had secret plans in their brief-cases most of the time. To Muggeridge, the physical presence of Burgess was maladorous and sinister, as though he had some all-consuming disease. He likened this 'complaint' to the ravaging consumption whose symptoms he had seen in his father's brothers and cousins, and leprosy as he remembered it in India. But he did not feel any kind of aura of conspiracy around Burgess; he simply exuded an odour of decay and dissolution, symbolizing the end of a class and of a way of life.

Muggeridge's first assignment, in October 1940, was to attend a unique trial that was held in camera at the Old Bailey – a trial that was to make a lasting impression on him because of its bizarre defendants and international repercussions. His role was as an observer: his new boss at GHQ Home Forces, Colonel Ross Atkinson, was very interested in the affairs of MI5.

An American diplomat, Tyler Kent, was appearing on security charges along with a Russian expatriate, Anna Wolkoff, whose father, Admiral Wolkoff, had been the last naval attaché at the Imperial Russian embassy. After the Revolution, father and daughter had come to England, where they ran a Russian tea-room opposite the Natural History Museum in London. Anna was a fanatical Fascist, while Kent was harbouring an anti-Soviet obsession after a spell of duty in the Soviet Union. He was also fiercely anti-Roosevelt. His alleged offence was to have removed secret documents from the American embassy, whose ambassador was then Joseph Kennedy, and to have shared them with Anna. She had then, apparently, passed some of them on to William Joyce (Lord Haw-Haw), who was delighted to receive them as fodder for his anti-Allies propaganda broadcasts from Berlin. Muggeridge saw Kent as a gentlemanly American who wore a well cut, tailor-made suit and drank 'wine instead of high-balls and easily became furiously indignant'. He also struck Muggeridge as being just a little mad.

Muggeridge told me that Maxwell Knight, head of counter-subversion at MI5 at the time, gave evidence against Kent in court, but did not strike him as a particularly convincing witness, and was certainly regarded by MI6 as 'an old has-been'. Another bizarre character in the case was Captain Archibald Maule Ramsay, who was to be interned by Knight on the Isle of Man because he, too, had seen the incriminating papers, which also contained an exchange of information between Churchill and Roosevelt. If this had been revealed, Roosevelt's chances of re-election would have been ruined, and America's entry into the war might have been prevented.

Ramsay was an unworldly Christian patriot who was convinced that the earth was threatened by a three-pronged conspiracy of Jews, Bolsheviks and Freemasons. In 1939, he had founded the Right Club, whose main aim was to infiltrate the City of London and Whitehall and to capitalize on the growing national antipathy to Jews and Communists. Muggeridge saw Captain Ramsay when he was questioned in court, together with a large group of fellow internees, about their association with Kent and Wolkoff. Of the internees, whom he found a pathetic bunch, Muggeridge said: 'they were of upper-class aspiration and the women were appallingly made-up.' Both Kent and Wolkoff were found guilty, with Kent receiving a seven-year sentence and Wolkoff ten years. At the end of the war, Kent was deported to America and released; Anna Wolkoff, having served two more years in prison, was released in 1947 and lived in London until her death in 1969.

In 1941 Muggeridge was transferred to 5th Corps HQ at Longford Castle near Salisbury, to take up a position as an Intelligence officer in Department 1(b), Security Intelligence. A few months later Muggeridge was delighted when one of the secretaries from the Secret Service phoned to say that an appointment had been made for him to come up to London and be considered for 'special' Intelligence duties. Muggeridge was interviewed at the Savage Club by Alan Williams, another thriller-writer, whose brother, Douglas, had been a colleague of Muggeridge's on the *Daily Telegraph*. Muggeridge later observed waspishly that writers of thrillers seemed to settle in the Secret Service 'as easily as the mentally unstable become psychiatrists, or the impotent pornographers'. Williams told Muggeridge what was expected of him and alerted him to the dangers involved; for instance, a blown agent, Williams warned, had to be discarded. Muggeridge wondered how.

It was not long before he was informed that he had been accepted as a fit person to work in the Secret Service, and was asked to report to an office in Broadway, just opposite St James's Park underground station in London. He was to join MI6. Here at last was his chance to be a spy – to manipulate the world of intrigue as Lockhart had done. Muggeridge was a wry, astute young man, and the thought of being licensed to break the rules, to be amoral in the line of duty, gave him a tremendous kick. As an avid reader of Maugham's *Ashenden*, he had been expecting a rather more professional atmosphere, however: 'It was all very boy scout – false beards were quite the thing.' At one point he thought he spotted one such beard in the office foyer. It was a luxuriant growth, worn, he later discovered, by a former Marxist trade union leader from the boiler-makers' union. It was he who was later responsible for giving Muggeridge security guidance in industrial matters. His beard was quite genuine.

Muggeridge's first contact in the Secret Service was Leslie Nicholson, who had been an agent in Riga. His manner was gentle, and he had something of a Bertie Wooster personality – altogether a rather unlikely ex-spy. It was Nicholson who told Muggeridge that he and Graham Greene were to be posted to Africa: he to Lourenço Marques in Mozambique, and Greene to Freetown in Sierra Leone.

To become a Secret Service officer, Muggeridge swiftly had to assume a civilian identity, and to this end Nicholson gave him a new passport, stamped so as to give the impression that he had

91

recently arrived in the UK and was staying at the St Ermin Hotel. Dropping in for a drink to familiarize himself with his new home surroundings, Muggeridge found the lounge dim and quiet, redolent of the aftermath of discreet conferences. Nicholson told him to take his passport to Caxton Hall and to apply for a civilian identity card, explaining, if necessary, that he had recently disembarked at Liverpool after travelling abroad, and that he was anticipating an early departure from the UK for the purpose of more travelling. Deceiving bureaucracy for the first time, Muggeridge began to grow tense. What would happen if anyone asked him the name of the ship on which he had arrived at Liverpool, quizzed him in any detail about his travels? The questions filtered through his mind unhappily as he imagined his stumbling, unconvincing replies. But when he had made his way in trepidation along the dusty corridors of Caxton Hall to his official reception committee, anti-climax was to replace anxiety. No one asked him anything at all. He had cleared his first hurdle as a spy.

Sir Stewart Menzies was Director of the SIS during this period and, as was the tradition, was known as 'C' throughout the organization. His preferred form of secrecy was exceedingly complex and highly melodramatic, Muggeridge recalled:

A green light had to show outside his door before anyone was allowed in. Also, during conversation, he would place his overcoat over the telephone. Apparently, and presumably with some difficulty, he even answered it that way – for security reasons . . . MI6 officers at this time never put the war into perspective, and compartmentalized everything. As a result there was never any particularly high level of personal intelligence in the security services. For instance, a course on writing in secret ink was organized, and one particular formula – ludicrously – used milk.

Muggeridge once found a paper with invisible writing on an international boat train. Unfortunately, after he had duly processed the material, its message turned out to be useless. 'We were all fouled up by the boy scout element. We were carrying out exercises in mystery.'

SIS policy seemed to Muggeridge to be based on the premise that 'nothing should ever be done simply if there are devious ways of doing it.' He soon discovered that it was second nature to older SIS personnel to communicate in code, and to use an accommodation address for perfectly innocent and unimportant communications. Kim Philby, for example, sent his wife loving messages on tiny fragments of tissue paper. He explained that these could comfortably be swallowed, when required for security reasons. 'Secrecy,' wrote Muggeridge in *The Infernal Grove*, 'is as essential to Intelligence as vestments and incense to a mass, or darkness to a spiritual seance, and must at all costs be maintained, quite irrespective of whether or not it serves any purpose.'

At St Albans, the headquarters of Section 5, which was responsible for counter-espionage abroad, Muggeridge renewed his acquaintance with Kim Philby, at that time head of the Iberian sub-section. They had met briefly when Muggeridge was on 'Londoner's Diary' at the *Evening Standard*. Philby, just down from Cambridge, had been working for W. T. Stead on the *Review of Reviews*. The two men had been introduced by the editor, Wilfred Hinde, who had added in passing that Philby's father was the distinguished Arabist, Sir John Philby. In Muggeridge's opinion, Philby was wholly influenced by his father; he had an appalling stammer and an equally appalling drink problem, and by evening was usually drunk. Muggeridge remembers Ben-Gurion, the Israeli leader, once remarking to him: 'If Kim's father became a Mohammedan, why shouldn't Kim become a Communist?' Yet Philby was held in great respect by MI6. 'He dazzled them,' Muggeridge feels. And it was due to the impenetrable awe in which Philby was held that he found it easy to be a traitor. Muggeridge also knew that Philby was much liked because he had fought for Franco in the Spanish Civil War. This admiration was taken to the point of adulation by Dick Bruman White MP, who was then number two at the Foreign Office. Bruman White was to die suddenly and mysteriously at the time of Philby's abrupt departure to Russia.

Without doubt, Philby was a dominating presence at St Albans, entirely overshadowing Felix Cowgill, who was head of Section 5. A man of great drive and determination, Philby was not inhibited by his stutter: in fact, it seemed almost an asset. Muggeridge detected in him a naïve boyishness, and wrote in *The Infernal Grove*:

> As I think of him now, in Moscow, in what must be rather melancholy circumstances, no doubt returning to the vodka bottle for solace, studying cricket scores in old copies of *The Times*, managing to get supplies of Player's Cigarillos sent over from London, and listening clandestinely, whenever possible, to the Overseas Service of the BBC, I see him rather as a boy scout who lost his way than the cool, calculating player of a long drawn-out traitor's role, which, I am sure, is how he would like to see himself.

Philby's office garb was an old army officer's tunic that had belonged to his father in the First World War, which contributed to Muggeridge's conviction that he would rather have been a soldier than a member of the Secret Service – but presumably his stutter had prevented it. At this time, Sir John Philby was interned on the Isle of Man under Regulation 12B. He had told King Saud of Saudi Arabia, a personal friend, that he had better keep out of the war, as Hitler was bound to win. Naturally enough, this had not gone down too well with the British authorities.

Years later, Muggeridge still wonders about the true reasons for Philby's defection. He hardly ever discussed politics, although Muggeridge assumes that he took the leftish position that was fashionable amongst the bourgeois intelligentsia of his generation. He was more certain that Philby had a strong veneration for buccaneering. The company he kept, Muggeridge thought, very much substantiated this argument, for he found violence and recklessness in all their forms quite irresistible. This, he believes, is why he was drawn to Guy Burgess.

Strangely, at the time of Burgess's defection, a photograph was published showing Philby at the annual dinner of the Anglo-German Fellowship, a society that sought to promote cultural relations with Germany. Most people assumed that he was building up cover, but Muggeridge suggests that he attended as a genuine member and is sure that he joined the Soviets when it became clear that the USSR was to be on the winning side. Muggeridge claims that Burgess admitted it was the debility and malaise of his own country that made him defect, and Burgess's great friend, Goronwy Rees, asserts that he was enraged by the winding up of the British Raj. Muggeridge considers that there is still an abnormal amount of mystery surrounding the Burgess/Maclean/Philby/Blunt affair, and to illustrate this he relates an extraordinary anecdote concerning Maclean. Apparently, Maclean and journalist Philip Toynbee attended a party held by King Saud in Cairo, during which, at some point during the evening, the inebriated Maclean urinated on the carpet. Then, towards midnight, he fell over and broke his ankle. (A few days later Muggeridge was lunching with Anthony Powell in the Travellers' Club in London, when Maclean arrived with his leg in plaster.) Having committed such a dramatic social and diplomatic blunder, he should have been severely reprimanded. Instead, he was made head of the American desk in the Foreign Office. Later still, he took high office in the US embassy, briefing journalists. Who was his protector? wonders Muggeridge.

Muggeridge spent the first few weeks in his new job familiarizing himself with how agents were directed in the field, creating deception material or liaising with other counter-intelligence agencies that were attached to governments in exile such as the French, Polish and Czech. He soon discovered that cracking enemy ciphers was central to MI6's day-to-day work, and formed the basis of most of its more effective activities. After having been taught code-cracking by an elderly lady who had

95

gained her experience of ciphering at embassies throughout the world, Muggeridge was to be given lessons in the use of invisible ink.

When he presented himself for the first lesson, at an innocent-looking house in Hans Crescent in London, a Signals NCO opened the door. Having checked his identity, the man took him upstairs to a room in which sat a jaundiced-looking man with thinning black hair – an old SIS professional who, having come down in the world, was reduced to teaching. Muggeridge's lesson went on into the early evening, as the sad old veteran showed him how to mix his inks, once again using milk, and even wine, plus a variety of different chemical substances including a well known brand of headache tablet. The last of the secret substance was referred to by the instructor as 'BS'. It was regarded, he said, as a last resort, only to be fallen back on in an emergency, particularly as acquiring supplies could prove problematical. The instructor told him that he himself had had to resort to this ingredient on an assignment in The Hague, and had scattered crumbs on his balcony in the hope that the birds would reciprocate by supplying what he needed. But this was not to be. The birds arrived, ate the crumbs and flew away. Eventually, he had taken a doleful walk in the park, from time to time dropping his handkerchief as if by chance, and scooping up the BS as nonchalantly as possible. Muggeridge attempted to enthuse him by expressing admiration for his technique, adding that he was sure it would prove useful when he was posted to Mozambique. But his mentor merely nodded sadly, pointing out that tropical birds might not prove adequate donors.

In the event, Muggeridge proved ham-fisted at invisible-ink writing, and his instructor told him testily that he would never make a spy unless he mastered the craft. As they sat there forlornly in the black-out, Muggeridge was struck by the total absurdity of his situation. How could two grown men spend their time like this?

In 1942, Muggeridge set out in a flying boat from Poole harbour in Dorset to Lisbon, on the first leg of his journey to

Mozambique, with a passport describing him as a 'government official'. Lisbon, with its blazing lights, was a magnificent spectacle after two years of black-out. For the first few days he wandered about the streets, glorying in the shops and restaurants after the drabness of London. Lisbon was rich and busy: a sophisticated city untouched by the war.

Reporting at the British embassy, he was directed to the section that dealt with the affairs of the SIS. Here he discovered a rather different atmosphere from that of the other departments he had known, and eventually came to realize that this one was typical of SIS sections in embassies. The office was extremely relaxed, with all its personnel in shirt-sleeves. The older, pre-war brand of Secret Service personnel were more formal, given to wearing spats and monocles; but the new brigade, recruited during the war, were determined to present as unconventional an image as possible, wearing sweaters and grey flannel trousers, and drinking in bars and night-clubs rather than at the traditional diplomatic cocktail parties. They openly boasted of their underworld life. Philby was of this new order, explained Muggeridge, and was viewed as a model to be copied and admired.

When, on 9 May, Muggeridge's visa arrived for Lourenço Marques, he sailed from Lisbon, taking with him a number of diplomatic bags which were to be handed over to the British representatives at the various ports of call. He was under strict instruction not to let them out of his sight.

His first impression of Lourenço Marques was of a run-down Mediterranean resort, with the usual jaded assortment of beaches, postcards, souvenirs and restaurants. At night there were cabarets and casinos. The only different between Lourenço Marques and the Mediterranean was that the sun was fiercer and the air far more humid. He stayed at the new Polona Hotel, finding himself immediately immersed in the kind of tense, understated atmosphere that Graham Greene was to write about so evocatively. Both of Muggeridge's opposite numbers were also temporary residents of the Polona – Leopold Wertz, the German consul-general (and secret agent) and Campini, the

Italian consul-general (and secret agent). Wertz was pink, bespectacled and earnest, while Campini wore a cloak and was given to dramatic gestures and rhetorical speeches. None of the three spoke to either of the others, but bowed politely when they passed in the corridors. Yet Muggeridge felt he shared a kind of unspoken intimacy with them.

Keeping the tools of his trade – a typewriter and a safe in which he kept invisible inks and cash – in his office at the consulate-general, Muggeridge began his work immediately. His brief was to obtain information about the torpedoing of Allied convoys by German submarines as they sailed up the Mozambique Channel to North Africa. The torpedoing was being carried out on a massive scale, and Muggeridge found his task very daunting as he had no local contacts and did not speak much Portuguese.

The British consul was a pleasant enough man named Ledger, who was nevertheless sceptical about Muggeridge's usefulness – just as the British ambassador in Russia had been about Maugham's. Other members of his staff regarded the new recruit with similar reservations. Meanwhile, Muggeridge was busy decoding cables from Philby (now his boss) – an extremely tedious process. First of all he had to subtract from the groups of numbers in the telegram corresponding groups from what was called a 'one-time pad'. Then he had to check what the resultant groups signified in the code-book itself. Mistakes in subtraction or in the groups subtracted would ruin the whole project, and would necessitate starting again. The first of Philby's cables provided a brief résumé of the state of espionage in Lourenço Marques. The information was taken from the intercepted telegrams of Wertz and Campini, and then passed on by MI6 to General Montgomery, Commander-in-Chief of the Allied troops in North Africa. The first cable from Philby suggested that it would be better to infiltrate the Campini camp rather than Wertz's, as Campini seemed at the time very much more vulnerable.

Muggeridge gave considerable thought to his first attempt at infiltration, eventually deciding to focus upon Signora Campini

98

as a possible chink in the already wafer-thin Italian armour. She was short, not very beautiful, but vivacious. Gradually, he began to think of her in an almost amorous light, wondering if he should be seducing her, getting her to blurt out, in his narrow hotel bed, what she knew of her husband's secrets. After dinner he would surreptitiously follow the Italian party when they went for a night-time stroll. But he always followed so cautiously, at such a distance, that he failed to catch the merest hint of what they were saying. Muggeridge knew that he had not done very well at his first exercise in surveillance, and was equally unsuccessful at obtaining information from contacts. In his first few days, the only intelligence that he was able to discover about Wertz was that he wore a hair-net in the privacy of his bathroom. It was an interesting revelation, but not exactly the sort of material that Philby would welcome having ciphered back to him.

With a view to improving his local contacts and working from a more satisfactory grass-roots level, Muggeridge recruited a local agent. He was a Polish Jew named Camille who had successfully made his escape from the Gestapo in Germany, finishing up at the unlikely location of Lourenço Marques and promptly joining the prosperous bridge-playing circles there. These were a source of useful information to Muggeridge, because they included certain high-ranking policemen as well as local Portuguese officials. Camille had assumed the highly fictitious role of a dashing cavalry officer who, having been forced to keep alien company earlier in the war, now took a stance of tolerant condescension and expected Muggeridge to realize his 'true' social status. Muggeridge played the game according to Camille's rules, growing very fond of him as he did so. Camille soon rewarded him by introducing him to his first local contact – a police inspector. Muggeridge asked his tame inspector to report on anything he came upon in the course of his duties that might be of interest to the British consulate-general. He was prepared to pay 'expenses', but his initial proposal of one hundred escudos was met with scorn. Camille discreetly made it clear that Wertz paid three times as much, and

Campini was liable to pay even more. Eventually, the inspector was pleased to accept five hundred escudos. He turned out to be a valuable contact, particularly when safe-conduct arrangements had to be made for a number of South African troops interned in Mozambique to be taken into the then British territory of Swaziland.

The troop ship, en route for North Africa, had been torpedoed off the Mozambique coast, and Muggeridge accompanied the consul-general and his staff to meet the survivors as they came ashore. The night was moonless and the sea turbulent; little could be seen, apart from the flickering lights of the rescuers and the pounding white surf. The survivors were in a bad state and made a haunting spectacle. As belligerents landing in a neutral country, they were immediately impounded by the Mozambique authorities in the Assistencia Publica, a particularly squalid prison. But eventually with the help of Inspector Y (as he was now designated), Muggeridge hired a fleet of taxis, engineered the release of the prisoners and hurried them over the border.

Not all Muggeridge's cases had such buccaneering overtones; others were grubby and devious, and he was soon to discover that Intelligence work involved considerable betrayal and deceit. Another case involving his 'bought' police inspector concerned a local resident who was discovered to be a vital provider of shipping intelligence for Campini. MI6 decided that the man should be removed forthwith and taken across the border to Swaziland for interrogation. The problem was how to achieve his speedy dispatch, and it fell to Muggeridge to find a solution. So, approaching the man's white South African girlfriend, Muggeridge arranged for her to induce her boyfriend to take her for a drive. Her reward was to be her own return to South Africa. Everything went according to plan: the inspector stopped the car at a certain point, and briskly transferred the offending and by now protesting spy from his car to another. He was then taken rapidly across the border to Mbabane, where a search of his pockets revealed notes of Allied shipping movements. His abrupt disappearance from Lourenço Marques was claimed by the authorities there to have been caused by 'financial problems'. But this was not the end of the case for Muggeridge, who was determined to keep his bargain with the girl. He approached the South African consul-general, and after much tortuous negotiation succeeded in getting official permission for her to return to Johannesburg. Although the ending was a happy one, Muggeridge realized that it had been on the cards for the consul-general to have refused to cooperate, rendering the girl a victim of typically callous SIS manipulation. More by luck than judgement, Muggeridge had succeeded in doing the honourable thing.

He soon settled into an Intelligence routine. He began his day by opening the mail and deciphering Philby's cables at the consulate-general. He then returned to the Polona for lunch, to keep an eye on Wertz and Campini. In the afternoon he would stroll by the sea-shore and then return to his office. Various social functions took place in the evening. Away in the distance, far from Mozambique, the Second World War continued to rage. Hitler had marched against Russia, and in Asia the Japanese were increasingly in the ascendent. But in Lourenço Marques the three Intelligence combatants – Wertz in his shorts, Campini in his cloak and Muggeridge in his tropical kit – played a watching, waiting game in the tropical heat. It was farcical yet tedious. Occasionally the monotony was broken by a visit to Cape Town to liaise with a representative of MI6 – who were not allowed to operate personally in a British dominion, though they could be represented there – or by some interesting information gleaned from Camille. By this time he had taken on a local agent – Serge, an Eastern European Jew. Through Serge, Muggeridge embarked on his most successful case.

A Greek sailor had confided to Serge that the captain of his ship was working for the Axis, and that he had a rendezvous with a German U-boat operating in the Mozambique Channel, when vital stores and equipment would be handed over. (This clandestine meeting was later revealed by the code-breaking centre at Bletchley, where Wertz's cables had been decoded; one of these referred to a Greek boat that Wertz was to keep a special look-out for.) Serge told Muggeridge that there was only one place where he could be sure of running into the Greek sailor: Marie's Place, the local brothel.

The traditional red light was glowing over the door when Serge and Muggeridge arrived. Inside, Muggeridge was somewhat surprised to meet the eminently bribable inspector, who explained his presence by remarking blandly that inspecting brothels was one of his 'less pleasant' duties. Later, one of the prostitutes introduced Muggeridge to his Greek informant, and together they made plans to take over the ship and imprison the captain. The detention of the captain was to be the duty of the crew – who were all more than willing to cooperate; Muggeridge was to arrange for the ship to sail into Durban. The sailor promised to bring his first officer to see him at the consulate-general the next morning, as they were due to sail in forty-eight hours. The first officer duly arrived, whereupon they worked out the final details of the plot. He also gave Muggeridge the exact bearing of the ship's rendezvous with the U-boat.

Everything went smoothly and according to plan. The ship arrived at Durban with the furious captain locked securely in his cabin, together with his associates. The rendezvous was kept, the submarine was captured, and Muggeridge realized that he had pulled off a considerable coup. Despite his success, however, he was reprimanded by MI6, with typical Secret Service petty bureaucracy, for having gone straight to Naval Intelligence rather than to them. Nevertheless, Muggeridge received a congratulatory telegram from C – a considerable accolade in Secret Service circles.

But despite the excitement of his coup, and the fact that he could regularly correspond in code with Graham Greene who was still in Freetown, loneliness was becoming an increasing factor in Muggeridge's life and was beginning to influence his choice of friends. Anna, the Portuguese wife of a local German businessman whose marriage was breaking up, was a typical example. She and her husband came to stay at the hotel, occupying separate rooms. She sat at Wertz's table, but in private conversation with Muggeridge made it clear that she was anti-German and, in particular, anti-Wertz. Muggeridge saw her at once as a useful contact, and requested London's permission to continue seeing her. They acceded, but it was not long before Muggeridge began to view his relationship with Anna as almost schizophrenic. Double agents, he reflected, were quite liable to be driven mad by their multiplicity. He saw them fitting into one another, like Russian dolls, getting smaller and smaller, until, right at the centre, there was nothing.

Muggeridge's outpost at Lourenço Marques was suddenly invaded by a Miss Steward, who took over the ciphering and re-ciphering. She was a most welcome addition: by being given a secretary, Muggeridge felt, he had at last won his MI6 colours. About this time, another secret agent, called Steptoe, was seconded to him. Short, and with a bristling moustache, a high voice, a monocle and a vast range of suits, ties, hats and shoes, Steptoe claimed to have been interned since Japan had come into the war – which made his elaborate wardrobe all the stranger. Muggeridge considered that Steptoe was either a real professional, or highly paranoid, or both, for he was under the impression that all occupants of cafés, railway carriages and hotels, and even passers-by, were perpetually keeping him under surveillance. He conscientiously burned every communication he received, and told Muggeridge that before the Japanese took him into custody he had swallowed his code-book page by page, and that he was about to eat his 'one-time pad' when he was arrested. Muggeridge introduced Steptoe to Anna and her South African friend Johann. The four of them would meet clandestinely in Steptoe's room, and he would turn his radio up to full blast in case of hidden microphones.

The Office of Strategic Services was the American counterpart to MI6; it was later to become the CIA, and during the Second World War sent its raw new agents to learn the ways of the British Secret Service. The majority of the early arrivals were Yale or Harvard dons who, having read Somerset Maugham's *Ashenden*, imagined that they would be able to pen similar literary masterpieces when the war was over. But Huntington Harris, the OSS agent who arrived at Lourenço Marques, was very far from being a Yale or Harvard don, as well as being wholly unmilitary. The offspring of rich parents, he was extremely well funded, so that Muggeridge was soon able to make use of the extra cash to increase the fees of Camille, Serge and Inspector Y. Muggeridge had decided to leave the Polona Hotel, and, finding Harris a pleasant enough companion, soon moved with him into an apartment on the outskirts of the city, which had a door in the garage permitting visitors to come and go undetected.

Soon after the arrival of Harris, Muggeridge was summoned to Cairo, where, in Shepheard's Hotel, he met Peter Fleming, brother of Ian and an MI6 operative. The discussion centred on the possibility of using MI6 contacts in Lourenço Marques to disseminate deception material. Later, Fleming's boss, Colonel Dudley Clark, arrived, and told Muggeridge that he wanted rumours circulated in Lourenço Marques to the effect that the Allies had plans to land in Africa. This, it was hoped, would fool the Germans and distract them from the Allies' actual intention: the landings in Normandy. When, next morning, to his great satisfaction, Muggeridge saw in the Egyptian *Gazette* the headline AFRICAN CORPS IN FULL RETREAT, he guessed that his job in Lourenço Marques must almost be over, because troop ships would now be able to use the Mediterranean again instead of diverting round the Cape and up the Mozambique Channel.

Despite the prospect of his imminent return home, Muggeridge arrived back in Lourenço Marques feeling depressed and anti-climactic. Then, quite suddenly, he became involved with Hélène, a dancer at the Café Penguin. He had been introduced to her by Serge, who thought she might prove to be a good contact, for she associated with a number of dubious underworld characters and useful officials, and she could speak Spanish, Portuguese and French. Muggeridge saw Hélène, in spite of her brassy exterior, as a brave gamine. For her part, Hélène was delighted to be of use, particularly when financial reward was in the offing, but was surprised when Muggeridge made a drunken pass at her. When she explained that she respected him too much to have an affair with him, he experienced a wave of self-loathing. But he still felt unable to let her go, contriving romantically to view her as two people – the serious person in the hard, professional shell of the 'good-time' girl. But the doomed obsession was not without portent. While he and Hélène were out on a jaunt, his car careered out of control across the road. Fortunately, both they and the vehicle were undamaged. Muggeridge put the incident down to bad maintenance, but later he discovered an essential part of the steering had been removed when the car was being serviced at a garage run by an Italian, and he was forced to the depressing conclusion that Campini had sabotaged his car. Suddenly, the Ruritanian farce seemed at an end.

A prey to increasing depression, Muggeridge now lay miserably on his bed thinking of Kitty and of how he had mentally betrayed her. Suddenly suicide seemed the only way out. Rejecting pills or bullets as too barbaric, he drove to the furthest point possible along the coast road from Lourenço Marques, left the car, undressed and walked into the sea. Slowly he swam out of his depth – and then changed his mind. As he began to swim back towards the lights along the coast he experienced an overwhelming joy, and his depression lifted for the first time in weeks. Returning to his car as dawn broke, he rejoiced exultantly at still being alive. That morning he reported back to London that he had made a pretence of drowning himself so that Wertz and Campini would think he had cracked. Wertz soon picked up the rumours on the grapevine, and, sure enough, Bletchley deciphered a message from Wertz to Germany concerning Muggeridge's suicide attempt. Wertz explained the attempt as a demonstration that Muggeridge had finally realized that he was inferior to him as an agent. Graham Greene, who was back in London now and monitoring Muggeridge's telegrams as well as the Wertz intercepts, minuted that he was sceptical that the suicide attempt had been staged; he considered it to be genuine – perhaps his writer's perception told him so. He, like Muggeridge, suffered from depression in his posting, and largely for the same reasons: they had left England not primarily to fight for a cause but, at least partly, to escape their own responsibilities.

En route back to London, Muggeridge was rushed into hospital in Kampala for an emergency appendix operation, and it was some months before he returned to Section 5, which was now ensconced in Ryder Street off Piccadilly, with Philby dominating the office. Muggeridge soon discovered that his work in Lourenço Marques was well regarded and had earned him prestige. Nevertheless, he was uneasy, feeling an outsider when with Philby and his friends. Muggeridge noticed that although political arguments occurred in the office, Philby rarely joined in. There was, however, one exception, which occurred when a colleague was complaining that important Bletchley Intelligence concerning the order of battle operations on the Eastern Front was being withheld from the Russians, in case the source was compromised. Muggeridge agreed with the suppression, largely because the Russians had given the Germans information about British intentions during the Nazi–Soviet pact. He argued that, on the other hand, Stalin was bound to disbelieve anything that came officially from the Allies, assuming it to be provocation. Even details that Stafford Cripps, Britain's ambassador in Moscow, had given to Stalin about the time and place of a German attack on the USSR had been discounted. The present discussion appeared to goad Philby into surprising fury. He stuttered with rage, declaring that Britain was duty-bound to do everything in her power to support the Red Army, even if there was a risk of exposing Bletchley material. When Philby's double cross became public knowledge, Muggeridge considered that it might well have been over this issue that Philby for the first time gave secret documents to the Russians.

Muggeridge visited Philby at his home in Chelsea – a home which struck Muggeridge as too well appointed for wartime conditions. At the time he assumed that Philby's wife, Eleanor, had private means, but this later proved not to be the case. All SIS salaries were secret and tax-free, so even the all-knowing Inland Revenue had no idea of the Philbys' means. The grapevine, however, gave everyone in Muggeridge's department an accurate picture of what everyone else was earning. With hindsight, Muggeridge realized that Philby's income must have been supplemented by the Soviets. He was naturally hospitable, generous and over-extravagant. No doubt the Russians had been quick to take advantage of his constant desire for funds. Philby seemed happy enough at this time, but Muggeridge detected that Eleanor was under stress. Later he heard that she had had a breakdown. Muggeridge found her as uneasy as he himself was in the company her husband kept, but Philby told him that he and Eleanor would shortly be moving to the country, in common with other MI6 families, as Bletchley had prior information of a new and lethal addition to the German armoury – the V weapons.

Some months later, Muggeridge was asked to go to Algiers to take over liaison duties with the Sécurité Militaire. For this purpose he donned the uniform of a major. He discovered that Algiers had all the atmosphere of a boom town. The people in the streets seemed energetic and assertive, and he often spent the sultry summer nights drifting amongst the crowds. The SIS occupied a large house, high above the city, and from here they sent operations into Italy, Yugoslavia, Greece and other neighbouring territories. Muggeridge's Section 5 office was in the rue Charras, and it was here that he grew to know the extraordinary personality of the British agent, Trevor Wilson. Wilson had been a bank manager in France and spoke the language fluently, but in a sort of muttering whisper, and he thrived on noise and confusion. Despite these eccentricities, Muggeridge found him to be one of the ablest Intelligence officers he had met; he seemed to have an instinctive flair for the devious.

At that time, the SIS in Algeria was making good use of several turned-round enemy agents. One, a French colonel stationed near Algiers, functioned successfully right up until the end of the war, and another, an upper-class English beachcomber in Tangier, was so trusted by the Germans that they regarded his reports as credible even after he had persuaded them that the Allies' North African Expedition was heading in the direction of Dakar. Muggeridge's French colleagues were particularly keen on such agents, as they could be made to work for profit. For example, they would ask the French colonel to apply to the *Abwehr* for money, to be parachuted down in bags of specie rather than notes, which were dangerously detectable. The *Abwehr* would immediately oblige. A little later on, when the French ran short of motor tyres, they asked the colonel politely to point out to the *Abwehr* that if he were to buy tyres locally at such rocketing prices he would immediately draw attention to himself. Once again the *Abwehr* rushed to oblige, and parachuted a set down to him. They were later discovered to be manufactured by Dunlop. Muggeridge suggested that the malleable colonel should tell the *Abwehr* that he was sexually frustrated, that he could no longer concentrate on his work, and that he did not wish to use the local brothels in case he gave himself away. Muggeridge had a fantasy of parachuting Rhine maidens, but his French colleagues felt that the *Abwehr*'s only response would be a supply of bromide.

Before returning to England, Muggeridge was posted to Brindisi in Italy and then, on 12 August 1944, to France. Liberation was in progress, and he soon became infected with the exultant atmosphere. Much of his work here was concerned with trying to define the situation of alleged British agents who had been arrested by the French police on charges of collaboration. It was a complicated situation because the Allies had depended on the luckless agents cultivating good relations with the German regime, but now, with Liberation, they were in serious trouble and could well be executed. Trying to help them, Muggeridge now considers, was about the only worthwhile thing he did in the war. Muggeridge later wrote a play called *Liberation*, based on one of his cases, in which a French girl agent, who has fallen in love with a German soldier billeted on her family, is informed on. Her soldier disappears; liberation has merely turned her into yet another war victim. In real life, Muggeridge was able to protect her, but in his play the German lover remained behind in Paris, to be shot with the help of her brother, while the girl was left alone with her grief.

While he was in France, Muggeridge was also asked to keep the British writer, P. G. Wodehouse, under surveillance. Foolishly, Wodehouse had made broadcasts from Berlin that had caused a storm of controversy, and Muggeridge was curious to see how a much loved and celebrated writer could have been reduced to the status of national villain. Criticism of Wodehouse for his broadcasts had been very heavy indeed, ranging from an angry attack by Cassandra in the *Mirror* and expulsion from the Beefsteak Club, to removal from the roll of honour at his old school, Dulwich College. Muggeridge's first impression of him at the Bristol Hotel, Paris, where he and his wife, Ethel, were staying, was of a pleasant prep school master – large and bald, wearing grey flannel trousers, golfing shoes and a sports jacket, and smoking a pipe. Despite Muggeridge's uniform and the ominous reason for his presence, Wodehouse seemed very much at ease, and they spent many sessions piecing together the curious circumstances that had overtaken him during the war years.

Wodehouse and his wife had been living in a villa at Le Touquet when the Germans arrived in the summer of 1940. They were taken into custody and interned, at Tost in Poland, in a prison camp that had originally been a lunatic asylum – an irony which Wodehouse had relished. During his incarceration, Wodehouse wrote five novels, all well up to his usual standard, and produced an account of life at Tost which he gave Muggeridge to read at this first meeting. Muggeridge considered it unique in prison literature in minimizing the rigours of captivity and emphasizing the harmonious relationship the prisoner had had with his guards, as well as with his fellow captives. Certainly, Wodehouse had not been imbued with the Colditz spirit, for he had no burning desire to escape. Released through the influence of friends a little before his sixtieth birthday, he went immediately to Berlin and broadcast his prison-camp reminiscences on the German network. He seemed to have no idea that he would thereby be seen to be serving Nazi propaganda.

Muggeridge was certainly convinced that Wodehouse had simply made a very foolish error, and that it was unlikely he had actually made a bargain with the Nazis to broadcast propaganda in return for his release from Tost.

Wodehouse and his wife were arrested by the French police after an English guest at a dinner party given by the police chief had protested about the presence of two such notorious English 'traitors' who were living so pleasantly in Paris. Muggeridge managed to rescue Ethel, but Wodehouse's extrication proved more difficult. Eventually the decision was taken to transfer him to a clinic, despite the fact that he was not ill, but as there were no beds available he ended up in a maternity home. Removed fairly speedily from this bizarre setting, he was then, with Ethel, transferred to a quiet hotel in Fontainebleau where they remained until the end of the war, eventually accepting exile in America. When an MI5 barrister, who had been sent from England to advise on the case, told Muggeridge that Wodehouse must remain abroad, Muggeridge realized how heartbreaking this decision must have been for Wodehouse.

Inadvertently, however, Wodehouse had struck a blow against German Intelligence, who thought that his literary fantasies represented British life and that Blandings Castle was a typical ancestral pile. With incredible naïvety, the *Abwehr* used Wodehouse's writings as briefings on British life for their agents, even dropping one luckless victim into the Fens wearing Berti Wooster spats. He was quickly arrested.

At the end of the war Philby sent Muggeridge a directive concerning a new MI6 department that had been created to deal solely with Soviet Intelligence activities, including both sabotage and subversion. Muggeridge was asked two principal questions: Who was the head of the French Communist Party, and where was its headquarters? The simple answer was that the address of the headquarters could be found in the Paris telephone directory, and it seemed likely that the most casual inquiry would produce the name of its head.

When Philby arrived in Paris to survey the creation of the

new department, he and Muggeridge spent a bizarre evening together, dining in the department's headquarters in the avenue Marigny, where Muggeridge was staying. As Philby was very much a gourmet, the dinner was exotic, and although Muggeridge was more abstemious, neither stinted the alcohol. After dinner they took a stroll by the Seine; then, somewhat abruptly, Philby suggested they walk to the rue de Grenelle where the Soviet Embassy was situated (although at that moment Muggeridge was unaware of its location). He clearly remembers, despite the drinks, being amazed when Philby started to talk about penetrating the Soviet embassy. He explained that the embassy presented unique difficulties, as there was little chance of planting spies among the staff; since even the lowliest Soviet officials were imported from the USSR, their loyalty was beyond question. He went on to rage about the equal impossibilities of bugging or of maintaining observation posts, shouting and gesticulating dementedly in front of the embassy itself, and as he continued to unleash his drunken invective, Muggeridge grew increasingly anxious. He was sure that at any moment the two policemen standing in front of the embassy would step forward to investigate this extraordinary barrage of indiscreet rhetoric. But, miraculously, nothing happened, and they both staggered home. When Muggeridge awoke the next morning he half-wondered if he had dreamt the whole business, for he just could not understand Philby's dangerous, histrionic behaviour. In retrospect, he could only hit on one explanation: possibly Philby was literally seeing double in the role he had taken on. To a lesser degree Muggeridge had experienced the same problem in Lourenço Marques: being able to see the point of view of both sides with disturbing ease.

In his autobiography, *My Silent War*, Philby took a somewhat wary view of both Graham Greene and Muggeridge:

[MI6] even survived . . . corrosive imports, such as Graham Greene and Malcolm Muggeridge, both of whom merely added to the gaiety of the service . . . He was despatched to Lourenço Marques, too far away for my liking, where his principal adversary was the Italian consul-general, Campini, an assiduous reporter of British shipping movements. I was glad when our interest in Campini died, and Muggeridge was brought back to deal with various aspects of French affairs. His stubborn opposition to the policy of the day (whatever it was) lent humanity to our lives.

Returning from Paris in 1945, Muggeridge took a civilian job in Fleet Street, without asking MI6 for permission. In retrospect he considered Intelligence work to be 'a silly thing'. Certainly, the form in which he practised it is now outdated. He had seen soldiers playing at being spy-masters, and finding it much more fun than conventional warfare. He singled out Sir Dick White, head of MI5 from 1953 to 1956, as a particularly good example. There was no high level of intellect at work in MI6, he considered – just the boy scout element. As to popular fictional Secret Service heroes, he found James Bond nauseating, once describing him in a review as an 'Etonian version of Mickey Spillane'.

Muggeridge's Secret Service experiences have influenced the whole of his life: he has always clung to the belief that it was impossible to overestimate the stupidity of MI6. In Page, Leitch and Knightley's study, *Philby: The Spy Who Betrayed a Generation*, we read: 'As Muggeridge is known to be a man of caustic views on almost every subject, it might be possible to discount his opinions of the SIS. But they are corroborated, if not in detail at least in general spirit, by numerous other people we have interviewed.'

In Muggeridge's novel, *Affairs of the Heart*, published in 1949, one of the characters says: 'Don't even your nostrils catch the stench of decay, everywhere and in everything?' The other returns: 'Yes . . . as a matter of fact they do.' This was how Muggeridge saw the fading British Empire and its murkier subjects such as Burgess, Maclean and even Philby. He believed this decay had spread to the Secret Services as a whole, and was as irreversible as a terminal cancer.

Muggeridge is remarkable for not having used his Secret

112

Service experiences in his fiction, but only in his autobiography. The reason is clear: the stench of decay was too strong, too permeating for him to be able to distance himself from it. He had been changed by his period in Intelligence, and his restless nature made him search for inspiration in more spiritual fields.

CHAPTER SIX

GRAHAM GREENE:
THE ABRASIVE SPY

In 1923, Admiral Hugh Sinclair succeeded Captain Sir Mansfield Cumming as head of MI6, but as he grew older the department gradually came to be dominated by his deputy, Stewart Menzies, and by Valentine Vivian and Claude Dansey. Graham Greene served under Menzies, the most important of the three. Kim Philby was recruited and promoted to high office under his command, and Menzies remained at his post throughout the Burgess and Maclean defection. He was a reasonably efficient Intelligence officer, but he belonged to the old school and did not move with the times.

> 'I only know that he who forms a lie is lost. The germ of corruption has entered into his soul.'
> Joseph Conrad, quoted by Greene in the epigraph to *The Human Factor*

In the winter of 1939, Graham Greene was asked to go before the draft board for the Emergency Reserve (personnel to be drawn on if the war were to go badly). Although he had passed the medical inspection, the board, consisting of a major-general and two colonels, had no idea where to place him. Greene's statement that he had experience of journalism provoked little interest. Tentatively, and without much enthusiasm, he suggested he might join the infantry. This seemed to cheer the major-general and his two colonels, and he was told to keep fit until June, when he would be conscripted. It was with a sense of relief that Greene took his leave of the draft board.

114

But the infantry was not to have him after all; instead he was asked to join the Ministry of Information's wartime staff. In his department, Greene found that he had access to a file of letters from successful writers such as Hugh Walpole, Michael Arlen and Geoffrey Winn, offering their pens for king and country; reading through these afforded both Greene and Malcolm Muggeridge, who was also working for the MOI at that time, considerable amusement.

Greene's work in the Ministry of Information and later in MI6 only served to intensify an obsession with the theme of betrayal that had begun at school. His father, Charles Henry Greene, was headmaster of Berkhamsted School in Hertfordshire, and although Greene had been happy enough in the junior section, he soon found life in the senior house intolerable. He wrote in his autobiography, *A Sort of Life* published in 1971: 'I had left civilization behind and entered a savage country of strange customs and inexplicable cruelties; a country in which I was a foreigner and a suspect, quite literally a hunted creature, known to have dubious associates. Was my father not the headmaster? I was like the son of a quisling in a country under occupation.'

Greene's elder brother, Raymond, who was not only a prefect but also head of house, without doubt slipped easily into the role of quisling's collaborator. Greene felt surrounded by the forces of the resistance, yet he could only join them if he betrayed his father and brother. His cousin Ben, one of the 'rich Greenes' and a junior prefect, did not have the same inhibitions, and Greene claims he worked clandestinely against Raymond. As a result, Greene was not as sympathetic as he might have been when, during the Second World War, Ben was unjustly imprisoned under Regulation 18B.

Escaping into books to alleviate the miseries of school life, Greene became entranced by John Buchan's hero, Richard Hannay. He would hide out on Berkhamsted Common, imagining that he was one of Buchan's heroes 'making his hidden way across the Scottish moors with every man's hand against him'. His isolation increased as the terms rolled by, and

115

he felt betrayed by his inability to take sides. The theme of betrayal, therefore, had been implanted in Greene from an early age, and it was this that underlay the writing of *The Confidential Agent*, published in 1939. One of the greatest admirers of this novel, in which the hunted are very much to the fore, was Kim Philby. Though a lacerating critic of his own books, Greene has always liked it for its treatment of the dilemma of the foreign agent with moral principles.

Greene's first real experience of espionage was a little out of the ordinary. In 1924, while still an Oxford undergraduate, he read a book of short stories by Geoffrey Moss called *Defeat*, which was about the occupied zones of Germany. Moss described an unofficial attempt by the French authorities to organize a separatist Palatine Republic between the Moselle and the Rhine. Apparently, German criminals had been transferred from Marseilles and other ports, and from French prisons, to support the French authorities, but the British and American authorities had opposed the idea and the move was suppressed. Nevertheless, rumours continued to circulate in Germany that an uprising was to occur.

Partly because Greene enjoyed anticipating dangerous experiences, and partly because he was concerned about the situation, he wrote to the German embassy in Carlton Gardens in London, offering them his services as a propagandist. He put forward his credentials as a communicator and his current editorship of the *Oxford Outlook*. It was probably the editorship that impressed the Germans; in any event, he had not really expected a reply and was therefore amazed to receive an immediate response. Returning one evening to his rooms in Balliol, he discovered a stranger there, consuming his brandy. The fat, blond man identified himself as Count Von Bernstorff, First Secretary to the German embassy. Greene later authenticated this, and also discovered that Von Bernstorff was a luxury-loving homosexual who regularly visited the Abyssinia, a rather shady Soho club. But Von Bernstorff was no mere hedonist: during the Second World War he was to run an escape route from Germany to Switzerland for Jews. He was eventually executed in Moabit prison.

Greene's Oxford rooms were soon regularly frequented by other German nationals as well as Von Bernstorff, many of whom bore a marked resemblance to characters in a musical comedy. Amongst these were an attractive cousin of Von Bernstorff's who left a scented glove behind in his room, a young man with a complicated title, and an ancient, scar-faced mystery man called Captain P, who cut a bizarre figure for a German Intelligence officer. Greene's experiences of MI6 were to lead him to conclusions similar to Muggeridge's: Intelligence was a game and its players were often exotic. A few weeks later Greene was summoned to Carlton Gardens and there handed a packet by Count Von Bernstorff himself. Inside were twenty-five old pound notes – expenses for a 'holiday' in Germany. Predictably, Von Bernstorff told Greene to burn the envelope.

Greene's father, disturbed at the strange company his son was keeping, offered to pay for the holiday himself. Greene refused. He was still in love with the thought of the danger he was possibly about to plunge himself into, and set off for Germany with the writer Claud Cockburn. They were joined by Greene's cousin, Tooter (Edward Greene) – a useful travelling companion, since neither the would-be propagandist nor his friend could speak German. Their journey had a suitable melodramatic beginning: when they were safely ensconced in their railway compartment on the train to Harwich, the door suddenly opened and Captain P slid in beside them, his duel scar looking even more sinister than before. Greene wrote later in *A Sort of Life*: 'Our laughter broke abruptly off and we tried to appear the serious observers we were meant to be. I was very sea-sick on the crossing in spite of Mothersil [a preventive tablet] and saw no more of Captain P – perhaps he was sea-sick too.'

Disappointingly, the party were to experience little of the dangerous world of intrigue and espionage, despite the mysterious arrival of Captain P who was, perhaps, on some other errand. They had a comparatively uneventful holiday. In Cologne they met a political organizer and an industrialist, and

117

in Essen they witnessed the silence of a factory whose workers were on strike. They began to collaborate on the plan of a Buchan-style thriller, but nothing came of it. Edward Greene remembers the trip as a bewildering experience: 'We sat in the board room at Krupps and were lectured at, while Graham took notes. He was a good companion during our holiday, but moody – always up and down. We stayed at some luscious hotels and were very well treated. I couldn't help noticing throughout the trip what a shrewd observer Graham was.'

It was only when the trio arrived in Heidelberg, outside the occupied zone, that their hoped-for-experience of the espionage world showed faint signs of materializing. Visiting the Society for the Relief of Exiles from the Palatine, they discovered that it was none other than a front for kidnapping, run by a man in plus-fours named Doctor Eberlein. Eberlein recruited young men to drive cars as fast as possible across the frontier. Once in the French zone, they seized officials who were alleged to be collaborating with the French authorities, and bundled them back into Germany to be tried at a kangaroo court for high treason. When Greene returned home to England, he wrote to Count Von Bernstorff suggesting that there could be some difficulties in getting funds through to the occupied zone from the secret nationalist organizations. He also pointed out that an Oxford undergraduate would be a very unlikely suspect as a courier. Von Bernstorff replied that they were experiencing no difficulties in this direction at the moment, but that he had been asked by 'friends' in Berlin whether Greene would be interested in returning to the French zone, contacting the separatist leaders and trying to discover their future plans. Greene was delighted by this suggestion, feeling that at nineteen he was finally moving in the direction of espionage – an experience that would combine escape from the common round with the 'dangerous edge of things' that was to preoccupy him so much in later life. He wrote in *A Sort of Life*: 'I suppose . . . that every novelist has something in common with a spy; he watches, he overhears, he seeks motives and analyses character, and in his attempt to serve literature he is unscrupulous.'

Throughout the autumn term of 1924 Greene continued to receive strange foreign visitors and to lead something of a double life. On one level he went to tutorials, and socialized. On another, he finished an unpublished first novel and planned espionage with Bernstorff. Then, rather to his own surprise, he became a double agent. Writing to the *Patriot*, a right-wing journal owned by the Duke of Northumberland which had supported the separatist republic, he politely suggested that he should become their correspondent in Trier. They were delighted by this offer, for he required no fee and was a Balliol student. Providing Greene represented their point of view – and no one else's – the *Patriot* would be delighted to take him on. Greene then wrote to the French embassy in London, informing them that he would be reporting from Trier for the *Patriot* and would be pleased to receive any introductions they could give him.

Unfortunately, his attempt at double-agenting was destined to failure. The Dawes Plan – which set about solving the problem of Germany's war reparations debt – was drawn up, agreements were made between the European countries concerned, and with these improved relationships Greene was no longer required. Marie-Françoise Allain, in her book *The Other Man: Conversations with Graham Greene*, reported him as saying: 'I should have preferred the role of double agent to that of spy, but I was advised that my services would not, after all, be needed. The mysterious Germans, who were such a feature of my student days, vanished as if by magic.' And he commented in *A Sort of Life*: 'Espionage is an odd profession – for some it is a vocation, with an unscrupulous purity, untouched by mercenary or even patriotic considerations – spying for spying's sake.'

Graham Greene was recruited into MI6 by his sister, Elisabeth, who was still a high-ranking personal assistant in the Secret Service. When the summons came it seemed all too easy – which is why Greene has always felt that Philby's account of his own smooth entry into the British Secret Service was perfectly accurate. In Philby's case the only inquiry made into his past was the routine references to MI5, who passed his name through their records and came back with the statement: 'Nothing recorded against'. He was luckier than Greene, who already had a police record as a result of a libel action brought against him by the film star, Shirley Temple, resulting from a review he had written in the new literary magazine *Night and Day*. Greene's papers had been sent to the Director of Public Prosecutions, as well as having been submitted to C (Menzies). Greene believes that there was a moment when Philby wondered if he had actually entered the Secret Service at all. Indeed, his first reports made his Soviet contact conclude that he might have ended up in the wrong organization.

Greene liked *My Silent War*, commenting in his introduction to it: 'We were told to expect a lot of propaganda, but [the book] contains none, unless a dignified statement of his beliefs and motives can be called propaganda.' Nevertheless, Greene viewed Philby's domination – and eventual removal – of Felix Cowgill, head of Section 5, in a highly critical light, seeing it as one of a number of self-indulgent power games. And it was because of this that, in the end, Greene resigned rather than accepted Philby's offer of promotion. But in *My Silent War* Philby admits that his elimination of Cowgill makes for 'sour reading just as it makes sourer writing', and Greene now considers he was wrong in seeing him as an egocentric manipulator. Philby, he now thinks, was simply serving a very different cause and had no personal ambitions in MI6 whatsoever.

Greene looks back with pleasure to the long Sunday lunches they shared at St Albans, when the sub-section would spend hours relaxing and drinking. They would also meet in London over a drink at a pub behind St James's Street, while firewatching. Greene remembers that if any of them made some error of judgement, Philby was sure to minimize it or cover it up, without criticism, with a halting, stammered witticism. 'He had all the small loyalties to his colleagues, and of course his big loyalty was unknown to us.'

Greene, like Muggeridge, was to be sent abroad by Philby as an MI6 case officer. In the winter of 1941 he left for Sierra Leone on a small Elden-Dempster cargo ship, sailing through the North Atlantic in a very slow convoy, on a particularly devious route to West Africa. He was to go to Lagos, via Freetown, for training. (This was not his first trip to French West Africa – he had paid a visit there in 1934.) Greene passed the time writing a short book called *British Dramatists*, taking his turn on watches and reading voraciously through the ship's library. He had brought with him a trunk of books, but as those would have to last throughout his sojourn in Sierra Leone he was loath to dip into them. Later in the voyage, Greene conceived the plot for *The Ministry of Fear*. He had just read and rejected as unrealistic a book by the detective writer, Michael Innes. Lying in his bunk, desperate to return to England, Greene suddenly decided to write an escapist thriller of his own.

On 30 December 1941, the long and boring voyage was suddenly punctuated by the sight of the blazing lights of a Portuguese liner. Such neutral liners were to dominate Greene's life in Freetown, for they were involved in smuggling commercial diamonds, and he was to use them in the plot of *The Heart of the Matter*.

Finally, on 3 January 1942, Greene's convoy arrived at Freetown. He noted in his diary: 'Very hot. About 10 a.m. in the mist and heat the hills behind Freetown. Before noon we had entered the boom. The great bay crowded with shipping. The strange bubble-like mountains, the yellow beaches, the absurd Anglican cathedral built of laterite bricks in the shape of a Norman church.' He was sent immediately to Lagos for three months' training; there he struggled with coding and decoding, while living with a colleague in an ex-police bungalow on a creek that was plagued with mosquitoes. At night they used to hunt cockroaches by torchlight, turning the activity into a game, awarding one point for a death and half a point if the cockroach was flushed down the lavatory.

After his training, Greene returned to Freetown and moved into a house on the flats below the hill station, in the European quarter. It was situated opposite a transport camp which attracted an alarming combination of flies and vultures. The house, which had been build by a Syrian in a land of bungalows, had the advantage of both a staircase and a first floor. At first Greene found it strange that the house had been condemned by the local medical officer, but the reason soon became clear with the coming of the rainy season, when the ground on which it stood rapidly turned into a swamp. Nevertheless, he soon settled into a routine, spending what little free time he had in writing *The Ministry of Fear*.

Breakfast was at six, and at seven Greene would drive his Morris into Freetown, where he would shop and collect coded telegrams from the commissioner at the police station, with which he was connected through his cover employment with CI0 Special Branch. He would then drive home, decode his telegrams, draft replies, write his reports, have lunch and take a siesta. After tea at half-past four, he would walk along an abandoned railway track, once used by European officials, that was situated half-way up the slopes below the hill station. From there he could view Freetown bay, where the *Queen Mary* sometimes rode at anchor and the *Edinburgh Castle* rotted on a reef of empty bottles. At dusk he would return home to take his bath, timing this moment to pre-empt the appearance of a vast colony of rats who enjoyed emerging for an evening airing. Once, to his irritation, he arrived home late, only to find a rat on the edge of the bath. Worse still, there was no avoiding the rats' nocturnal antics, and he would often wake to find members of the rodent colony happily swinging on the bedroom curtains, with only his mosquito net screening him from their gambolling. It was incidents like this, Greene felt, that made *The Ministry of Fear* less humorous than it might have been.

Despite these drawbacks, Greene, now thirty-eight, had lost his heart to Africa, and he was happy. The only problem was that he was desperately short of time in which to write. Nevertheless, he somehow finished *The Ministry of Fear*, typed the manuscript and sent it off to his publisher. Now and again his routine was broken by a trip into the interior, one of his most pleasurable experiences. On his first visit, in 1934, he had taken the narrow-gauge line that ran up to Pendembu, near the Liberian and French Guinea border, which he had described in *Journey without Maps*. He now discovered that nothing had changed in the intervening years. He took his 'boy' chair, bed, oil-lamp and a supply of food. The train stopped for the night at Bo – the passengers were to stay at a government rest-house there. Next morning it steamed slowly uphill to Pendembu. Because he was doubtful about the chef at the guest-house at Pendembu, he ate a tinned evening meal in style beside the railway line, with his camp table neatly erected on the track itself.

Greene lived as well as possible in Freetown, and was soon in trouble over his expenses. One cable from London brusquely pointed out that the correct allowance for an officer away from his station was three guineas a day – a suitable amount with which to pay his hotel bills. The cable went on to ask him to confirm that his expenses would be duly adjusted: Greene's reaction was to open his office safe, transfer forty pounds in notes to his own pocket and then cable back that the adjustment had been made.

His relationship with his immediate superiors in Lagos was disastrous, for they had disliked each other on sight. His boss was a sick man with no knowledge of Africa, and he found Greene a tricky and, indeed, abrasive agent to deal with. A note of pithy sarcasm had entered Greene's reports, and so much did the man fear him, that he would not open the Freetown bag for days in an attempt to delay as long as possible reading Greene's sniping comments. He saw Greene as a rank amateur, and found him a difficult man to discipline; he even went to the extent of trying to cut off his funds. Greene, however, was able to borrow from his friend the police commissioner, so the ploy did not work. When Greene wanted to travel to Kailahun on the Liberian border, the conflict became more open. He was immediately sent a telegram, insisting that he remain in Freetown because a Portugese liner was about to arrive. All Portugese ships coming from Angola had to be searched for either illegal communications or industrial diamonds. Greene, however, seeing this as entirely the police commissioner's job, refused to comply. He even wrote to London, tendering his resignation; but it was refused and Philby freed him from the control of his Lagos superior.

This sudden release gave fresh impetus to Greene's writing, which had been abandoned in face of the conflict. In fact, diamonds were rarely found on the ships, and the mail always seemed innocent. The only episode of any note occurred when the Colonial Secretary ordered the Navy to intercept a liner that was already beyond the boom and therefore on the edge of the statutory three-mile limit. A suspected spy was alleged to be on board, but no arrest was made. Strangely, the address book of one of the passengers under suspicion contained the name of Greene's French friend, translator Denyse Clairovin, who was later discovered by the Germans to be a British agent and eventually died in a concentration camp.

The difficulty of writing a book in Freetown was bad enough, but sending the manuscript home was also a problem. With the danger of submarine attack, Greene realized, he could lose the entire work if he were to send the only handwritten manuscript. So each evening after dinner, he laboriously typed out copies with one finger. Fortunately, he finished the book before the North African landings threatened the coastline.

The Ministry of Fear was bought unseen by an American film company on the strength of its title alone, although Greene was not pleased with the end result, wishing that he had handled the espionage sequences in a less fantastical way. He thought, however, that the character of Mr Prentice of the Special Branch, who was based on someone he had known while working for MI6, was satisfactorily realized.

Indeed, Greene was later to make extensive use of his Freetown observations. He kept a small notebook of incidents that occurred during his work there, that he thought might spark off ideas for future novels. Some of them were to appear in *The Heart of the Matter*, which was set in Freetown. He noted enigmatically: 'The German agents' letters. The list of ships which have called. Tell so-and-so he's too optimistic when he says no ships can call here.' The touch of pacifism: 'What would Livingstone have said?' Then sharp images: 'The small brown kid dead in the middle of the road between the shops, and the vulture hopping round, hopping back towards the gutter when cars came by . . . The suitcase of the suspect – the squalor and intimacy of a man's suitcase.'

Many of the things that happened in his life of duty either irritated or nauseated him, and in particular the case of a young Scandinavian seaman who was suspected of being a German agent. Greene's job was to interrogate him, but he was also briefed to blackmail him in a particularly unpleasant way. The young man had a lover in Buenos Aires, and if he confessed, he would be able to return to her. If he did not, Greene was forced to tell him, he would be interned for the remainder of the war. Greene was furious because he knew this was another police job that had been palmed off onto MI6. He did not consider that he had been employed to operate this kind of sordid blackmail, and he gave up the interrogation prematurely, without gaining any result.

Seeking relief in companionship, he often corresponded with Malcolm Muggeridge in Lourenço Marques by means of coded messages. They had never been close, and indeed were wary of each other in England. Yet here, where both were enduring a certain isolation, the fact of being in the same predicament was a considerable comfort, even a bond. Throughout the three months he spent in Lagos and the year in Freetown working for MI6, Greene did not, for security reasons, keep a journal. Although he still kept up his notebook, he now bitterly regrets having no fuller record of such a strange period in his life, and only half-remembers such episodes as the police commissioner being driven out of his mind by well-meaning MI5 agents, and his own argument with his superior officer two thousand miles away. He did not realize that a novel would emerge from those years, and when he began to write *The Heart of the Matter* five years later, his lack of detailed notes was a source of considerable frustration to him.

In that book, Major Scobie, a police officer in a decaying West African colony, is passed over for promotion and borrows money from Yusef, a Syrian trader, to send his disillusioned wife, Louise, back to London on a holiday. Scobie, a Catholic, is self-sacrificing, and will do anything to make his wife happy. Then he philanders and falls in love with a young girl, and his conscience, together with his genuine love of God, plunges him into crisis and eventual disaster. Greene was able to draw substantially on his Freetown experiences. Yusef tells Scobie:

> 'I want to talk to you as a friend, Major Scobie. There are diamonds and diamonds and Syrians and Syrians. You people hunt the wrong men. You want to stop industrial diamonds going to Portugal and then to Germany, or across the border to the Vichy French. But all the time you are chasing people who are not interested in industrial diamonds, people who just want to get a few gem stones in a safe place for when peace comes again.'

When Greene returned to London in 1944, he found himself out of place in the offices of MI6. Philby's section, which he was rejoining, was responsible for counter-espionage on the Iberian peninsula, and Greene's own particular responsibility was to be Portugal. Philby commented in *My Silent War*: 'Happily, Greene was posted to my section, where I put him in charge of Portugal . . . His tart comments on incoming correspondence were a daily refreshment.'

In Portugal, certain *Abwehr* officers had been sending home entirely fictitious reports based on information from imaginary agents. They did this for personal financial reasons: there was a mass desire to feather their own nests, to ensure the continuing flow of salaries and expenses, now that the German government was in such jeopardy. At the time Greene reflected how easy it would have been to have played the same game in West Africa, if he had not been satisfied with his own small salary. One incident that he could definitely have turned to his advantage concerned a report on a Vichy airfield in French Guinea. The agent who wrote the report was illiterate and innumerate, and entirely unfamiliar with the points of the compass. He claimed that a certain concrete shed housed a tank, but Greene had already received a report from another agent saying that it only contained old boots! Knowing from his own experience that the prosaic explanation was more likely, Greene was sure the latter account was the correct one. Despite Greene's assertion that the agent was incompetent, his superiors rated the agent's report as 'most valuable'. Greene knew that there was no rival organization with whose reports the agent's could be compared, except the Special Operations Executive. But he had no more confidence in SOE reports than in the agent's, because there was little doubt that they came from the same source. Clearly, this had merely enabled somebody in an office in London to write some words on a blank card. The idea of falsifying reports for money finally culminated twelve years later in one of Greene's finest novels, *Our Man in Havana*.

As a result of what Greene thought at the time were Philby's power games, he rejected promotion, left the Secret Service in 1945, and joined the Political Intelligence Department of the Foreign Office, hoping to be sent to France after the invasion. But the PID failed in their promise to send him there, and he joined the publishing house of Eyre & Spottiswoode in Bedford Street. Greene feels his only legacy to MI6 was the 'Who's Who' he left behind him – a volume that was limited to only twelve copies. Greene had compiled the work himself; it contained a list of German agents in the Azores, together with two short pieces on the administrative and agricultural situation of the islands. He also included an essay by Kim Philby on radio communications, designed to be of assistance to British invasion forces.

At Eyre & Spottiswoode he shared a room with Douglas Jerrold – like Greene, a Catholic convert – who had moved to the extreme right, supporting General Franco. Greene, meanwhile, had moved further to the left, as an advocate of Catholic Marxist dialogue. The two men made a particularly volatile combination.

When, in 1946, Greene began writing *The Heart of the Matter*, he soon found that writing and decoding innumerable secret cables in Sierra Leone had stunted his ability to write creatively. He also found the writing of this book emotionally difficult, for his private life was far from easy. He wrote in *Ways of Escape*, published in 1980: 'I had always thought that war would bring death as a solution in one form or another, in the blitz, in a submarined ship, in Africa with a dose of black-water, but here I was alive, the carrier of unhappiness to people I loved, taking up the old profession of brothel-child.' Edward, his cousin, told me that it was through his wife Vivien, whom he had married very young and from whom he had separated, that Greene became converted to the Catholic faith.

Greene's technical dilemma in the initial stages of writing *The Heart of the Matter* was that he did not have the confidence to decide how to remove the character Wilson from the balcony in the West African colonial hotel from which he was watching his police officer hero Scobie. Clearly, two very different kinds of novels could begin on the balcony, and Greene had to choose which one to write. Finally, he decided to write a serious novel rather than an entertaining one, but the end product did not please him. The book was to prove more popular with Greene's readers than with Greene himself, who felt that the plot was overloaded and the religious morality too extreme. He denies that Scobie was based on his valued friend, the commissioner of police in Sierra Leone. He also denies that Wilson was based on any of the MI6 agents he knew on the West African coast. The only real contributors from the experiences of his Secret Service days were the Portugese liners and their smuggled diamonds and letters.

In 1948, Greene researched a film scenario in Vienna for Alexander Korda, which eventually became the novel *The Third Man*, published in 1950, as well as the very memorable and atmospheric film of the same name. *The Third Man* is not really a spy story, but it is highly evocative of Vienna, a city with a strong tradition of espionage. Vienna had been occupied after the war by the Four Powers, each with its own separate zone. Greene arrived in the city in February 1948 with one sentence playing on his imagination: 'I had paid my last farewell to Harry a week ago when his coffin was lowered into the frozen February ground, so that it was with incredulity that I saw him pass by, without a sign of recognition, among the strangers in the Strand.' Although the Strand became in the film a more exotic location, the character of Harry Lime was to survive intact. Greene had lunched with an Intelligence officer who had told him about the 'underground police' who patrolled the vast network of sewers that catacombed the divided city. This unorthodox police force aimed to intercept agents travelling from the four sectors. Another factor that fired Greene's imagination was that entry to the sewers could be gained from innocent-looking advertisement kiosks on the pavements.

In response to a request from Alberto Cavalcanti, the Brazilian film director, to write a film for him, Greene decided to plan a Secret Service comedy based on his experiences of *Abwehr* deceits in Portugal. The central character of *Our Man in Havana* is Wormold, a financially insecure vacuum cleaner salesman who has an expensive daughter. He is recruited by MI6 and, to maintain his improving finances, he takes on imaginary sub-agents about whom he relays back to London a chain of false stories. Before Cavalcanti would start work on the film, he decided to try to obtain clearance from MI6. This was a disastrous move, as he was immediately told that no film that made fun of the British Secret Service would ever receive a certificate. At least, that was what Cavalcanti told Greene, who wondered if he had not simply made up a good excuse to relinquish responsibility, having tired of the whole enterprise. But Greene had no intention of shelving such an irreverent idea, and when he later visited Havana he knew that here was the right setting for such a bizarre comedy. Wormold is a purely fictitious character, but the habit of the recruiting officer, Hawthorne, of giving directions to his cook from his bed by telephone was a practice of Admiral Sinclair – the story had been told to Greene by Sinclair's niece.

The Russians were extremely suspicious of Greene's arrival in Vienna, knowing of his SIS background and assuming that he had come to take over the MI6 section there. They also knew that Greene had very briefly been a member of the Communist Party. One KGB man is reported to have told his opposite number in the CIA that it was a pity Greene was in Vienna only in his capacity as a novelist, for he now knew more exactly what went on in the sewers than did the head of the British Secret Service section there.

The Quiet American (published in 1955), while using as its background CIA manipulations, is basically a plea for the use of common sense to prevent a small-scale massacre becoming a holocaust. A shrewd novel, it could only have been written by a highly perceptive ex-Intelligence officer.

Years later, but before the Blunt exposure, Greene wrote *The Human Factor*, set in the Soviet Union, and one of his bleakest novels about the Secret Service. Maurice Castle, the anti-hero, is a double agent. The development of the plot is extremely subtle, with the net eventually closing around Castle with inexorable precision. One of Greene's post-war literary ambitions had been to write a spy story that contained none of the gratuitous violence later to be found in the adventures of James Bond. Greene wanted to reveal the Secret Service as an unromantic, office-bound, pensionable profession. He admits, though, that he based *The Human Factor* on outdated material, as he had originally begun the book years before its publication in 1978. He had abandoned the project after two or three years' work, largely because of Philby's defection. Although neither his double agent, Castle, nor any of the other characters bore the slightest resemblance to Kim Philby, Greene was extremely concerned that the general public would consider that he had drawn inspiration in *some* way from Philby's character. He writes in *Ways of Escape*:

> I know very well from experience that it is only possible for me to base a very minor and transient character on a real person. A real person stands in the way of the imagination. Perhaps a trick of speech, a physical trait may be used, but I can write no more than a few pages before

realizing that I simply don't know enough about the character to use him, even if he is an old friend. With the imaginary character I am sure – I know that Doctor Percival in *The Human Factor* admires the painting of Ben Nicholson, I know that Colonel Daintry will open a tin of sardines when he returns from the funeral of his colleague.

In a rare interview for the *Sunday Telegraph* at the time of publication, Greene told his niece, Louise Dennys: 'Of all the books *The Human Factor* has probably been the most difficult to write – that and *The Honorary Consul*. It's an albatross off my neck. He added that *The Human Factor* contains a strong element of fantasy, which is inevitable when writing about the Secret Service. In this same interview, he confirmed again that he liked Philby personally, and had often asked himself what he would have done if he had discovered at the time that he was a secret agent. But as they were then both up against the common enemy, Greene thought that 'perhaps if in a drunken moment he had let slip a hint, I would have given him twenty-four hours to get clear, and then reported it.' Greene's views on loyalty are apparent in his writing:

> The subject of divided loyalty is one that I've dealt with a lot and which is psychologically important to me . . . The human factor is in this case the effect of family life on a man working day by day in the Secret Service, which draws him in a completely different direction from what the authorities would like. I mean love for his wife, love for his adopted child. I mean a greater loyalty than the loyalty of country, as it were.

Greene had written twenty-five thousand words of *The Human Factor* when he shelved it, but its memory continued to nag at him, and it was reluctantly and with many doubts that he decided to continue. Yet although he considered the Philby scandal to be an affair of the past, he still did not send the manuscript to the publisher for some time, toying with the idea of having it published posthumously. There was an additional reason for these delays: Greene was no longer satisfied with the book. Violence had crept in, with the murder of a central character, Davis, and he did not consider Doctor Percival a realistic member of the British Secret Service. But eventually he decided that the novel did have one saving grace – its title – and he later ascribed its success to the fact that it is the love story of an elderly man.

Kim Philby's reaction, when Greene sent him a copy of the book in Moscow, was that Castle's Russian environment was far too bleak. Philby felt he would have had much more provided for him, as he himself had, although he classed himself as a much more important agent than Castle. As for Doctor Percival, he felt that he must have been recruited from the CIA. Percival had been loosely based on a Doctor L, whom both Philby and Greene had known in MI6; his diagnoses were notoriously inaccurate, but he was not capable of murder. Professor Valentina Ivasheva, another friend of Greene's in Moscow, wrote to tell him that central heating was everywhere now, and the day of the Russian stove was past. When the book was reprinted, Greene changed 'stove' to 'radiator', but he did not alter furnishings in Castle's flat, for he had based these on descriptions in Eleanor Philby's book, *The Spy I loved*, published in 1968.

Sir Maurice Oldfield, an old friend of Greene's, was amused to discover that, in *The Human Factor*, Greene had used – quite accidentally, as it turned out – the cover name of one of Oldfield's agents.

Duplicity is a subject that fascinates Greene. In *The Human Factor*, Castle is visited in Moscow by Boris, his ex-control in London, who tells him that the information Castle has been passing on is of no value. He continues:

I know I am not very clear. I am not used to whisky. Let me try to explain. Your people imagined they had an agent in place, here in Moscow. But it was we who had planted him on them. What you gave us he gave back to them.

132

Your reports authenticated him in the eyes of your service, they could check them all the time he was passing them other information which we wanted them to believe in.

Although it is clear that Greene did not base Castle on Philby, he certainly drew considerable inspiration from his motives and the way he operated.

Malcolm Muggeridge says in his autobiography *The Infernal Grove* that Greene 'characteristically took a highly professional view of what was expected of us, coolly exploring the possibility of throwing stigmata and other miraculous occurrences into the battle for the mind in Latin America to sway it in our favour.' In his foreword to Philby's *My Silent War*, Greene wrote: 'Espionage today is really a branch of psychological warfare. The main objective is to sow mistrust between allies in the enemy's camp.' He considered Philby a first-class chief, and found that he worked extremely hard – far harder than his associates – and was entirely unflappable. Though at first he was fighting the same war as his fellows, the real stress must have come later when he was creating the new section to fight Russian espionage.

Soon after Philby's clearance by the British Prime Minister, Harold Macmillan, Greene and Muggeridge went to Philby's home at Crowborough in East Sussex on an unannounced visit. They did not know at the time that they had arrived on a particularly unpropitious day. The garden was overgrown, there was no answer to their ring on the bell, and when they peered through the windows they could see the floor was littered with unopened post and brochures. In the kitchen they could see some empty milk bottles, and a single dirty cup and saucer in the sink. Greene thought it looked more like an abandoned gypsy encampment than the home of a man with a wife and children. Although neither knew it at the time, Philby had already left for Beirut – the last stage of his journey to Moscow.

Greene, a highly atmospheric writer, was impressed by this homely desolation and it was the domestic life of his central character Castle that was a vital aspect of *The Human Factor*.

CHAPTER SEVEN

IAN FLEMING:
THE DASHING SPY

Code-breaking has always been a naval tradition, and although Naval Intelligence may well have bungled in their reaction to the early warnings of Erskine Childers before the First World War, over the years they had become a highly efficient department under the leadership of Admiral Sir Reginald 'Blinker' Hall. One of their early First World War coups had been to decode the Zimmerman telegram. This was a radio telegram from the German Foreign Secretary, Arthur Zimmerman, which offered Mexico the return of her lost territories of Texas, Arizona and New Mexico in exchange for their help against America in the event of America entering the First World War. The telegram was intercepted in February 1917, and eventually only served to precipitate America into the war. The Navy code-breaking team went under the name of Room 40, the number of their room at the Admiralty.

In 1939, Admiral John Godfrey was appointed Director of Naval Intelligence. The department had lost initiative during the preceding peacetime years, and had faded to a mere shadow of the verve and efficiency that had characterized it under Admiral Hall. Hall had been an unorthodox director, perceiving that Intelligence departments needed to recruit unusual and imaginative minds. Following in Hall's tradition, Admiral Godfrey had been searching, ever since his appointment, for just such recruits among journalists, lawyers, dons, scientists and writers.

'Throughout all Bond's adventures nobody English does anything evil.'

Kingsley Amis

Ian Fleming's adventures in Naval Intelligence during the Second World War were infinitely more exciting than anything his fictional creation, James Bond, ever undertook in all his many books, and Fleming himself employed far more ingenious strategies than the hedonistic Bond could ever manage. Fleming brought charm and style to his work in Naval Intelligence. Thirty-one at the time of his appointment, he was strikingly good-looking, possessing a lively authority that pleased everyone, from his driver to the First Sea Lord. One post-war director of Naval Intelligence, Admiral Sir Norman Denning, who knew him well, commented: 'Ian had enormous flair, imagination and ability to get on with people. He would have been no use in a routine Admiralty appointment, but he was perfect for this job. He could fix anyone or anything if it was really necessary.'

Born in London on 28 May 1908, Ian Lancaster Fleming was the son of Major Valentine Fleming, Conservative MP for South Oxfordshire, and Evelyn St Croix Fleming. As a child, Fleming was far from conformist, and did not take to his family's obsession with the traditional country pursuits of hunting, shooting and fishing. Luckily, however, he went to an idiosyncratic prep school in Dorset called Durnford, where the headmaster and his wife were genial, outgoing people who ran the school on family lines – even if some of their activities were a trifle unusual. For instance, on Sunday evenings, the headmaster's wife, Mrs Pellatt, reclining on a sofa in her drawing-room, would ask one of the boys to stroke her feet while she read aloud. But she also encouraged the boys to read as much as possible themselves, and soon Fleming was devouring Sax Rohmer, Buchan, Poe and Robert Louis Stevenson.

Throughout his childhood, Fleming remained at odds with his family's interests. He disliked dogs and horses, and had a particular distaste of family gatherings, especially those that occurred at Christmas. He seemed inhibited by the Flemings' Scottish origins, and went out of his way to avoid crossing the border at any time, complaining: 'All those wet rhododendrons and people with hair on their cheeks sitting round peat fires

135

wrapped in plaid blankets.' Gradually, he developed two passions of his own: shooting and walking. His biographer, John Pearson, exactly caught his personality when he described him as having 'one of those natures for which the world is uncomfortable in whatever shape they find it'.

In the autumn of 1921, Fleming went to Eton. He was already conscious of his good looks and took considerable trouble with his appearance, even going to the lengths of using a rather extravagantly scented hair oil. At first he stayed under the shadow of his elder brother, Peter, who won many prizes and became captain of the Etonian Sports society, the Oppidans, but soon Fleming was able to establish himself in his own right by emerging as one of the best marksmen in the school team and as a first-class athlete. He had the distinction of being the only boy to be victor ludorum two years running.

But sporting success did not make him any more conformist and, perhaps predictably, he left Eton under a cloud, owing to the double sin of owning a car and having 'relationships with girls'. Leaving Eton a term earlier than he would normally have done, he went to a crammer where he was prepared for Sandhurst, joining the Royal Military College in the autumn of 1926 as a gentleman cadet. But once again he seemed restless, so he resigned from Sandhurst, and after some desperate research by his mother, was sent to the Austrian Tyrol, where he joined a further education establishment that was as unconventional as Durnford. Run by A. E. Forbes Dennis and his wife, the novelist Phyllis Bottome, the school based much of its general policy on the philosophy of Alfred Adler, who held that a child's first five years were of extreme importance in forming the character. It might have seemed rather late in the day for Fleming to benefit from this particular theory, but here, at last, he had found an educational and social setting that was totally right for him – even if this had far more to do with sympathetic and perceptive teaching than with the educational theories of Adler.

Fleming clearly benefited from his Tyrolean 'finishing school'. In 1963 he wrote to Phyllis Bottome: 'Looking back, I am sure

Erskine Childers   *Photograph: BBC Hulton Picture Library*

Somerset Maugham *(above)*
Photograph: BBC Hulton Picture Library

John Buchan *(left)*
Photograph: BBC Hulton Picture Library

Compton Mackenzie *(above centre)*
Photograph: BBC Hulton Picture Library

Ian Fleming *(above right)*
Photograph: Popperfoto

Malcolm Muggeridge *(right)*
Photograph: BBC Hulton Picture Library

Graham Greene, right, with
François Mauriac (*left*)
Photograph: Associated Press

Tom Driberg (*below left*)
Photograph: BBC Hulton Picture Library

John Bingham (*right*)
Drawing from a private collection

Dennis Wheatley (*below*)
Photograph: BBC Hulton Picture Library

E. Howard Hunt *Photograph by Bob Sherman*

John le Carré (David Cornwell)   *Photograph: Camera Press*

Len Deighton   *Photograph by Mark Gerson, FIIP*

that your influence had a great deal to do with the fact that, at any rate, three of us later became successful writers. I remember clearly writing a rather bizarre short story which you criticized kindly and which was in fact the first thing I ever wrote.' Forbes Dennis commented: 'Ian was inclined to do anything to excess, in a desperate attempt to get through to a mythical place where everything would be all right at last, where nothing could ever let him down again. And of course it never was and never would be.' Goldeneye, Fleming's house in Jamaica, was perhaps the nearest he got to his mythical place.

After a year in the Tyrol, he went to Munich University, and it was here that he witnessed the first stirrings of the Nazi movement. He also began to study Russian. He then continued his studies in Geneva, returning to England in 1930. Fleming had a great facility for mastering foreign languages, and it was this that prompted him to sit the Foreign Office examinations in the summer of 1931. Unfortunately, the results were so disappointing that he abandoned any idea of entering diplomatic life, and instead took a post at Reuters News Agency in London. And it was Reuters that provided Fleming's first major adventure. In 1933 he was sent to Moscow to cover the trial of six British engineers of the Metropolitan–Vickers Electrical Company, who had been arrested on spying charges. Russia made a profound impression on him, but because he saw Moscow from the isolation of the British Press compound, and had only limited opportunity to meet and talk with the Russian people, he was forced to focus on the empty shops, the long queues, the ubiquitous portraits of Lenin and the badly dressed Muscovites. It was a one-sided picture, that led him to see Russia in terms of stereotypes. To make matters even more subjective, Fleming was not in a very confident mood, for as well as making him financially dependent on his mother, failing his Foreign Office exams had badly shaken him. It was thus a matter of urgency that he should succeed as a journalist, and he saw his Moscow assignment as the potential proving ground.

In fact, Fleming *did* prove himself, showing what a resourceful journalist he could be, particularly as he had to write a number of dull news stories while awaiting the results of the trial. Nevertheless, his flair for originality could bring even the most potentially boring piece of information to life. Then, with the aid of the chance opening of a hitherto non-existent telephone line, he managed to scoop his colleagues on the trial's verdict, and spent his last remaining week in Moscow trying to interview Stalin. In the event, he returned home with nothing more than a signed letter from Russia's leader, declining to be interviewed. Many of Bond's future battles with SMERSH (its title was a contraction of *Smyert Shpionam* which, roughly translated, means 'Death to Spies') were to be based on the dour pictures of Moscow that Fleming took back to England with him, for although he was a good journalist, he was unable to perceive a deeper meaning to Russian life – a failure which tended to tinge Bond's encounters with Russians with a rather jingoistic prejudice.

Fleming's experiences in Russia and his skilled reporting of them gave him considerable distinction at Reuters, and as a result he was offered the plum job of Reuters Far East correspondent. This was an enormously flattering offer for a young man of twenty-five and Fleming would have had no doubts about taking it up had not another more financially rewarding opportunity, outside the world of journalism, cropped up. The offer came from Cull and Co., a firm of London merchant bankers. The money, considerably more than Reuters could afford, was the main attraction, but he was also subjected to family pressures: his grandfather had been a merchant banker, and it was the kind of profession that the Fleming family thought far more in keeping with a solid future than the sordid world of journalism. He was to work for Cull and Co. for two years.

In October 1933 Fleming joined the stockbrokers, Rowe and Pitman. But, very predictably, he soon lost interest in stock-broking, and its substantial financial rewards no longer appealed to him. One of his colleagues, Hugh Vivian Smith, remembers: 'As a stockbroker old Ian really must have been among the world's worst.' Feeling directionless, Fleming spent much of his spare time enjoying gourmet food and playing golf and bridge. As a games-player he contributed a schoolboy energy, but he took too many risks in bridge to be a satisfactory partner. All the intellectual alertness that his sojourn in the Tyrol had taught him now seemed to have dissipated. Subconsciously he was aware of the problem, and he increasingly found his hedonistic lifestyle purposeless.

Meanwhile Admiral Godfrey, Director of Naval Intelligence, busily recruiting throughout 1939 very much in the tradition of his predecessor, Admiral Hall, had already been looking carefully at the stockbroking world and taking a particular interest in this young journalist turned stockbroker. He invited Fleming to the Carlton Grill where, without explaining his intentions, he gave him a good lunch. At the table was Admiral Aubrey Hugh-Smith – brother of Lance Hugh-Smith, the senior partner of Rowe and Pitman – who was clearly acting as both observer and referee. In fact, Godfrey was recruiting at a very high level, for he wished to appoint a dynamic and imaginative personal assistant. It was a key post, requiring someone with the right chemistry and initiative, and Fleming had come highly recommended by no less a person than the Governor of the Bank of England. All Godfrey was prepared to tell Fleming at the lunch, however, was that he should hold himself ready to fill a post that would be 'exceptionally important in time of war'.

Fleming began to visit the Admiralty at least three or four afternoons a week, while continuing to work in the mornings as a stockbroker. He would arrive at Room 39, which was to become a historic nerve centre for the Navy throughout the war, and walk through to Room 38, where Godfrey sat in isolated splendour. The two of them would then discuss the part Fleming would play as Godfrey's personal assistant – and just how influential that role might be. Almost at once, Godfrey began to appreciate why Fleming had been so highly recommended. Not only was he brimming with ideas but he had a direct, confident manner that Godfrey knew would be acceptable in even higher echelons of the Admiralty.

One major weakness in Naval Intelligence during the early years of the war was the lack of a Combined Operations policy. Many of the Navy's top brass were highly antagonistic to ideas put forward by the Admiral of the Fleet, Sir Roger Keyes, who wanted to combine units of the Army, Navy and RAF under a single command, so that amphibious and airborne offensives could be more efficiently organized, with the overall aim of preparing for the eventual invasion of Europe. Unfortunately, the Admiralty decided to show its insular hostility towards this idea by making the Combined Operations Department the runt of the service, stocking it with officers of poor stature whom the Navy wanted to lose anyway, and with ratings weak or even violent. Later, Fleming was to rectify this situation with considerable verve.

On 26 July 1939 Fleming was appointed lieutenant in the Royal Naval Volunteer Reserve. Admiral Godfrey explained his original brief: 'From the beginning, my idea was that I would tell Ian everything so that if anything happened to me there would be one man who would know what was going on – he could ensure the continuity of the department. I also used him a lot to represent me on important routine interdepartmental conferences.' The latter would cover such essential topics as the media, propaganda, political warfare and subversion.

To a man like Fleming, this new appointment brought together the unpredictability of journalism with the power of the Stock Exchange – a combination that sent his adrenalin surging. He was a born fixer, although bully-boy tactics were not in his style. He was exceptionally tactful, but had no particular veneration for senior officers, whom he treated as he treated everyone else. Admiral Godfrey commented: 'He learned perhaps sooner than I, that Intelligence may be a sticky commodity which sometimes needs sugar-coating, and that the purveyor of bad tidings is unwelcome. How to reconcile sugar coatings with bad tidings with speed is an aptitude possessed by few.'

Fleming was to have more power as Godfrey's personal assistant than he at first realized. He knew more secrets and had more real influence than many of the senior officers in the three services. Consequently, Godfrey ensured that he was quickly promoted to lieutenant-commander, and then commander. Godfrey now had considerable faith in Fleming, and after his death Godfrey was to say: 'I once said that Ian should have been the D.N.I. [Director of Naval Intelligence] and I his naval adviser. If he had been ten years older and I ten years younger, this might have had the elements of a workable proposition.' But although the job fulfilled Fleming's drive and aborted any question of boredom, he was still restless and 'uncomfortable'. He shared with Graham Greene a great melancholy, but whereas Greene's would often disappear when he was 'on the dangerous edge of things', Fleming's aura of inner restlessness and isolation seemed to remain with him. Colleagues in Room 39 noticed that he did not take part in light-hearted jesting, and indeed refused to fully join in any group movement or mood. He was apart, and he made them very conscious of this. Edward Merrett, Admiral Godfrey's secretary, who sat at the next desk to Fleming in Room 39, was in a good position to observe his behaviour. He recalled:

> The first time I saw him I put Ian Fleming down as a withdrawn and unhappy man, and I never changed my mind about that. I thought his attitude was very much that of the typical old Etonian, the same withdrawn superiority, and I have never forgotten how he used that remark of his, 'Well, there it is.' Anything he was bored with or tired of would be terminated with, 'Well, there it is.'

Godfrey, meanwhile, was coming to the conclusion that his resourceful personal assistant *did* have a weakness: he was poor at following things through – a man with brilliant ideas, but inclined to let other people tackle the routine hard work of checking detail. Godfrey, however, was a strong enough personality to insist that Fleming leave no loose ends.

Some aspects of his work in the department reminded Fleming of Buchan. In particular, his imagination was exhilarated by the contacts he made through Naval Intelligence in the Special Operations Executive, the organization that had been created to carry out special missions such as the parachuting of personnel and supplies to Resistance fighters in Occupied Europe. This was to be marvellous material for Bond. Naturally, Fleming also had close contact with MI6 as well as MI5, where he first met Maxwell Knight. The character of M, James Bond's shadowy boss, was said to be based on an amalgam of Godfrey and Knight.

Fleming was to draw inspiration for the James Bond stories from the adventures of his brother, Peter, who had been recruited by SOE to work in the Middle East. Another powerful influence at this time was Erskine Childers; after reading *Riddle of the Sands* Fleming had initiated an undercover venture of his own which was partly fantastic, partly real. In 1960 he drove up the coast of North Germany past the strange landscape of the Frisian Islands – a trip about which he later wrote:

> The last time I paid serious attention to those island names – Wangerooge, Spiekeroog, Nordeney, Borkum – was when, as a young Lieutenant R.N.V.R., I had studied them endlessly on Admiralty charts and put up a succession of plans whereby I and an equally intrepid wireless operator should be transported to the group by submarine and there dig ourselves in, to report on the sailings of U-boats and the movements of the German fleet.

But nothing came of Fleming's dream, for Godfrey was not prepared to risk his valued assistant in such a reckless adventure. Admiral Denning considered that some of Fleming's ideas were almost insane, but had to admit that:

> a lot of his far-fetched ideas had just a glimmer of possibility in them that made you think twice before you threw them in the waste-paper basket. Just before the Dieppe raid, for instance, he had the idea of sinking a great block of concrete with men inside it in the English Channel

to keep watch on the harbour through periscopes. We never did it, of course, but it might have worked.

Despite the exhilaration he experienced in his work, Fleming was beginning to resent being so desk-bound, becoming more and more anxious to take a more involved, perhaps even more dramatic role in the war. His chance finally came in June 1940, just as the French surrendered to the German Army. Paris was expected to fall at any moment, but the French Navy, under Admiral Darlan, was still a force to be reckoned with, being the fourth largest in the world, with a fleet of modern ships. Churchill's plan was that Darlan should order these ships to sail into British ports, to be utilized by the Royal Navy. But Darlan showed no sign of agreeing, and communications between France and England were in the process of becoming cut off as the German Army swept into Paris. Godfrey began to despair that the order would ever be given, particularly as Darlan had confided to him some months before that his great-grandfather had been killed at Trafalgar – which hardly boded well for a hand-over of his ships to the British. Fleming then suggested to Godfrey that he should be flown into France with a wireless operator, so that he could stay as close as possible to Admiral Darlan until he came to a decision – preferably the right one.

Godfrey was desperate enough to agree to the idea, and on 13 June Fleming and his operator were flown to Le Bourget, when they made their way to Darlan's headquarters at Montbazon. Unfortunately, Darlan did not seem to realize the urgency or the danger of his position, and gave no indication of moving, despite instructions from London that he should come to a decision about the handing over of his ships and be prepared to leave immediately. Just as Darlan was telling London that he considered their view a little too pessimistic, German planes attacked his headquarters, which necessitated an undignified retreat to Bordeaux. There Fleming discovered that the estuary of the Gironde was offering one of the best possible escape routes from Western Europe, and the town was crammed with refugees. While the British continued attempting to make

143

Darlan see sense, de Gaulle made his escape via the Gironde to England.

Meanwhile, Fleming had received instructions over his private radio to ensure that a large cache of aircraft engines and spares did not fall into German hands. With great alacrity, and with the captain in total ignorance of his cargo, he loaded them onto a ship bound for England. He also spent a considerable amount of time burning documents that he considered should not be allowed to fall into German hands, but his most audacious coup was to persuade the captains of some neutral ships that were standing out in the Gironde estuary to evacuate the refugees. Amazingly, they agreed, probably semi-hypnotized by a barrage of authoritarian Fleming charm. Indeed, not only did Fleming manage to organize this sizeable evacuation of officials and civilians, but he also included in the mêlée a distinguished refugee, King Zog of Albania. The king, together with his family and retinue, had arrived on the quayside at the last moment with a cavalcade of limousines and in a mood of mounting agitation. He had brought with him a vast amount of luggage, amongst which were the crown jewels of Albania. Never had Fleming spent such a glorious hour as when he shepherded these regal refugees on board his flotilla of ships. With great panache, he had masterminded the entire operation from the quayside.

Carried away by the success of this venture, he then made a somewhat over-ambitious suggestion aimed at remedying the stalemate over the still-procrastinating Darlan. He recommended to the British ambassador in France that His Majesty's government should offer the Isle of Wight to Admiral Darlan for the duration of the war, and for him to take his ships there, making the island French territory. His suggestion was greeted with icy outrage. Two weeks later Admiral Sir James Somerville, in a desperate attempt to prevent the intransigent Darlan letting his ships fall into German hands, began to bombard them off the coast of Oran, where they had now gathered.

Once the reluctant Fleming had returned to his London office, Godfrey resolved not to let him off the leash again. Although Fleming had pulled off some great entrepreneurial feats, he relied too much on luck and cheek, a combination that might easily run out at the wrong time. Fortunately, being imprisoned behind a desk did not entirely cramp Fleming's style, for he was still able to produce some extraordinarily original ideas.

Early in the Battle of Britain, Naval Intelligence received details of a new, high-powered launch that the Germans were using to pick up the crews of both German and Allied planes that had been shot down along the coasts of Holland and northern France. Fleming suggested that one of these launches should be captured, so that the ciphers on board could be studied. His idea was approved, and he decided to set a highly imaginative trap which needed a captured German aircraft, a resourceful, German-speaking British air crew and the opportunity of staging a dummy crash that would lure the Germans towards its location somewhere in the Channel, near the French coast. The counterfeit crew would then overpower the Germans in the launch and capture it for subsequent investigation.

Fleming took a somewhat bemused Naval Intelligence officer named Peter Smithers on a search for German guns and an authentic German flying kit. These props were eventually discovered in an RAF hangar used specifically for storing captured German uniforms. With typical dash, Fleming tried the outfit on for size, and strode about impersonating a German airman, asking for a Major Fleming. In fact, Major Peter Fleming was then based in nearby Canterbury. Making his brother the subject of this rather alarming practical joke was typical of Fleming's humour. But eventually the project was cancelled, not on the grounds that it was a bad idea but because intact captured bombers were in short supply.

Much of Bond's delight in lethal gadgetry was inspired by Fleming's own interest in these deadly toys. For instance, he was particularly attached to a fountain pen that was able to eject a substantial cloud of tear-gas when the clip was pressed, and he often carried it around with him. Various other deadly items, such as a cyanide cartridge, could be carried in the pen.

145

But if Godfrey continually managed to exploit and delight in Fleming's talents, his secretary, Edward Merrett, remained a stern critic, although there is a strong element of sour grapes in his comments:

> You mustn't get the wrong idea about Ian's service with N.I.D. He wasn't James Bond. He was a pen-pusher like all of us . . . Of course, he knew everything that was going on, but he never seemed to show any real inclination to take part in it. If he was secretly longing for action I never saw any sign of it. In short, Ian's war had plenty of sweat and toil and tears but no real blood.

This is an unfair conclusion, considering Fleming's activities in France, and even if he was now operating from behind a desk he was certainly capable of pulling off some important coups. Several of these emanated from his own personal contacts. By introducing Sefton Delmer of the *Daily Express* to Godfrey in 1939, he had prepared the ground for the radio station called the *Atlantiksender*, which was set up by Delmer in his war-time role and the Naval Intelligence Department to feed disinformation to German U-boat crews. Fleming was also heavily involved in the Naval Propaganda Section, which Godfrey created to harass the German Navy. The propaganda group was liberally staffed with writers: its head, Donald McLachlan, was later to become the editor of the *Sunday Telegraph*, and his one-time deputy, Robert Harling, was a novelist who became editor of *House and Garden*. Other literary figures such as William Plomer and the novelist Charles Morgan were also responsible for writing the propaganda reports.

Although Fleming was rightly renowned for his imaginative schemes, many of them still penetrated too far into the realms of fantasy. One such scheme involved the unlikely combination of Rudolf Hess and Aleister Crowley, and depended for its success on the main protagonist's faith in the power of astrology. When Hess made his parachute descent into Scotland in May 1941, in his crazy plan to make peace with Britain, Fleming drew up a plan to enlist the services of Crowley, an acquaintance of other Intelligence figures such as Tom Driberg, Dennis Wheatley and Maxwell Knight. Like them, Fleming had been fascinated by the dubious activities of Crowley, and his self-vaunted reputation of being a black magician. Having tracked Crowley down to the seaside resort of Torquay in Devon, he asked the old reprobate if he would help with the interrogation of Hess. Crowley would have been delighted to oblige, but his services were turned down by the rest of the NID, so Fleming merely filed his name away for reference; after all, self-styled black magicians might well have some future role to play. Many top-ranking Nazis were preoccupied with astrology and the occult, and Fleming felt sure that Crowley, with all his knowledge on the subject, could be of use at some point.

There are claims that Fleming himself was responsible for luring Hess over to England in the first place. He had certainly been studying a dossier on Admiral Sir Barry Domville – given to him by Maxwell Knight, head of MI5's counter-subversion department – who had been a particularly pro-German head of Naval Intelligence between 1927 and 1930. He had founded an organization called The Link, which Knight's department had recently been investigating. Fleming had the original idea of resurrecting this banned pro-German organization, by hinting that, although it had gone underground, it had acquired some powerful new members who would pave the way towards the overthrow of the Churchill government and a negotiated peace with Germany. What Fleming wanted to do was to leak this disinformation to the Nazi leadership in the hope of provoking it into making contact, or even that German invasion plans might be temporarily or even permanently shelved. He knew, however, that this extraordinary plan was unlikely to be well received, even by Godfrey, for it was clearly far too risky and the potential for it to back-fire on its organizers was enormous.

It is claimed that Fleming entrusted the machinations of the plan to two trusted friends, one of whom was in another branch of British Intelligence and the other a contact in Switzerland who was an authority on astrology. Apparently Fleming had decided that Hess was by far the most likely candidate for the key role in his plan, and he was later delighted to receive confirmation from his contacts that Hess was without doubt the keenest of all the Nazi leaders to make peace with Britain. He was also heavily addicted to astrology and the occult. Fleming's Swiss contact was able to plant a British agent who was also an astrologer in Hess's department. The plant arranged to obtain two horoscopes from astrologers who were known to be trusted by Hess, so that he could produce a fake horoscope that would be similar to the ones Hess was used to and that would therefore not arouse his suspicions. The fake horoscope would tell Hess the 'right' time to plan his journey to Britain, where he would attempt to make peace through the help of sympathizers there.

None of this can be proven in detail, and there is no real evidence to suggest that Hess's dramatic flight to England was brought about by Fleming's plans. However, Richard Deacon, author of *A History of the British Secret Service*, feels that the story is likely to be true in some details. His opinion of Fleming's ingenuity is high – particularly his 'uncanny skill when briefing people to give less than the information required, thus completely disguising the purpose of an operation, yet cajoling the mystified subordinate into doing the right thing without his knowing why he was doing it'.

In 1941, Fleming began a journey that was later to be used as background material for his first thriller, *Casino Royale*. British Naval Intelligence had decided that they needed to create better contact with their American counterparts, and to this end Fleming and Admiral Godfrey flew to Washington for secret talks with the American Office of Naval Intelligence. En route their Sunderland landed for an overnight stop at Lisbon, which, Fleming had been informed by MI6, along with its neighbour Estoril was crawling with German agents. Learning that the most senior of these gambled feverishly every night in Estoril with his two assistants, Fleming decided to combine business with pleasure, and somehow he managed to wheedle Admiral

Godfrey into joining him. Fleming later insisted that he gambled against the Germans himself:

> We went there, and there were the three men playing at the high *chemin de fer* table. The D.N.I. didn't know the game. I explained it to him, and then the feverish idea came to me that I would sit down and gamble against these men and defeat them, reducing the funds of the German Secret Service. It was a foolhardy plan . . . I 'bancoed' and lost. I 'suivied' and lost again and 'suivied' a third time and was cleaned out. A humiliating experience.

But Admiral Godfrey claims they spent a particularly slow and dismal night at the casino. He had noticed a glaze come over Fleming's eyes as he sat down and began to play for the first time since the beginning of the war. But the stakes were low, because only a handful of Portugese happened to be in the casino that night. Fleming whispered to Godfrey that they might bring off quite a coup if the Portugese were German agents in disguise – and they then managed to clean them out completely. But Godfrey thought his supposition unlikely, and merely longed for his bed.

Dusko Popov, code-named 'Tricycle', a double agent working for the British XX organization, (so-called after the roman numeral version of the Twenty Committee, the responsible body) was also in Lisbon during Fleming's visit. He has his own anecdote about Fleming at that time. He had just received, the same night, $80,000 from the Germans for services rendered, which he was due to hand over to MI6 the next morning. He was certain that Fleming knew about the money and that he was following him to ensure he handed it over. The evening began to assume the characteristics of farce when Popov, having encountered Fleming in the lobby of his hotel and then in a café before dinner, found him in the restaurant where he was dining. Popov later wrote in his book *Spy-Counter-Spy* (1974):

> British Intelligence had enough confidence to entrust me with 80,000 dollars. The secrets I carried in my head were

worth much more. We strolled through the halls of the casino, my shadow and I, observing play at the different tables. A favourite *bête noire* of mine was there – an insignificant but wealthy Lithuanian named Bloch, who attempted to compensate for his tiny stature by arrogant play . . . I don't know what the devil was behind me, perhaps Fleming or the knowledge that he was there, but when Bloch announced 'Banque ouverte' I announced 'Fifty thousand dollars'. I glanced at Fleming. His face turned bile green. Obviously the Lithuanian didn't have that sort of money on him. He squirmed in his chair in embarrassment.

Eventually the bet was not taken, and presumably Fleming recovered his nerve. Perhaps Popov's story is a little implausible, though.

When Fleming arrived in the States he met Canadian millionaire Sir William Stevenson, who was responsible for representing British Intelligence in America through the organization, British Security Coordination. Stevenson was an ex-First World War fighter-pilot who had been highly decorated. He was also a European lightweight amateur boxing champion, and Fleming saw him as the classic hero. Stevenson also specialized in mixing particularly large martinis, which he apparently served in quart glasses. He was reputed to be a man of few words, but this might have had something to do with his substantial martini intake. There was much in his personality and way of living that Fleming was to extract for Bond. He was especially interested in the sophisticated gadgetry that comprised the coding equipment that Stevenson had been amassing, and he used to spend happy hours watching how it worked.

In May 1941, Fleming began work on his most important and most imaginative contribution to the war. After the German invasion of Crete, he began to take an interest in the activities of *Obersturmbannführer* Otto Skorzeny, who was to inspire him to create the character Sir Hugo Drax in *Moonraker*. Skorzeny, who was in his early thirties, had risen to power in the Nazi Party through the *Studenten Freikorps* and the illegal peacetime Austrian Nazi Party. Now, he had raided the British headquarters at Maleme and Heraklion in Crete, where his objective had been to remove British secret papers. He and his men seemed to know exactly what to look for, and Fleming suddenly realized that he had discovered the first German Intelligence commandos. As he studied their methods, he came to the conclusion that British Naval Intelligence could well learn from the Germans and create such a unit themselves.

His first attempts were modest and naïve; they were also disastrous. He took the extraordinary step of lunching some German prisoners-of-war at Scott's restaurant in Piccadilly, with some British colleagues. His idea was to inebriate the German captain and navigator of a captured U-boat to the point where they would give away the secret of how they managed to avoid Allied minefields in the Skagerrak, the strait between Norway and Denmark, linking the North Sea and the Baltic. Fleming had artfully arranged for them to be allowed out of their prison camp for a day's 'sightseeing'. He and his conspirators played the role of brother officers who had been forced to fight by politicians and were anxious to be friendly. But before the alcohol could work its effect, one of the waiters noticed the Germans' ill-fitting clothes (not to mention their accents), and Special Branch were called to the restaurant to investigate and eventually arrest the whole party. It was not one of Fleming's more successful ideas, and it caused Admiral Godfrey considerable embarrassment.

Unabashed, the nonchalant Fleming then put another, similar, plan into operation. Having made a chance encounter with a gunnery officer from the sunken *Bismarck*, he set about planning a night out which would remind the German of the old and elegant London he had known and loved before the war, in the hope that he would reveal some Intelligence information over his liquor. This time the drink *did* have the desired effect – but to the extent that the German officer ended up too incoherent to speak, let alone to divulge any secrets. This was all a great pity, because Fleming had taken the trouble to arrange the perfect nostalgic evening: a meal at the Écu de France with a couple of German-speaking British naval officers, and then on to a delightful house in Sloane Square for coffee and indiscretion. Gradually, even Fleming began to realize that these outings were too unpredictable to have much chance of real success.

In early 1942, Fleming's thoughts returned to Skorzeny and his Intelligence commandos. As it happened, Naval Intelligence was currently planning to carry out some raids on the French coast, and Fleming put forward the proposition that they should be accompanied by a specially trained team of what he called 'Intelligence scavengers', who would go in with the first wave of conventional commandos. After a lot of thought, Godfrey eventually agreed to give Fleming his head, and the scheme was launched in conjunction with the big raid on Dieppe of August 1942. It was made clear that this was to be a pilot project for Fleming's initiative, but the go-ahead was announced too late for him to think the scheme through – which may have been a deliberate ploy to try and keep him in check.

When the time came for his assault on the French coast, Fleming selected two naval lieutenants, and gave them a covering force of ten particularly efficient marines, ordering them to fight their way through to German headquarters. As he had before, Fleming asked Godfrey if he could go with them – but he knew it was a vain hope, for he was far too valuable to lose. Nevertheless, he was given permission to play an observer's role on one of the invading ships. Unfortunately, owing to delays with Canadian troops, his small Intelligence team were unable to leave the ship.

Nonetheless, Fleming now felt that his idea was being taken seriously, and that he would be given another chance. This finally occurred later in the summer of 1942, when plans were going ahead for the Anglo-American invasion of North Africa. For this attempt Fleming had adequate time to set up his Intelligence assault unit in more detail, and he was given responsibility for their training. He chose his two leaders carefully: Quentin Riley, the Arctic explorer, was made joint commanding officer with Duncan Curtis, who had commanded the leading ship on the previous raid on St-Nazaire. Fleming was also supplied with seven Royal Marines. These good men and true were known officially as 30 Assault Unit, and unofficially as Fleming's Private Army. Curtis relates: 'Ian was immensely excited. You'd have thought he was the one going on the trip. It was an enormous adventure for him.' To train his men, Fleming took them to Scotland Yard, where they learned safe-blowing techniques as well as picking locks and breaking and entering. Once they were schooled in these arts, he took them to a house in Buckinghamshire to learn about small-arms weapons, radar sets, booby traps, minefields, gelignite and plastic explosives, as well as the more sophisticated techniques of how to crack ciphers and code-books and interpret Intelligence reports. All this was to provide a vital store of specialized information for the adventures of James Bond.

Once on the ground in Algiers, Fleming's men immediately proved themselves worthy of their desk-bound leader. Within minutes of landing, they commandeered a French truck and its startled driver and undertook a hit-and-miss exploration through Algiers until they discovered the house that the Italians had been using as their naval headquarters. Surprised by the invasion, the Italians had not had time to burn their secret documents, and Fleming's Private Army gathered a generous harvest of files and code-books as well as the current German and Italian ciphers and the order of battle of the enemy fleets. It was a tremendously important haul, and a great coup for British Intelligence.

Now Fleming's 30 Assault Unit had more than proved themselves for future action, and he was arguing an effective case for their expansion. This came with their reinforcement by a squad of Royal Marines, to provide both defence and fire power. Fleming's Private Army was also given its own transport and status, symbolized by their own particular uniform – khaki battledress and naval caps – a visible retort to the original Admiralty critics of Combined Operations.

But this was to be Fleming's last military achievement, for

153

Admiral Godfrey had now been made Flag Officer of the Royal Indian Navy, and his successor, Commodore E. G. N. Rushbrooke, did not see Fleming in the same kind of role. Yet despite his reduced influence, the Private Army went from strength to strength, with Fleming still firmly at the helm. When, in April 1943, the Anglo-American forces met Montgomery's Eighth Army on the North African coast, 30 Assault Unit had a complete and up-to-date picture of all defences and minefields on the Sicilian coast – a vital contribution towards the successful invasion of the island. Eventually the unit was divided into two, one division accompanying the Allied invasion of Sicily and Italy, and the other returning to England for further training under Fleming's leadership. The Private Army was now further expanded, and Fleming took on Robert Harling as the unit's expert on mines; another recruit was broadcaster and writer, Ralph Izzard. The division trained for D-Day, and their numbers swelled to 150 as they prepared to land at the Arromanches beach-head with the objective of reaching the huge German radar station before it could be destroyed. Thanks, once again, to Fleming's careful planning, the raid was a success, but the over-confidence and debauchery that went with it annoyed the tidy-minded Fleming. His biographer, John Pearson, writes:

> For when the men in his Unit were behaving with a dash and independence which would have done credit to James Bond himself, Fleming reacted with all the touchiness and exasperation that old M was to show when the best-laid plans were disregarded by bungling subordinates. Beneath the exasperation there seems to lie the passionate disappointment of the symmetrist whose tidy vision of things has once again been reduced by reality to chaos.

In fact, Fleming was beginning to wonder if his Private Army was slipping out of his control, hampered as he was by being stuck at his desk.

Fleming was not the soul of tact when he met his men in

154

action. On one occasion, sitting on the roadside at Carteret on the north coast of France, drinking captured enemy cognac while the Allied armies regrouped before they pushed north-east, he complained to Robert Harling: 'This stuff's undrinkable.'

As the war drew to a close, 30 Assault Unit continued to round up vast quantities of captured top secret German equipment, including the first German one-man submarine. As the Allied armies tore their way into Germany itself, Fleming's Private Army raided the submarine works in Hamburg and the torpedo experimental station at Eckernforder, and finally reached a castle at Tambach in the Württemberg Forest where they discovered a cache containing German naval archives dating back to 1870, as well as more interesting modern material. Fleming himself brought the documents back to England on board a fishery protection vessel, together with the old German admiral who had been trying to burn them. Fleming's last signal to 30 Assault Unit read: 'Find immediately the twelve top German naval commanders and make each one write ten thousand words on why Germany lost the war at sea.' This last touch was typical of Fleming's imaginative flair – a flair that had more than paid off.

It was with this last glowing tribute from Admiral Godfrey that Ian Fleming left Naval Intelligence on 4 November 1945: 'His zeal, ability and judgement are altogether exceptional, and have contributed very largely to the development and organi-zation of the Naval Intelligence Division during the war. Any further words would be superfluous.'

After being demobbed, Fleming returned to his pre-war occupation of collecting rare books and bought Goldeneye in Jamaica, the property that was to become his writing retreat. Goldeneye was, in fact, the code-name under which Naval Intelligence had planned to seal off Gibraltar if Franco had decided to join the Nazis. Fleming, however, insisted that the name came from the novel *Reflections in a Golden Eye* by Carson McCullers. He was also offered a high-powered job by Lord Kemsley as manager of the foreign news service for his newspaper group. The position offered a large salary and plenty of free time in which to travel – in particular, to his beloved Goldeneye.

Once asked by Robert Harling what he intended to do when the war was over, Fleming had replied that he was going to write the spy story to 'end all spy stories'. In January 1952 he fulfilled that promise, and began *Casino Royale*, the first adventure of James Bond. The sales phenomenon of the Bond books has been much discussed, and it is unnecessary to analyse their success here. Fleming's Russian trip, together with his amazing wartime exploits, gave him excellent material for all Bond's adventures. Bond himself is an amalgam of Dusko Popov, Sydney Reilly (the Russian master-spy) – although Fleming thought that Bond never really reached his heights – and, of course, Fleming himself, with his dislike of flowers in rooms and his appreciation of caviare and dry martinis. But, despite the commercial success, Bond remains a pale, one-dimensional figure, a more sophisti-cated version of Richard Hannay or Bulldog Drummond. Nevertheless, he caught the mood of the fifties: although he was deeply patriotic, Bond slaughtered foreigners and went to bed with women whether they stood for good or bad. He represented for that era a kind of amoral physical freedom that was some people's pipe-dream. Yet Fleming's own adventures were much more exciting and original than Bond's.

Despite Bond's lightweight personality, the Russians took him as a serious threat, seeing his battle against SMERSH as positive anti-Soviet propaganda. To counteract this the KGB commissioned Bulgarian writer A. Gulyashi to write the *Zakhov Mission*, in which Bond is beaten at the hands of a Communist hero. The book was serialized in *Komsomolskaya Pravda* under the title *Avakum Zakhov Versus 007*, and a translation was eventually published in this country in 1968, some four years after Fleming's death. He would have been amused at the joke.

CHAPTER EIGHT

TOM DRIBERG:
THE DECADENT SPY

Tom Driberg worked as an MI5 agent in the Communist Party of Great Britain in the early part of the Second World War. He was eventually exposed as an agent by Anthony Blunt. Driberg had been recruited by Maxwell Knight, the veteran MI5 officer who had himself been one of Vernon Kell's earliest employees. Knight headed an MI5 department known as B5(b), which was responsible for infiltrating agents into Communist or Fascist groups.

'I'm just a girl at MI5, and heading for a virgin's grive
My legs it was wot got me in – I'm waiting for my bit of sin.'
MI5 typist's lament

Tom Driberg's wake at the Clergy House in Westminster in 1976 was a noble farce. He had left money for his mourners to indulge in unlimited drinks – an invitation which was readily accepted. Amongst the revellers were ex-convicts, Greek and Turkish Cypriots, representatives from the Russian embassy and a number of young men who had been amongst his much favoured 'rough trade'. There was total drunkenness, and fighting broke out. The funeral in his home village of Bradwell in Essex was a more restrained and dignified affair. His coffin was draped with a specially made red flag, over a purple pall, and the mourners were more respectable, including such distinguished figures as Michael Foot, then deputy leader of the Labour Party, and Lady Diana Cooper. His wife, victim of a marriage of convenience, was conspicuous by her absence.

Born in 1905, Tom Driberg was a self-confessed homosexual. He was also a Communist. Having joined the Brighton branch of the Communist Party while still at Lancing College in Sussex, he remained a member throughout his years at Oxford and as a journalist on the *Daily Express*, despite the obvious discrepancies between his private convictions and his lifestyle.

Driberg endured a lonely, confined childhood. In his autobiography, *Ruling Passions*, published in 1977, he quotes part of Philip Larkin's poem from his collection, *High Windows*:

> They fuck you up, your mum and dad.
> They do not mean to but they do.
> They fill you with the faults they had
> And add some extra, just for you.
>
> But they were fucked up in their turn
> By fools in old-style hats and coats,
> Who half the time were soppy-stern
> And half at one another's throats.

Driberg's father, a former chief of police in India, had died when he was fourteen, and he remembered him only as an anonymous Edwardian figure with bad health; but he loved his elderly mother passionately. He became increasingly solitary as he grew into adolescence; his mother had been thirty-nine when he was born, and his two elder brothers were both in their early twenties by the time he was five. Driberg felt he had been 'born out of due time'. His committed – and, later, public – homosexuality began to develop while he was at prep school – which he detested – and he started to make casual encounters in public lavatories when he was an adolescent. He also had a passion for churches – either High Anglican or Roman Catholic – where he discovered religion in an aesthetic sense, loving the mysticism of the mass.

At Lancing, Driberg had a brief courtship with the Labour Party and then, in frustration, joined the Brighton branch of the Communist Party. His membership of the CPGB continued while he was at Oxford, and it was about this time that he first encountered the alleged black magician, Aleister Crowley. They met for lunch at the Eiffel Tower restaurant in London, where Driberg remembered Crowley as wearing well cut plus-fours of hand-woven green tweed, and greeting him donnishly and somewhat inhibitingly with: 'Pardon me while I invoke the moon.' Driberg, however, loved the bizarre, and maintained a friendship with Crowley for many years.

When he left Oxford, Driberg's predilection for the 'rough trade' continued in his frequent sexual encounters with young working-class men that he picked up wherever he could find them. Gravitating naturally to the more eccentric boundaries of London's bohemian life, he attended Edith Sitwell's penny-bun tea-parties, where he met T. S. Eliot and Aldous Huxley. It was through the influence of the Sitwell brothers that he got a job on the *Daily Express*. Beginning as a reporter, he was soon transferred to the 'Talk of London' gossip column, where it was clear that his talents could be usefully deployed. When the column was killed by Beaverbrook, he became a reporter on the sharper William Hickey column.

Driberg first came to Maxwell Knight's attention when he became William Hickey, and Knight lost no time in recruiting him to infiltrate the circles of what Beaverbrook termed 'the Café Communists'. Driberg, who loved intrigue of any kind, was all too anxious to comply. But his use as an infiltrator was questionable: he was far too skittish in his contacts to be 'serious' as an agent. For Knight's sake – and perhaps, also, because of his considerable skill as a journalist – Beaverbrook not only tolerated Driberg's membership of the CPGB but, surprisingly, turned a blind eye to his promiscuity. Driberg wrote satirically about the 'Café Communists' in the 'Londoner's Diary' of the *Evening Standard* of 19 May 1938 (but the piece was not entirely Driberg's, for Beaverbrook had a hand in the writing himself):

The Café Communists are one of the more recent products of our modern social life. They are the gentlemen, often

159

middle-aged, who gather in fashionable restaurants, and, while they are eating the very fine food that is served in those restaurants and drinking the fine wines of France and Spain, they are declaring themselves to be of Left Wing faith.

Among the Café Communists was the distinguished left-wing publisher, Victor Gollancz, who, while not a member of the CPGB, was sympathetic to their views and had, with fellow CP member John Strachey, formed the Left Book Club in March 1936. Knight was interested in the club, as it represented a specific attempt to unite the Communists, Socialists and Liberals of Great Britain. Although its purpose was fronted by the wider ideal of opposing Fascism, Knight had seen behind this from the beginning. During its first year the club had published Palme Dutt's *World Politics 1918–1936*, among a selection of other books that actually promoted Communism, and over the next eighteen months Gollancz and his Left Book Club had reached an amazing subscription figure of fifty thousand. Right up to the beginning of the war, public meetings were frequently organized. Knight was particularly anxious to monitor the actions of Harry Pollitt, the General Secretary of the CPGB, who spoke at some of the meetings. This Driberg was well able to do.

Beaverbrook, in the same 'Londoner's Diary', mischievously commented – enabled to do so by the traditional anonymity of the column:

> Another [Café Communist] is Tom Driberg, the columnist. When taxed with this incongruity between his views and his surroundings, Mr Driberg retorts that he does not see why he should also be a victim of the malnutrition which is an endemic disease of capitalism; that clear thinking need not imply poor feeding; that since the most painful part of his job is to associate occasionally with the rich and powerful, he naturally, on such occasions, needs an anaesthetic; and that he has yet to discover a really 'fine' Spanish wine anyway.

Knight's next step was to ask Driberg if he would report back to him on anything he discovered at the CPGB that would affect the security of the country, and this he promised to do. He was not asked to spy on any one individual or to set up an arrest, but simply to observe. Driberg was not a serious enough party member to regard this behaviour as disloyal, but there was another important factor in his acquiescence. Driberg needed Knight's help to conceal his promiscuity, which was becoming so increasingly public that even Beaverbrook's whitewashing might prove inadequate. When Knight learned that Driberg favoured a particular male brothel in Essex, he gave him a telephone number so that if he ran into problems there he could call for assistance. Knight enjoyed Driberg's company as well as his first-rate journalism, for he was an engaging and witty companion. As an agent, however, he was hardly reliable, regarding the whole business as an exercise in skulduggery. Nevertheless, he had his uses, for he was friendly not only with Harry Pollitt but also with Douglas Springhall, a prominent office-holder in the party, who in 1943 was to be convicted of spying for the Soviets. And quite unwittingly, Driberg served the wider purpose of alerting Knight to the increasing Soviet infiltration of MI5.

It was Anthony Blunt who brought Driberg's work as an MI5 agent to an abrupt end. Blunt was at this time responsible for checking the diplomatic pouches of neutral countries and was part of B1(b), a position he held until 1944. He also represented MI5 at the weekly meetings of the Joint Intelligence Committee. Blunt, although not a member of B5(b), had seen a copy of one of Driberg's reports in someone else's office in St James's Street in London, and at once noted that it referred to Communist knowledge of a secret British aeroplane. It was not possible at that moment for him to identify the writer of the report, as it was signed only by the code-name, M8. Blunt showed the content of the report to his Soviet case officer, who instructed him to discover the identity of M8. Because of the independence of Knight's department from the main body of MI5, this was difficult to achieve, and six months were to pass before Blunt

161

could make any progress. It was when he saw another report from MS which mentioned a book that Driberg had recently published, that Blunt was able to identify him at last.

Retribution from the CPGB came swiftly. Driberg was en route to a branch meeting with a print worker named Harry Kennedy, an old and trusted friend. When they stopped at a pub, he clumsily blurted out that he had been instructed to inform Driberg that he had been expelled from the Communist Party. Considerably shaken, Driberg angrily asked for a reason, but Kennedy replied that he was only a messenger and did not know the exact reason. Horrified, Driberg later went to see the most influential party members he knew – among them, Robin and Olive Page-Arnot and Douglas Springhall. He asked each in turn why he had been expelled, but they were as negative in their responses as Kennedy had been.

There was only one silver lining to the situation: in 1942 Driberg was able to stand for parliament as a left-wing independent, as he could honestly claim to belong to no party. Blunt, however, was furious, for the unsubtle expulsion might have undermined his own position, as it was clear to everyone involved that the denunciation could only have come from MI5 sources.

In March 1981 the British investigative journalist, Chapman Pincher, laid claim to facts concerning Driberg's espionage career, which he published in the *Daily Mail* of Wednesday 23 March and in his book, *Their Trade is Treachery*. Pincher alleged that Driberg was one of the most extraordinary agents that MI5 had ever recruited; his cover was excellent, as no one had ever suspected that the man who was to become chairman of the Labour Party was also employed by the security services.

Pincher claimed that Knight had recruited Driberg much earlier, when he was at Lancing College, and that it was Knight who had told him to join the Brighton branch of the Communist Party. His account of events surrounding Driberg's expulsion from the CPGB tallies with what I have just described, and he goes on to state that although the Russians knew of M8's identity, MI5 continued to employ him when he entered parliament in June 1942. He reported to Knight on the activities of MPs on both sides of the House. After the war, Pincher claimed, the KGB tried to get Driberg to feed false information to Knight. To engineer this, the KGB apparently ordered Harry Pollitt to re-subscribe Driberg as a secret member – a role which, Pollitt assured him, several other MPs were playing. Driberg, however, went to Knight and told him about the offer. Knight instructed him simply to keep his contacts with Pollitt open.

After Driberg had visited Moscow in 1956 to see Guy Burgess about the biography he was writing about him – to be published later as *Guy Burgess: A Portrait with Background* – he informed MI5 that he had been asked by the Russians to give them regular information about the inner workings of the Labour Party. As it happened, he was in a particularly good position to provide this material: he had been elected to the National Executive in 1949, and was to serve on the NEC until he retired from Westminster in 1974. As Labour was currently out of office, MI5 agreed that Driberg could report back as much as he chose, since no official secrets were involved. In return, Driberg guaranteed to use his KGB contacts in MI5's interests.

Pincher further claims that the KGB gave Driberg two identical brief-cases, so that when he handed one with his reports to the Russians in London, they would give him the other, containing bank-notes in payment for the information, in exchange. Driberg was instructed by MI5 to hand over this money, plus copies of his reports. Although he handed over several thousands of pounds, there would appear to be little doubt that he also kept some for himself. Since his reports to the KGB were alleged to contain information on the private lives of senior ministerial colleagues, the KGB could use the material for recruiting purposes – particularly as this information included some salacious and incriminating details. Driberg was reputed to have lent his London flat to parliamentary colleagues for lunchtime assignations with prostitutes, all of which was grist to the mill for his reports to the KGB.

When Driberg travelled to Moscow to see Burgess, in order to work on the biography, he did so with the blessing of both MI5 and the KGB. MI5 apparently understood that his book would be a disinformation exercise, controlled at both manuscript and proof stage by the KGB. MI5 also knew that Driberg would submit the proofs to them for vetting, and that it would be able to 'share' the KGB monitoring of the book. In Driberg's book Burgess denies that he spied for the KGB, and Driberg claims to believe this. MI5, apparently, wanted harder evidence against Burgess, to prevent him from being tempted to return to England, and Pincher believes they instructed Driberg to try to induce him to recollect details of his brief time in the secret wartime Special Operations Executive. They also wanted him to name some of those who had worked with him. Burgess fell neatly into the trap, and Driberg's publishers, Weidenfeld and Nicolson, unaware of the part they were playing in the game, were warned they risked prosecution under the Official Secrets Act unless they removed certain parts of the manuscript before publication. Innocently, they complied, but MI5 had already obtained enough information against Burgess to ensure that he never entered the country again.

In the meantime, Chapman Pincher was approached by 'an outsider' to write a story in his newspaper stating that because of what Burgess had told Driberg, evidence had now been gathered which, since he had committed a provable breach of the Official Secrets Act, could lead to the arrest and prosecution of Burgess, should he ever return to Britain. As a result Burgess was frightened off, and received a triple pay-off from Weidenfeld and Nicolson, MI5 and the KGB, who were equally anxious to keep Burgess out of the United Kingdom.

But MI5, Pincher states, did not trust Driberg, for they suspected him of giving rather more to the Soviets than he admitted in his reports to MI5. In 1969 this suspicion was reinforced, when the Czech director, Josef Frolik, gave information against several Labour MPs, and in particular against a senior Labour MP who was reputed to be a homosexual and who had been recruited by Czech Intelligence and given the code-name 'Crocodile'. Frolik later identified Crocodile as Driberg, from photographs shown to him by MI5. When interrogated, Driberg told his case officer that he had merely written a few articles for Czech journals. After more questioning, however, he revealed that he had sold them additional information about internal squabbles in the Labour Party and various personal scandals. 'All useless stuff,' he claimed, further admitting that he had continued to do this while chairman of the Labour Party. There was little that MI5 could do about these revelations, apart from warning Driberg about the dangers of passing on information that had not been vetted by them. The very last thing they wanted to do was to make it public knowledge that they had employed the chairman of the Labour Party as a double agent. Despite his unreliability, MI5 continued to use him, even when he had been elevated to the Lords as Baron Bradwell – whereupon he came to be known in MI5 circles as 'Lord of the Spies'.

After Driberg died in 1976, MI5 became convinced that he had been controlled by the KGB since the end of the war. Although he had moved further to the left, there was also the strong possibility that he might have been blackmailed. Certainly, he had left himself wide open to such a move. Pincher claims that the KGB had a large number of incriminating photographs of Driberg, including some of him in a homosexual situation with Burgess.

As a result of Pincher's claims, Michael Foot sprang strongly to Driberg's defence, describing the accusations as 'one of the most extraordinary allegations in the British Press in recent times'. Speaking at the annual Press awards of Mirror Group Newspapers, Foot added:

No more serious accusation has been made against the Secret Services of either country. I am not sure which must be the most offended. It is a more extraordinary fact that this allegation never came out in his lifetime. You could

165

have transformed Tom Driberg into one of the heroes of his time . . . right from his early public school days he risked his career at every stage in order to serve the one true love of his life, the Secret Service.

In 1981 Michael Foot praised Margaret Thatcher for her criticism in the Commons of *The Trade is Treachery*, the book in which the allegations against Driberg were published. In denying the allegations, the Prime Minister stated in the House on 26 March of that year that 'parts of the book contained unsubstantiated claims, were inaccurate or distorted.'

When Driberg returned to Moscow in 1956 to go through the proofs of his biography with Burgess, he spent time both in a flat in Moscow and in Burgess's dacha, which was carefully guarded by security men. Burgess was lonely, and was working part-time for the Foreign Literature Publishing House, which he had just persuaded to publish Graham Greene's *The Quiet American*. He also sat on various committees connected with Western policy in international affairs. Driberg had first met Burgess before the war when the latter was editor of 'The Week in Westminster' on BBC radio; he had chosen Driberg several times to present the programme. In his autobiography, *Ruling Passions*, Driberg writes:

Neither the British nor the Soviet Secret Service need feel disturbed by my reference to the private and, we believed, unmonitored talks I had with Guy. We traded no national secrets. We gossiped about life in London; he gave me messages for former lovers. The theme that he constantly reverted to was the possibility that he might some day be able without danger to come home to England.

According to Pincher, Driberg betrayed Burgess for money and effectively prevented him from ever returning. Driberg, for his part, claims that Burgess asked him to negotiate a safe-conduct return for him. But Driberg insists that he always told him the same thing, either face to face or on the telephone from

England when he had to ask for him by his Russian name, Jim Andreyevitch Eliot – that no British government could possibly give that kind of assurance in advance, and that any possible hope of returning entirely hinged on the prevailing international climate of the time. Also – Driberg posed the dreaded question – would the Russian authorities let him go, anyway?

Pincher's allegations that Driberg betrayed Burgess are unlikely to be correct; he was too humane a man to prevent Burgess' possible return, however pressing his own financial problems were. But there is always the possibility that, knowing Burgess' return was impossible unless there was some massive *détente*, he *did* accept MI5 money for encouraging Burgess to break the Official Secrets Act.

On 15 September 1956 the *Daily Express* reported: 'Mr Tom Driberg, former Socialist MP for Maldon, Essex, said when he arrived at London Airport from Russia last night that it was "utter nonsense" to label the missing Foreign Office diplomat Guy Burgess, now in Moscow, as a traitor.' Driberg told the *Express* that he was convinced Burgess had acted in good faith, and had done nothing contrary to British interests. He went on to state that Burgess had gone to Moscow with Donald Maclean because of his political beliefs, and that he entirely denied any allegations that he was a Communist agent or had ever given any secret information to the Russians. When asked how he had contacted Burgess, Driberg replied that he had merely written to him and, to his astonishment, had received a reply. He added that he used to know him 'slightly'. In his letter Driberg had told Burgess that he was coming to Moscow, and that he would like to see him to talk over the whole story. Burgess had agreed to the meeting. When Driberg got to Moscow, Burgess had informed him that he hoped to come back to England in due course. When asked by the *Express* when this might be, Driberg replied that he had no idea, and that Burgess found the job he was doing in Moscow both satisfying and interesting. Somewhat disarmingly, Driberg admitted: 'He realizes, being a realist, that he would not get another job with the Foreign Office, and he is not the sort of person who would do any work of which he was

167

ashamed.' He went on to explain that Burgess worked in a foreign languages publishing house, which published translations of Soviet books, and that there was no question of him drafting important speeches for Soviet leaders. He concluded his interview by pointing out that he did not agree with the action that Burgess and Maclean had taken, because 'I believe there are other ways of doing it.' Nevertheless, he also considered that Burgess was 'perfectly right to do what he did, feeling as he did'.

Predictably, Tom Driberg's marriage of convenience to Ena Binfield, when they were both forty-six, was not to last. A widow, Ena was the secretary of the Marie Curie Hospital in Hampstead and had been a Socialist member of the West Suffolk County Council. She originally regarded Driberg as a confirmed bachelor reprobate in need of reform, and it is likely that she briskly dismissed rumours of his rampant homosexuality. But her campaign of reform was disastrous; within months Driberg disliked his new wife so much that he moved into a separate wing of his country home at Bradwell. Soon he would not even drink out of the same cup, and eventually Ena moved out of the house and into a cottage at Chorley Wood.

Driberg noted in his diary in June 1951: 'Married today, at the age of forty-six, for the first (and, I feel sure, only) time in my life ... When I woke this morning, I didn't feel so much frightened as dazed – dazed and rather unreal, and as if my bones were not quite solid. I couldn't eat any breakfast.' His best man, John Freeman, then a television presenter and later a television executive, called for Driberg in good time, bringing dark-red carnation buttonholes. Fortunately, Driberg still had half a bottle of brandy which he had recently brought home from France, and after a few nips he felt a little stronger. Their car stopped at the sacristy door of the church and they looked in: there at the far side, in the half-light, stood an Oxford contemporary of Driberg's, Cyril Eastaugh, Bishop of Kensington, a tall figure in purple, who was to perform this travesty of a marriage service. Between them, the bishop and Canon Frederic Hood of Pusey House in Oxford took Tom and Ena through the essential part of the ritual. Ena told the *Express* afterwards: 'When that frightful moment of tension – ". . . or else hereafter for ever hold his peace" – had passed in silence, I puffed a "Phew!" of relief which made the flames on the altar candles flicker.' Only some of the guests knew that poor Ena, who was of Jewish parentage but who had lapsed in the faith, had become a Christian only a few months before.

As to the wedding music, Driberg decided to play a trick on his newspaper colleagues. He wrote in his diary:

The final item on the music paper . . . read:

ORGAN MUSIC
Choral Prelude on an old German tune
('O Tannenbaum', Benjamin Frankel (1906–   )

He wanted to find out how sharp-eyed and well educated modern newspapermen were – for this was the tune of the Red Flag. He knew that by playing the Socialist anthem at his wedding in a well known London church he was providing material for the sort of story that popular newspapers loved. Also, he was thinking what a wonderful Hickey column he could have written about the wedding!

The twenty-five years between wedding and funeral were a time of great suffering for Ena, but she remained studiedly loyal to Driberg until the end. It was she who requested that a red flag should cover his coffin. The reason she gave was that the Red Flag had been sung at their wedding and that as she could not expect to have it sung at his funeral, she was doing the next best thing. But finding one was easier said than done. The Labour Party was contacted, Transport House was scoured – but no red flag could be found. Eventually, one was made overnight by a London company of flag-makers, and draped over the coffin the next day.

Sir John Betjeman read the address, and Dr Mervyn Stockwood, Bishop of Southwark, conducted the service. Michael Foot, Geoffrey Bing QC and Lord and Lady Gordon-Walker occupied the extreme left wing of the church, while other mourners included Joan Littlewood, Lord Strabolgi, Labour Party Secretary, Ron Hayward and Mr Isaac Berman, a survivor from Buchenwald who had been befriended by Driberg. Driberg had given strict instructions that the service should be conducted in the High Anglican tradition that he had loved since his schooldays. An 'antipanegyric' was delivered by the Vicar of St Matthew's, Westminster. Driberg had specially requested that this should be performed by a 'discreet, learned and godly clerk of my acquaintance'. The service was conducted by Trevor Huddleston, Bishop of Stepney. Driberg had wanted it to be in Latin, but this was eventually vetoed as being too complex an undertaking. In an address, Dr Stockwood described Driberg as 'a gadfly, a searcher for truth':

> Of his loyalty to the Socialist cause there was no question. But the expression of that loyalty had led to the raising of eyebrows and perhaps to distrust that prevented him from achieving high office. I think the explanation is to be found in his fear – of an Establishment of any sort.
>
> Tom suspected that once a man, a party, or a cause became successful, visions perished and ideals were corrupted by expediency. That is why he criticized party decisions and refused to toe the party line. That is why he failed to conform.

Ena told the *Daily Express*:

> I only look pretty fit and remain upright because I'm living on a drug. Without it I'd be dead in a flash, and eventually it will kill me anyway. I've really come to the end of a useful life – and Tom's finished his. Though we lived apart since 1971, there was never any real animosity or bitterness between us. We had twenty years of marriage. I won't say what they were like, that would be disloyal. I always admired and had a huge respect for Tom's journalistic skills, political power and championship of the underdog.

If that admiration didn't extend to our personal life, well, that's a purely private matter.

She added caustically that she did not want to be known as Lady Bradwell because she had always disapproved of the House of Lords, feeling that this august body should be abolished and replaced by a senate. Returning to the tragic theme of their private life, she said that she and Tom had parted without rancour. She had in no real way shared his life. He had taken a London flat in the Barbican, and she had gone to live with her sister. She was deeply concerned that it was somehow demeaning and squalid to die, as her husband had, in a London taxi. She added that, although she had known that Tom had been writing his memoirs and she had heard that they were revealing, she had never read them, nor seen the manuscript. In fact, Robert Boothby, the journalist, MP and peer, had advised Driberg against publishing his memoirs until after his death, because the contents would be so inflammatory.

Gerrard Irvine, a priest and a long-standing friend of Driberg's, had as vivid a memory of the funeral as he had of the man himself. One of the ushers, another friend of Driberg's, an antique dealer called Brian Bell, had kept putting people in eccentric positions and 'camping up the way the seating was arranged'; Michael Foot as a Chapel man, had been shocked. During the sixties, Driberg had moved into the clergy lodging house while selling his house, but he had failed to look after himself there, and would eat cold soup from a tin. He was, nevertheless, socially very fussy about food, and would crusade for the reform of London restaurants. He lived expensively, and his favourite restaurant was The Gay Hussar in Soho. 'Yet he was very unpleasant to waiters and I avoided going to restaurants with him. He was also utterly ruthless in the sense that he would always get what he wanted.' Irvine's reminiscences built up a very exact picture of Driberg's personality: as well as being promiscuous, he was generally self-indulgent, histrionically religious and highly intolerant. Yet, at the same time, he was a very warm person, 'witty, friendly and a very good constituency

171

MP with a deliciously dry sense of humour'. He shared the distinction, with his great friend John Betjeman, of having been contemporary prep school boys with foreign names. But Betjeman determined to conquer and charm, and Driberg to 'fuck things up'. He was, apparently, often personally funded by upper-class contacts and other friends and acquaintances, including Edith Sitwell, of whom he was a protégé; John Rainer, ex-editor of the *Daily Express*; Beverley Baxter, Tory MP and another ex-editor of the *Express*; and Maurice Oldfield, head of MI6 from 1973 to 1978. Irvine felt that Driberg was ambivalent, and went to extremes in everything. 'He was very patriotic, but would prefer England to be Communist-run. Yet he was dead against Russia or anti-libertarian policies. Tom failed to examine his conscience,' concluded Irvine. 'And, of course, any spy must be a double spy.'

Driberg was essentially a journalist, with no great wish to make creative use of the rich vein of MI5 and KGB material he had quarried for so long. He really did care about Communism, even though he was essentially a 'Café Communist'. Like Muggeridge, he could not take spying seriously, and played as many games with MI5 as he did with the KGB. Driberg loved a good gossip, and he found spying to be the stuff of which excellent anecdotes are wrought. Unfortunately, he was effectively prevented from publishing a lot of what he could have told, by a piece of legislation that has in recent years been singularly unsuccessful in muzzling so many others – the Official Secrets Act. But if he was unable to make use of his material, MI5 made very good use of him.

CHAPTER NINE

JOHN BINGHAM:
THE PATRIOTIC SPY

A dramatic change in MI5 leadership occurred in the summer of 1940, when the National Security Executive was created to officially supervise all British security agencies. Vernon Kell was forced to resign, and ex-policeman Harker was appointed in his place. In his turn, Brigadier 'Jasper' Harker was soon replaced by Sir David Petrie. Appointed by the chairman of the Security Executive, Lord Swinton, he revolutionized the organization. Petrie was determined to appoint officers from a variety of different backgrounds. Maxwell Knight's department, B5(b), was an example of this policy in microcosm.

'Good things of day begin to droop and drowse,
Whiles night's black agents to their preys do rouse.
Thou marvellest at my words; but hold thee still:
Things bad begun make strong themselves by ill.'

Macbeth, III, ii

John Bingham is not only a highly underrated writer of extremely authentic thrillers based upon his experience in MI5, but he is also one of the few public defenders of the British Secret Service. He takes great issue with John le Carré's sceptical view of MI5 and MI6, contending that he has done irreparable damage to the Service with his attitudes and his writing. Bingham's views on this subject are discussed more fully in chapter 12.

John Michael Ward Bingham succeeded to the title of Baron Clanmorris of Ireland in 1960. Born in November 1908,

173

Bingham was educated at Cheltenham and then spent three years in France and Germany studying languages. He began his working life as a journalist on the *Hull Daily Mail*, moving on to the *Sunday Dispatch*, for which he eventually became picture editor.

His wife, the biographer Madeleine Bingham, writes: 'Perhaps being on a newspaper filled with reports of the rise of the Nazis and the persecution of the Jews made us more politically aware than most people. More sensitive to the possibility of war. Besides, in 1936, we had been living in Chelsea, and we had seen Mosley's blackshirts marching down the King's Road.' Bingham was short-sighted and initially unable to join a regiment, but eventually, by learning the sight-testing board by heart, he managed to get into the Royal Engineers. At the time of his conscription, he and his wife started the British Democratic Party, which opposed the idea of appeasement, and it was through this new political group that Bingham enthusiastically tried to come to grips with his first spy.

When a German national named Schavroth applied for membership of the British Democratic Party, Bingham, brought up on a diet of Buchan and Childers, was immediately suspicious. He could not understand why a German should want to oppose his own country, particularly as Schavroth also happened to work for an armaments factory. Gradually, the hopeful Bingham made up his mind that Schavroth must be a spy. Determined to bring him to justice, Bingham wrote to his uncle, Herbert Dixon, a Westminster MP, asking to be put in touch with the Intelligence Service. But Dixon was more concerned with Bingham's involvement with the British Democratic Party. He summoned him to the House of Commons, and pointed out that it was forbidden for a Territorial Army officer to organize political parties. Although Bingham defended himself on the grounds that he was no more than a humble RE driver, Uncle Herbert was still not amused. But he did promise to have Schavroth investigated, and Bingham awaited the results with the calm certainty that he had done his duty – and that a major spy was about to be unmasked.

Much to Bingham's dismay, Schavroth turned out to be quite innocent. Nevertheless, the investigation provided an entrée for Bingham into security circles, for a few weeks later he was asked to go for an interview at MI5 headquarters. There he found himself in a bleak room, bare of furniture except for a desk, behind which sat Maxwell Knight, the veteran MI5 officer responsible for counter-subversion. Knight was an extraordinary character. Student of the occult, ardent cricketer, jazz musician and self-taught naturalist, he was in later life to become one of the best-loved naturalists on BBC radio Children's Hour and natural history programmes. He was also one of Ian Fleming's models for M, James Bond's boss.

Knight's work for MI5 had already been extremely successful; he had planted agents in the Communist Party of Great Britain and in the British Union of Fascists, as well as exposing the Communist-inspired Woolwich Arsenal spy ring in 1938. His private life, however, had been a disaster; his first wife committed suicide and his two subsequent marriages were tense. Knight was one of the most ambiguous and mysterious figures in MI5, gathering around him in the late 1930s an elite group of young case officers in Department B5(b), MI5's most secret outpost in Dolphin Square, an exclusive block of flats on the Thames Embankment. Bingham remembers his first encounter with Knight: 'He was good-looking in a hawk-like sort of way with a large, beaky nose. He laughed easily and could have been a model for one of Buchan's heroes. He was dressed in grey tweeds to match his hair and was aged about forty.' The interview was followed by anti-climax, and Bingham returned to his picture editor's desk in Fleet Street. Over the next few months Knight occasionally sent for him, asking him questions about Fascist-inclined journalists. Sometimes he could answer the questions, sometimes not, but gradually he realized that his role as 'spy' in the *Daily Mail/Sunday Dispatch* offices might have some importance, for at one time their proprietor Lord Rothermere had been a Mosley supporter.

Then, in the spring of 1940, Bingham received a letter from Knight asking him to consider a position in MI5 at a salary of

£400 a year. Madeleine Bingham remembered that her husband rang her from Aldershot and told her he had agreed to Knight's proposition and that the army were releasing him immediately. 'I couldn't believe it. Jack in the Secret Service – in wartime. It was the most marvellous thing I had ever heard. Jack had become one of Buchan's heroes – except that he didn't have a good club, or a home in Scotland. The Press Club would hardly do.' But Knight did not want a brood of Richard Hannays; he wanted a group of adaptable young men who could fit into most social backgrounds. Amongst his more recent recruits were Bill Younger, the stepson of the occult writer Dennis Wheatley, and a detective novelist in his own right under the pseudonym of William Mole; an ex-journalist named Norman Himsworth who was responsible for supervising anti-Communist operations; and the playboy Tony Gilson. Bingham began work at Dolphin Square immediately, discovering that one suite was used as an office and the other for sleeping and as a safe house. He was under the close supervision of Knight, who insisted that he tell Madeleine nothing. His comings and goings were as erratic as when he had been a reporter on the *Dispatch*, so he aroused no comment from friends or relatives.

It quickly became apparent to Bingham that Knight had chosen his trusted few with particular care, as he made no distinction between 'officers' and 'agents'. They had to be completely versatile, sometimes functioning as Intelligence officers in interviews with recruits or suspects, and sometimes acting as agents themselves. Knight took the view that in counter-espionage agents had to be a hundred per cent trustworthy; he could trust no man more than his own officers. The atmosphere was light-hearted, and there were frequent joking references to 'the constant coming and going of keen hawk-eyed men'. As all of Knight's case officers were on the short side, and none remotely resembled a hawk, their very ordinariness seemed hilariously funny. They also amused themselves with phrases from Buchan and his imitators.

Knight's greatest wartime coup was the arrest of Anna Wolkoff and Tyler Kent. The two had been implicated in

176

stealing copies of top secret correspondence between Roosevelt and Churchill which, if revealed, could have brought down the Roosevelt administration and prevented America from entering the war. All his department shared the honours for this feat, and Bingham now gained first-hand experience of how methodically Knight worked. But as his wife wrote later, Bingham himself had humbler tasks:

> Out in the darkness, in the black-out in his second-hand car, with the searchlights sweeping the sky, he went about doing his best with his small piece of war. One of the few things he prided himself on was that he was never late for an appointment with an agent, whatever the 'discouragement', as he called it, in the way of bombs or falling shrapnel. 'It would be awkward if the agent arrived on time and was killed and you were not,' he once said.

When hostilities started in earnest in 1940, Bingham began a round-up of suspect foreigners, arranging for those with apparent or alleged Nazi or Fascist leanings to be interned on the Isle of Man. Madeleine eventually went to work as a secretary at MI5's new headquarters at Blenheim Palace in Oxfordshire. There she would sit at her typewriter, surrounded by portraits of the Marlborough family on the panelled walls and warmed by a twentieth-century coal fire in an eighteenth-century grate. Some accounts of the offices in MI5's various outposts – Blenheim, the 'Scrubs' (Wormwood Scrubs, the prison) – give the impression that the typists, secretaries and registry girls (filing clerks) were all dotty debs who regarded security as something of a joke. But Madeleine found all the staff highly security-conscious. Most of them were the daughters or wives of servicemen (the men were mainly based at Wormwood Scrubs, which was known as the 'sharp end'). Most of her colleagues lived in the cheerless surroundings of Keble College, where a visit to the bathroom required a trek across a Victorian Gothic courtyard. But Knight and his staff were completely separate, and did not concern themselves with such mundane tasks as filing, vetting or checking. They operated entirely from Dolphin Square, and it was only when Knight had to attend a top-level conference at Blenheim that he would appear resplendent in the uniform of a major – a uniform he was not really entitled to wear. Bingham told me:

> Knight was a tremendous leader. He loved the intrigue of it all and we would follow him anywhere. When the bombs came, Max clucked round like a mother hen, for he regarded us as his family . . . we were all of different shapes and sizes – Max with his enormous nose and Bill Younger who was very short. We used to call ourselves Knight's Black Agents after the passage from Macbeth.

Bingham was to call one of his spy novels *Night's Black Agent*.

Salaried at £400 a year (free of tax because MI5 did not officially exist), Bingham worked with Knight until the end of the war. Then, in 1946, he went to Hanover as an Intelligence officer. His job was to investigate the hundreds of potentially dubious refugees that were milling rootlessly around the town. His first impressions of Hanover were hauntingly described in his journal:

> A grey picture of desolation. The wide streets of large houses are piled high on each side with rubble. All is grey, the streets with their potholes and tram-rails, the houses and often the sky. The iron girders in the dome of the great *Stadthalle* are half-exposed. The clothes of the inhabitants are colourless. So are their faces; so are, in many cases, the faces of the children. Or if not colourless then an unhealthy yellow. The people have no road sense. Pedestrians seem not to hear approaching cars, and rarely look before crossing a road. Cyclists put out their arms, and then turn left or right without a glance behind, seeming to imagine that they are magically protected by the mere act of putting out their arms.

Many buildings had glassless windows and bomb-splintered walls. The remaining houses had makeshift chimneys sticking out of the insides, as evidence of human occupation. There was a zoo containing a few miserable animals; one or two large factories were still functioning, such as the Hannomag motor-works and the Continental Gummiwerke. Enormous queues formed in the rain for the trams which always ran in threes. On the back of the last car was a notice which read in English: 'Do not pass a stationary tram. Do not pass on the left side.' But nobody took any notice.

Bingham watched the passers-by stare at him blankly, neither hatred nor curiosity in their eyes. If he spoke to them, they would react politely, helpfully, in a wholly depersonalized way. Some men wore overcoats that came down almost to their ankles; others still wore their *Wehrmacht* uniform, shabby and torn as it was. Younger women wore knee-length socks – usually white with garter tabs, like the boys. Others wore pathetic red skirts made from torn-up Nazi flags. Shops contained the bare minimum of goods, while cotton, needles, wool, combs, scissors, kettles, pots and pans were impossible to find. Matches were rationed to one box a month, and coats were often made out of old dyed army blankets. It took six months to get lenses made for spectacles, no coal was being issued, and wood stocks were either inaccessible or unavailable. As for the attitude towards the military government – it wavered between bitterness and an apathetic acceptance that although they might mean well, they were cripplingly incompetent.

Bingham's schedule was exacting, and he would often work on state papers until 3 a.m. Many dealt with the Russian occupied zone, and the fate of those suspected by the Muscovites of espionage for the English or Americans. Among the inducements to 'talk' employed by the Russians was the infamous *Wasserkarzer* – the pouring of ice-cold water over naked victims at ten-minute intervals. This might continue for two to fourteen hours, and was only used in winter, when a film of ice eventually formed on the body. At the time, Bingham felt there was an air of unreality about the Russian Intelligence

Service, who appeared to be using up vast resources spying on the British zone, where so little that happened could have been of any interest to them. Then he wondered if their presence was no more than some giant peacetime exercise – a training scheme. Eventually he came to the conclusion that the Russian was still 'a semi-Asiatic child who has now grown up, and to this child Security work and espionage is the essence of living.'

One of the Russians to be interrogated by Bingham was Florentski. He had been captured by the Germans and put to work with other prisoners; then when the Germans retreated, he had escaped to Czechoslovakia where he had lived and worked for a time. The Czechs had clearly stated that Russian ex-prisoners of war would not be forced to return to Russia; there was no doubt in his mind that he did not want to go back, and he had even felt sufficiently secure to plan to marry. He was an officer, he later told Bingham; the war had interrupted his law studies, and so he had registered with the Czech police. But then an ominous new law was introduced insisting that Russian POWs be returned to Russia. Florentski, flinging away his new life in a desperate instinct for self-preservation, fled first to the US zone and then to the British zone. In Hanover he went to the town hall, told the truth and asked for papers and ration-cards with naïve confidence, assuring the authorities that he wanted to live and work in Hanover. He was immediately arrested.

The directive that Bingham had received from the zone authorities was unequivocal:

> All Russian subjects who were members of the Russian armed forces on or after 22 June 1941, and who have not been officially discharged, will be handed to the appropriate authorities for repatriation.

When he asked Florentski what exactly happened to Russian prisoners of war who were repatriated, he told him that they, and their families also, received very bad treatment indeed, for the Russians took the line that any soldier who surrendered was a traitor, and he could be 'sent away' for many years. As to those who obviously had not wanted to return to Russia, their fate appeared to be far worse: Florentski told Bingham that he would be shot.

Bingham was horrified. For a while, he wondered if Florentski was exaggerating, simply in order to stay in the West and to marry. Certainly, that explanation was very likely. When Bingham told him that it was his duty to return him to Russia, Florentski retorted: 'If you send me back they will shoot me. Why don't *you* shoot me Herr Major?' Something in his eyes told Bingham that he could not take the moral responsibility of returning him to his own country. Without checking with his superiors, without any authorization, he gave Florentski a new identity and German papers. The man then disappeared into the devastated streets.

Another of Bingham's interviewees was a Ukranian called Nowosiliski, a massive figure dressed all in black, with a beret on his large bald head. He was extremely agitated, claiming to have been arrested while buying an accordion at a displaced persons' camp. Because they believed he had arrived there with Russian repatriation officers, the senior administrators at the camp had accused him of being a Russian agent. Nowosiliski appeared outraged at the accusation, claiming that he had been imprisoned by the NKVD (the People's Committee of Internal Affairs, the forerunner of the KGB) and that he had a wife and a child in a DP camp at Meerbeck; he said he was a musician and wanted to use the accordion to earn money to buy food for his family. It was all very suspicious, yet Bingham decided to release him. So he, too, disappeared into the streets, leaving Bingham wondering if he was either too gullible or too soft-hearted to stay on in his present job.

Writing with detachment yet with compassion, qualities which were later to be characteristic of his novels, Bingham's journal entries present some strikingly vivid images of post-war Germany:

> Out of the sleet and the biting cold into Hanover station –
> bomb battered, dingy, dirty from day and night use – come
> thousands of men, women and children – refugees from the

181

East. Businessmen in shabby, shiny suits, clutching attaché cases, women with mysterious, bulging clothes, bartering jewellery or blankets, or anything they possess, for food, for farmers don't want money.

Deep shadows, a few weak electric lights, draughts, the strange, musty smell formed by a mixture of German ration soap, German tobacco, and German perspiration.

In the main hall of the station, Bingham watched a mother with a cheap pram in which a young child lay. Two other children stood beside her. The family were isolated beneath the electric bulb, as if illuminated by an overhead searchlight. The woman was sallow and bovine, and wore glasses. Miserable and bewildered, she seemed to be searching for someone. The wide stairs leading down to the subways and the 'bunkers' – the former air-raid shelters – were choked with wandering people. Men, women and children sat on the steps, or on suitcases. Some lay asleep across boxes; others ate crusts of bread, and all wore the same sombre, dingy clothes that he had noticed on his arrival in the city. Motionless, with eyes that were dull and weary, they awaited trains that might be hours late. Once on board, they would stand packed tight in cold corridors, patient and inert.

Down in these bunker subways up to three thousand people huddled together; some were there because it was warmer than at home, and some because they had no home at all. Some were also there to trade on the black market. Inside the bunkers there were tables, chairs and a counter where hot drinks could be bought for coupons. One evening, Bingham saw three men with an accordion, singing, surrounded by a crowd who occasionally joined in. The familiar smell was omnipresent, hitting the newcomer in the face like a warm wall. He noticed one woman, perhaps seventy years old, with grey, streaky hair, squatting on a trunk. Her head was resting on her arms, her knees drawn up, her eyes closed. A child, one of many, lay sprawled across the end of the trunk, her yellow hair tangled and dirty – grotesque, like a doll tossed down by a giant.

182

In the middle of the room the air was so thick and foul that it threatened to choke him. He noticed groups of long-haired, grubby youths, plotting and trading in cigarettes and other unobtainable goods. They looked as if they would like to provoke an 'incident', to attack, rob and be gone before the *Bahnhofpolizei* could arrive. He knew they would boast of their exploits later.

Petty thieving was rife. Members of one of the larger gangs, who called themselves the Edelweiss Pirates, were interrogated by Bingham, who wanted to find out whether their stealing was casual, or organized as a subversive activity. One such pirate, who was just twenty, with a yellow-grey face, stubble chin, and a sullen expression, had not worked since the war ended, and because he was so used to being a gang member, was much discomfited at finding himself alone in a cell with Bingham. Claiming to be 'carrying on the fight against the Occupation', he and his gang stole spare wheels, luggage, cars – and resold them on the black market. They robbed and beat up Polish and British soldiers, and ran protection rackets on cafés. They were the typical residue of defeat.

Bingham was regularly involved in Intelligence raids on displaced persons' camps. The camps housed Ukrainians, Hungarians, Poles, Belgians, Czechs, Bulgarians and other displaced nationals. The huts had wooden floors and bunks. Some contained men only; others, with curtained-off bunks, were allocated to married couples.

The raiders, whose object was to round up security suspects and to try and discover any black-market operatives, would set out in trucks and jeeps at around 11.30 p.m. and arrive near the camp at midnight, leaving their vehicles about two hundred yards from the perimeter fence, with their lights out. Simultaneously, British Army soldiers, Intelligence officers and Kripo (German criminal police) would make their way to the camp on foot. Two soldiers would be sent to the entrance of each hut (which together housed two thousand or more), to prevent anyone leaving. Then Intelligence officers, NCOs and German police would check those inside and search their belongings.

These raids made a vivid impression on Bingham. He described one such in his journal. On the arrival of Bingham's team of investigators, everyone was ordered out of bed. Bewildered, people stirred, sat up. They were in pants and shirts, and some of the men wore night-caps, which somehow accentuated their vulnerability. The remains of simple meals lay on the tables; boxes of personal possessions – shoes and indescribable rags and odds and ends – littered the floor.

At the hut used by the camp police, Ukrainians in khaki with an armband marked CP – the commander wore a special one with 'Chief Constable' engraved on it in gold letters – everyone was standing around looking forlorn. One or two Intelligence officers were also waiting. Eventually, the suspects were shown in, usually singly, between soldiers with fixed bayonets. Amongst the haul that night were two girls from Berlin without papers; one woman whose husband had been admitted to hospital and had taken her papers as well as his own; a Frenchman whose papers were not in order; a jackbooted German youth, round-faced, red-haired, defiant, who had lost his papers. Bingham made notes of this last interrogation, recording each line of the truculent dialogue:

'Where are you from?'
'Halle.'
'Russian zone?'
'Ja.'
'Where are your papers?'
'I've lost them.'
'When did you arrive?'
'The day before yesterday.'
'How did you come to Hanover?'
'Over the frontier.'
'Why?'
'To get a job in Nordheim.'
'Where did you spend last night?'
'In Hanover.'
'Where?'

184

'In Kleefeld district.'

'Where?'

'I don't know the name of the street.'

'Yes you do.'

'No I don't.'

'How did you know there were jobs in Nordheim?'

'I read it in the paper.'

'Which paper?'

'*Hanover News.*'

'How?'

'It was sent to me at Halle.'

'By whom?'

'My uncle.'

'Jobs in Nordheim are not advertised in the *Hanover News.*'

'Yes they are.'

Bingham had had so much experience of interrogation by now that he intuitively knew that there was something very wrong about the replies that young German had been giving him. He could not define exactly what – he was relying on an old familiar feeling that he had come to trust. Perhaps the boy's answers were too glib, as though he had expected the questions; perhaps he was too self-possessed. Either way, Bingham made sure he was detained. In all, seven suspects were detained for further questioning that night, and four black-marketeers were handed over to the Kripo. In the early hours of the next morning the suspects were put into a truck and driven off under armed guard. The red-haired German boy took care to sit at the back, and when the truck slowed down at a corner, he suddenly dived out, turned a somersault in the road, and disappeared. Three shots were fired after him, but he got away. Bingham knew his hunch had been correct, but he was not too worried – the boy was probably only a low-grade Russian agent, anyway.

Amongst Bingham's fellow officers in the mess was 'B', an Austrian victim of the confusion of war. When Tobruk was about to fall in June 1942, he had had the choice of either escaping or of sacrificing the opportunity in order that a Czech officer on the German 'black list' might have the same chance. He chose the latter, despite the fact that his fiancée was waiting for him in Austria. His track record of sacrifice was to continue. When his fellow prisoners, denied water by the Italians, were dying of thirst, it was B, by now exhausted and himself ill, who halted a German column moving up the lines; the Germans gave the prisoners water from their bottles. And it was also B – who spoke fluent German – who liaised in the camps between the British and the Germans, and helped to organize escapes. When surrender came, it was B and an NCO who were detailed to go to the jail in Brunswick and liberate the political prisoners. Bingham described B in his journal: 'He would smile his slow, wide smile which stretched right across his parchment-like face and made his brown eyes gleam behind the spectacles; a smile which is so wide that, combined with wisps of hair which eternally stick up from the back of his head, it gives him rather the appearance of a newly hatched thrush.' But B's smile must have faded when he returned to Vienna and found that his fiancée had married while he was in captivity.

In 1948, Bingham returned to England. Maxwell Knight invited him to rejoin his old department at MI5, and he was to work in counter-subversion for the next twenty years. He never lost his humanity, treating his agents as a social worker would have done, and continuing to believe in the traditional methods. Unimpressed by MI5's growing dependence on bugs and electronic equipment, Bingham once commented typically to his wife: 'Nothing beats an agent in the right place. Bugs can't tell you who is sleeping with whom, who is jealous of his superiors and fed up with his job – and who is drinking.'

In 1952, Bingham published his first book, *My Name is Michael Sibley*; he went on to write more cool, highly credible and precise spy thrillers such as *Murder Plan Six* (1958), *Night's Black Agent* (1960), *The Double Agent* (1966) and *God's Defector* (1976). In his foreword to *The Double Agent* he spoke of his concern for the image of MI5.

There are currently two schools of thought about our Intelligence Services. One school is convinced that they are staffed by murderous, powerful, double-crossing cynics, the other that the taxpayer is supporting a collection of bumbling, broken-down layabouts. It is possible to think that both extremes of thought are the result of a mixture of unclear reasoning, ignorance and possibly political or temperamental wishful thinking.

Bingham's own view of MI5, as reflected in his novels, is an efficient service with its roots essentially in unswerving loyalty. He believed that intelligence gathering was slow, patient work and that the Russians were the first to appreciate this point, not minding if they took twenty years to put an agent in the right place. Bingham felt that their love of their country was their great strength and that lack of patriotism was correspondingly Britain's great weakness. His own principal quality as a writer is his understanding of human nature with all its failings. He always maintained that it would be the easiest thing in the world to be a traitor. A wife who trusts her husband can easily be betrayed, and the same applies to fellow Intelligence officers. Bingham used to tell his wife that the Russians had more defectors than the West, but didn't publicize them! What Bingham could never accept was John le Carré's 'Circus' (see chapter 12), with its manipulation, double standards and continual undertones of betrayal. From the moment *The Spy Who Came in from the Cold* was published, he vigorously campaigned against the erosion of the British Secret Service's image. But with the defection of Burgess and Maclean, and later Philby, that image was irrevocably tarnished.

CHAPTER TEN

DENNIS WHEATLEY: THE WOULD-BE SPY

At the outbreak of the Second World War, part of MI5 had been moved to the then abandoned prison at Wormwood Scrubs. It was a vulnerable target for bombs: one direct hit could have destroyed thousands of files on suspected persons. Later, when one section was moved to St James's Street in central London, Dennis Wheatley's wife, Joan, was put in charge of the allocation of petrol for the car pool, while his stepdaughter, Diana, worked as a filing clerk. His stepson, Bill Younger, was to work for Maxwell Knight's highly secret B5(b) department at Dolphin Square on the Thames embankment. It was becoming very much a family affair.

'I had the interesting experience of watching a real live Mata Hari knocking back our cocktails at No. 8.'

Dennis Wheatley, *Drink and Ink*

Dennis Wheatley was a prolific writer with a fund of good ideas spoilt by stereotyped writing. He was a self-publicist of considerable ability, sharing an interest in the occult with Maxwell Knight. The two men became close friends during the Second World War, when Wheatley continually pestered Knight to allow him to join his MI5 department, B5(b), where Bill Younger was already a case officer. But Knight, too wily to allow such a domineering character into the department, placated Wheatley by asking him to undertake certain outside jobs which at the same time fed him material for his books.

188

Wheatley was born on 8 January 1897, and was educated at Dulwich College and later on HMS *Worcester*, a training ship on which Maxwell Knight had also served. In 1914 he entered his father's wine business, but later that year he joined the Army. After being gassed in France, Wheatley was invalided out in 1919 and once again joined the wine business, eventually becoming managing director in 1926. He had considerable self-confidence, and a wilful, dominating personality. In 1931, when the family business ran into financial trouble, he was forced into what was to become a highly fruitful writing career.

Wheatley's first thriller was set in Soviet Russia and published in 1931 under the title *The Forbidden Territory*. This was followed by others which sold increasingly well, although the critics justifiably dismissed him as an outdated, boys' adventure paper writer. But although he wrote badly, Wheatley based his books on his own copious research, and in 1936, in association with journalist J. G. Links, he introduced his *Crime Dossiers*, in which he attempted to heighten the realism by including such material as police dossiers, letters and clues. This gimmicky technique commanded a good deal of public attention.

In the late thirties, Wheatley introduced his first spy hero, Gregory Sallust, many of whose adventures were inspired by MI5 anecdotes fed to Wheatley by Maxwell Knight. The character was based on Gordon Eric Gordon-Toombe, a First World War army friend of Wheatley's who met a mysterious end.

When peace was declared in 1918, thousands of claims began to come in from engineering factories for work on machine parts that were unfinished and no longer required in peacetime. Gordon-Toombe was an entrepreneur, and he saw his chance. He left the Army, but his friend Bill Dyer remained behind in the Air Ministry. Their plot seemed water-tight. Dyer's job was to vet the many claims and to ensure that they were cleared for settlement. Gordon-Toombe, meanwhile, began to set up a number of small-part suppliers in London and the provinces. The operation involved opening bank accounts, printing stationery, installing telephones and employing a secretary to staff otherwise empty offices. For each company he created, Gordon-Toombe sent a substantial financial claim to the Air Ministry, demanding compensation for work that had not even been started. Dyer passed the claim through, Gordon-Toombe would soon receive the cheque, and a few weeks later the firm quickly closed down. The risks that Gordon-Toombe ran, and the glamour of his personality, were later to make him the ideal *Boy's Own Paper* spy, and the MI5 gloss that Wheatley was able to add made the character all the more appealing.

Wheatley and Gordon-Toombe became very close, sharing girlfriends, visiting night clubs together and indulging in hedonistic twenties activity. Wheatley provided alibis for Gordon-Toombe's fraudulent adventures, successfully ignoring his own suspicions about their criminal nature. Then, quite suddenly, Gordon-Toombe disappeared, it seemed, from the face of the earth, and it was not until some time afterwards that Wheatley discovered the full extent of his clandestine affairs.

Some time after the Air Ministry fraud, Gordon-Toombe and his former conspirator, Dyer, had bought a derelict racing stable near Purley in Surrey, with a view to burning the premises down for the insurance money. One evening, the shadowy Dyer prepared the fire, while Gordon-Toombe established an alibi for himself by spending the evening at a party with Wheatley and his fiancée, Nancy. When the party was over, Gordon-Toombe drove to the stables and started the blaze. But despite such careful plotting, the insurance company were suspicious and refused to pay out. A few days later Gordon-Toombe revisited the burnt-out stables to try and discover why their suspicions had been aroused. He never returned.

Next morning, Dyer made an agitated appearance at Wheatley's office, anxious to discover why Gordon-Toombe had failed to keep an appointment with him the previous evening. Later the same day, Gordon-Toombe's girlfriend presented herself to Wheatley, frantically worried because he had not returned to her the previous night, and desperate to know where he could have gone. At her insistence, Wheatley reluctantly drove to Gordon-Toombe's bank where, after lengthy discussions with the manager, he discovered that Gordon-Toombe and Dyer had a joint account running to several thousand pounds. He also discovered that Dyer had not only taken the money out, but had also closed the account. Extremely disturbed, Wheatley went to the police, but found them of little help. People disappeared every day – and often of their own choice. In desperation, Wheatley employed a detective – although he did so with many qualms, for he doubted that Gordon-Toombe's past activities would bear much scrutiny. For some months, however, the detective agency drew a blank, and Wheatley irritably assumed that his dubious friend had gone abroad for his own nefarious purposes. This impression was confirmed when a mutual friend claimed to have seen him in Madrid.

Eighteen months later, Gordon-Toombe's father had a bizarre dream. In it, he saw his son's body lying in a well. So alarmed was he by the clarity of the vision that he insisted the police accompany him to the racing stables, where he was certain the well was situated. Sure enough, after a brief search, Gordon-Toombe's body was found, as depicted in the dream. He had been shot in the back of the head. The stunned Wheatley was certain the culprit was Dyer, who clearly had every financial motive. But there was no proof, and an arrest was declared impossible.

A year later, however, ironic justice was done. The police went to interview Dyer in connection with some minor local fraud. The guilty Dyer, imagining that they had come to arrest him for Gordon-Toombe's murder, fled upstairs, pulled out a pistol and shot himself dead.

The Press had a field-day with the case. The *News of the World* led with:

Fully clothed and bearing unmistakable marks of shot wounds, human remains have been unearthed by Scotland Yard detectives from a cesspool on a Surrey stud farm.

At yesterday's inquest it was definitely established that the body is that of a young man who mysteriously

191

disappeared from the farm early last year and has never been seen alive since.

Six months later, in a seaside hotel, his partner – a man with an amazing experience of life's ups and downs – was killed by a pistol shot he himself fired in attempting to resist arrest.

Before these two events, the stud farm had been destroyed by fire and the victim of the hotel shooting had failed in a heavy insurance case.

Fiction though it may appear to the incredulous, it is a fact, nevertheless, that the remains in the present instance were unearthed as the result of a father's presentiment.

Wheatley tells us in *Drink and Ink*, the second volume of his autobiography: 'Gregory Sallust was, physically at least, copied from my great friend of the First World War, Gordon Eric Gordon-Toombe, to whom I owe so much of my general knowledge . . . His physique and personality were based on those of my dear, unscrupulous friend.' Wheatley's first attempt at writing non-fiction was based on the Gordon-Toombe murder.

Towards the end of the manuscript, Wheatley describes Gordon-Toombe's practised plausibility in handling the reproaches of his devoted girlfriend:

No one could plead so eloquently as he. I could see him at it in my own mind – there would be tears, protestations, he would tell her all about his bouts of neurasthenia and anaesthesia, and sufferings he had undergone to reform his cravings, and finally she would forgive him, he would undergo a special course of psychoanalytical treatment with some big specialist, to exorcise the devil, then come to me and laugh like hell about it.

Wheatley tried to reassure her over Gordon-Toombe's disappearance, but she remained sceptical. 'The more I insisted that I was certain that he had not gone off with another woman, the more she became convinced that there had been foul play.'

In 1935, Wheatley's muse was again inspired by a friend – but a rather more formidable one than Gordon-Toombe.

George Hill was a highly accomplished spy, who has always been overshadowed by the notorious Sydney Reilly. Hill's father was a successful businessman working in Russia, where Hill spent his early life. He spoke good Russian, had travelled widely and had set up his own business in Moscow. When the First World War broke out, Hill was on a fishing trip in British Columbia. He thereupon joined the Canadian Light Infantry and was posted to do Intelligence work in France, where he was wounded by a grenade. He returned to the War Office in London. In 1916 he was posted to Salonika to report on enemy troop movements. He then learned to fly with the Royal Flying Corps, became one of the first pilots to land agents behind enemy lines, and eventually, in July 1917, was ordered to join the RFC mission in Russia. Discovering that the mission had withdrawn to Moscow and that action on the Eastern Front was diminishing, Hill went to the GHQ of the Russian Army at Mogilev. Here, the other powers were undertaking the delicate task of advising Russian generals on how to fight a war with demoralized troops.

During his spell in Mogilev, the romantically inclined Hill claims he was ambushed by members of the German Secret Service, but just as they were about to close in on him he swung round and flourished his walking stick. As he expected, one of his assailants seized hold of it, only to discover that he was gripping the sharp end of a sword-stick, which had been specially designed for Hill by Wilkinson, the sword-makers in Pall Mall in London. Hill recounts in his autobiography, *Go Spy The Land* (1932), that the moment his attacker had the scabbard in his fist,

> I drew back the rapier-like blade with a jerk and with a forward lunge ran it through the gentleman's side. He gave a scream and collapsed to the pavement. His comrade, seeing that I had put up a fight and was not unarmed, took to his heels while I withdrew and fumbled for my revolver.

Meanwhile, the man I had run through staggered off, leaving my scabbard on the pavement. I went back and recovered it. That sword-stick thereafter had a value in my eyes.

Hill's next task, together with a Canadian engineer, was to reorganize the Russian railway system. To effect this the two men were allocated headquarters in a luxurious railway carriage that had belonged to the Tsar's mother, Empress Maria Feodorovna. Carriage no. 451 was magnificently opulent, with a state bedroom and sitting-room, an observation/dining salon, a lavatory, a pantry and five couchettes with double sleeping berths. Using carriage 451 as a base, Hill and his engineer colleague travelled to Petrograd, becoming the first Allied officers to enter the Bolshevik headquarters. Then, with the help of a gang of workmen and passes given to them by Lenin himself, Hill began a mass clearance of the war-devastated railway system, even taking the dramatic step of tipping trains down embankments in order to clear the lines. As a result, food was able to reach thousands of starving Russians in Petrograd, and supplies could be sent through to the Russian Army, who were attempting to halt the German advance through the Ukraine.

Like Gordon-Toombe, Hill was a self-made entrepreneur who took great pleasure in boasting about his experiences. Wheatley, despite his own considerable ego, was a good listener. He writes in the third volume of his autobiography:

George H. Hill, known as Peter, . . . was one of the most interesting men I have ever met. He was an Englishman born in Estonia, his father having been a wood exporter there. As a young man he went into our Secret Service, where he was known as IK8, and, being bilingual, he was sent to Russia. When the Bolsheviks gained power first our Ambassador was recalled, and then that charming and gifted writer, Robert Bruce Lockhart, who had been left as British representative. Peter became the only source of

194

information that the British Government had about events in the Bolshevik-held territory. His adventures as a secret agent were fascinating.

They were also somewhat exaggerated, for Hill chose to give even the most exciting anecdotes his own fictitious gloss: he had once widely put it about that he was wholly responsible for smuggling the Russian crown jewels out of Rumania.

After the First World War Hill fell on hard times, and he and his wife, Dorothy, lived a less glamorous existence in a caravan in a Sussex farmer's field. His only substantial source of income was as adviser to film companies who were making films about Russia. It was in this milieu that Wheatley first met Hill, who had proffered his advice during the making of the film based on Wheatley's book, *The Forbidden Territory*, published in 1931, which has Istanbul, a city which Hill knew well, as its background. Hill used to lie on Wheatley's sofa drinking whisky and soda, while Wheatley sat a table taking notes about Istanbul and Mohammedan customs.

In 1941, Hill was returned to Moscow. He had been made a brigadier, and was given the job of liaising with the NKVD, with additional responsibility for preparing the reopening of the MI6 station in Moscow. '[He was] immensely paunchy, he looked rather like Soglow's king with a bald pate instead of a crown,' remembers Kim Philby in *My Silent War*. Wheatley recounts in *Drink and Ink*: 'He was later appointed head of the S.O.E. mission in Moscow, where the Russians hailed him with delight. They knew all about him. A very belated security check of his conference room in Moscow revealed a fearsome number of sources of leakage.

Hill claimed that he was very much a legend in Russia during the Second World War, recounting in dramatic detail his story about the Crown jewels. He had also, apparently, waded across a freezing Russian river to blow up a bridge, and later saved a beautiful Jewess from the Soviet secret police by concealing her in his bathroom. But there were also rumours that he had become a triple agent, feeding information to the

195

British, the Russians and the Germans. It was even said that, on one occasion, he had asked to be supplied with a £20,000 diamond to bribe a female NKVD agent, who was currently living with him. But much of this seems unlikely, particularly as no NKVD agent would have agreed to become Hill's mistress unless she was receiving particularly valuable information from him – and it is doubtful that the British would have entrusted him with anything important. It is, however, quite possible that he passed some information to the Germans at least, for he was made managing director of the Apollinaris Mineral Water Company in Germany, and was given a large house and a chauffeur-driven Mercedes. Three years later he was awarded the German Order of Merit for services rendered to industry, and he ended his life in comfortable decline surrounded by German luxury. To Wheatley, who remembered him in his Sussex field, this was an exotic ending to a chequered career. He saw Hill as a highly romantic spy – their relationship is reminiscent of Aubrey Herbert's and John Buchan's – and he imbued much of his spy fiction with Hill's heavily embroidered tales of intrigue and adventure.

During the Second World War, now married to his second wife, Joan, Wheatley became a regular visitor to Maxwell Knight's flat. Wheatley and Knight had a mutual interest in the so-called black magician, Aleister Crowley. Originally, Wheatley had met Crowley through Tom Driberg, and Crowley had dined with the Wheatleys several times, providing Dennis, who thought him interesting but harmless, with occult information for his books. Driberg had warned him that Crowley had been responsible for running a community in northern Sicily where a number of children had allegedly disappeared, after taking part in satanic masses. There had been another dubious episode in Paris, he said. Attempting to raise the pagan god Pan, Crowley had spent a night in a hotel room on the Left Bank with a man named MacAleister, who was one of his followers. In the morning they were both discovered naked – MacAleister dead, and Crowley howling in a corner. He was taken to an asylum and released four months later, but the cause of MacAleister's death was left undiscovered.

Driberg's story fascinated both Wheatley and Knight, but unfortunately Crowley in the flesh was something of a disappointment. He was well dressed and middle-aged, with the voice and manner of an Oxbridge don. He said his own grace, inflating Rabelais' *'Fay ce que vouldras'* (Do what you like) into 'What thou wilt shall be the whole of the law.' Knight clearly wondered how such scandalous rumours had come to surround such a seemingly harmless, if eccentric, academic, while Wheatley continued to hope that his black magician would show himself in a more satanic light. Nevertheless, both Knight and Wheatley did attend Crowley's occult ceremonies to research black magic for Wheatley's books. 'They jointly applied to Crowley as novices, and he accepted them as pupils,' Knight's nephew, Harry Smith, told me. 'But my uncle stressed that his interest – and also Wheatley's – was purely academic.'

Slowly, Knight's world of espionage began to penetrate Wheatley's life. They corresponded openly, apparently oblivious to the danger of exposure. One such letter discussed the surveillance of Dartington Hall, the progressive school and music centre in Devon run by Leonard and Dorothy Elmhirst, whose son by her first marriage, Michael Straight, was recruited as an undergraduate by Blunt in 1940 to spy for the KGB. The radical environment of Dartington was considered by Knight to be a breeding-ground for Communism. This inspired Wheatley to pen a Sallust novel that was never completed, although he used the idea later in *The Haunting of Toby Jugg*. Knight had given him a highly exaggerated account of day-to-day life at Dartington School, where, apparently, the pupils were encouraged to attend classes only if they particularly wanted to, and could equally well lie in bed all day. Knight also passed on to Wheatley rumours that the pupils were encouraged to attend satanic meetings in a ruined church. It was the ideal plot for Wheatley: Sir Pellinore, Sallust's boss, would have to send him down to Devonshire to investigate.

In early 1939, Knight asked Wheatley to employ an Austrian refugee, Frau Friedl Gaertner. She was to pose as a part-time research assistant to the Wheatleys, but in reality she had instructions to report back to Knight on the activities of various German nationals in Britain. Friedl Gaertner had a sister respectably married to Ian Menzies, younger brother of Major-General Sir Stewart Menzies (head of MI6), but Friedl was, in fact, a double agent, the *Abwehr* having recruited her in 1938 before she came to England. Knight was fully aware of this from other sources. His enjoyment of melodrama comes through in his letter to Wheatley about Friedl Gaertner:

> 38 Sloane Street
> SW1
>
> Dear Dennis
> Very many thanks for your most interesting letter of the 4th, which in itself might be quite useful, and if any further items of general news occur to you I shall be most grateful if you would let me have them.
> I am still very uncertain about the 11th, I am afraid, but at least you understand how I am placed.
> With regard to the particular business which we have been discussing, I should very much like to bring my friend along to see you early next week, but I rather feel we ought to have another talk before then, as it is absolutely essential for the scheme and for her own peace of mind that she should not suspect that the job is not an entirely genuine one. I will ring you up if I may in the next day or so and see what we can fix.
> Best wishes from us both for 1939.
> Yours ever
> Max

By 11 January Frau Gaertner had met the Wheatleys, and had been approved. Knight never told him that she was a double agent.

38 Sloane Street
London SW1

My dear Dennis,

I just want to write a line to thank you very much indeed for all the trouble you have taken in the particular matter we were discussing last night, and for the extremely able way in which you have cooperated. I must say, after last night's interview I came to the conclusion that when you turned your attention to literature the Intelligence department lost a great opportunity, though I fear the financial rewards in literature are greater than in the world of intrigue!

I do hope that the enterprise will actually be successful from your point of view. My only fear is that we may find some difficulty in getting hold of the references which are required. However, I have no doubt there is some way of getting round that.

In the meantime you have certainly earned my sincere gratitude, and in our friend you have acquired another Dennis Wheatley fan!

All the very best,
Yours ever,
Max

This kind of open correspondence underlines just how slack and amateurish MI5 could be.

By March 1939, Frau Gaertner was happily settled in the Wheatley household. Wheatley writes in the third volume of his autobiography: 'For many months afterwards she spent a good part of her time supplying me with translations of accounts of the Nazi leaders: their beginnings, background and rise to power. For my Gregory Sallust spy stories this data proved invaluable.'

Knight was also considering the possibility of offering a permanent job in MI5 to Bill Younger, already a part-time case officer and Wheatley's stepson by his second marriage. Knight wrote to Wheatley in July 1939:

There is a possibility of a vacancy in our own office, probably of a temporary nature, salary about £300 a year. This job would be for what one might term the duration of the crisis and/or war. It would be temporary in the sense that if suddenly there was a wonderful peace move and things really looked like settling down, it would of course be necessary for us to cut down staff and therefore the last to come would have to be the first to go. I think that the work would be exceedingly good training for the other job, and I have been given to understand that acceptance of a temporary job with us would not prevent Bill's name from going back on the rota for the other job later.

What do you think of this idea? The advantage is that Bill would feel that he was doing something useful and gaining experience, and of course it is impossible to say exactly when vacancies may occur in the other quarter. If you like to let me know by return what your personal view is – that is to say, that you and Joan have no objections – I will push on with the matter and put Bill's name forward.

With regard to our mutual lady friend: may I take it that if I send the usual cash to your house it will be opened and dealt with by your secretary, or shall I settle up direct with our friend, saying that you have asked me to do this?

I hope you are having a good rest and enjoying better weather than we are here, where it is beyond any description.

Yours ever,
Max

The friendship became even stronger as the war gathered pace, and Knight, perhaps as Wheatley's reward for providing a cover for Gaertner, arranged for the GPO to lay a direct telephone line into the Wheatleys' cellar, in case they had the misfortune to become entombed as a result of the bombing.

But Wheatley was still not satisfied with his role, and was anxious to have a more direct involvement with MI5. He knew Vernon Kell (MI5's Head) personally, for Kell had assisted him with his projected biography of Marshal Voroshilov. But Knight told him that no post 'suitable to his capabilities' was open. Nonetheless, Wheatley continued to hope: 'The time would surely come when I should be wanted, and perhaps quickly, for some post where my abilities could be used to best advantage.' Knight reminded him, however, that now that the war and the black-out had put an end to most normal forms of entertainment, thousands of people in camps, in hospitals, and at home would be depending upon him to maintain his output of thrillers. Wheatley was not appeased until a year later, when he submitted to the War Office his 'war papers', in which he outlined various tactical defence strategies in case of German invasion. The War Office took them very seriously, but not seriously enough to involve him in the theatre of war as much as he would have wished. Nevertheless, being so 'well' connected, Wheatley's fringe activities were enthralling.

Before Lord Haw-Haw (William Joyce) had fled to Germany late in August 1939, Wheatley had received him as a guest at one of his parties. He had been brought by a Fascist sympathizer, W. H. Tayleur, who used to assist Wheatley with proof-reading. Wheatley told Knight that Joyce had talked a good deal about Germany and expressed his disappointment that Wheatley's books were not published there. This, he said, was because in Wheatley's Duke de Richleau series one of the heroes, Simon Aron, was a Jew. But, despite this, Göring was a great fan and was anxious for Wheatley to come to Germany, preferably in Joyce's company, to meet the Nazi leaders.

When Knight raided Joyce's flat just after his escape, he found a file on Wheatley in which there were copies of various reports that Joyce had sent to Germany. In one of these Joyce noted that, as Wheatley had a number of Jewish friends, he might present something of a problem; but, this aside, he had potential as a collaborator after the invasion, and would make a first-class *Gauleiter* for north-west London. This testimonial would have made Wheatley suspect throughout the war, had he not been under Knight's protection.

In the autumn of 1939, Knight had asked Wheatley to keep

201

under surveillance a Hungarian lady known as Vicki, who was believed to be an enemy agent. Wheatley had already met her at a cocktail party, and, delighted at any opportunity to involve himself in MI5 affairs, accepted with alacrity. Knight told him that she had married a peer shortly before the war, and was at present living in Mayfair. Her husband, an RAF officer, was stationed in the country. Knight's reason for believing Vicki to be an enemy agent was that before the war she was said to have been the mistress of a wealthy Jewish armaments tycoon, who was now living on a neutral ship trading between England and the continent. Knight claimed that, although he had enough evidence to hang the tycoon, MI5 had no power to have him arrested, even when he was in a British port. All that could be done was to keep a vigilant eye on Vicki and prevent her from passing information to her former boyfriend.

Knight presented this somewhat unlikely story to Wheatley in his usual convincing style, but even if Wheatley found the connection rather far-fetched, he accepted it, as Vicki would provide just the kind of Mata Hari touch that he needed for his thrillers. Accordingly, under the pretence of trying to find a publisher for her memoirs, Wheatley invited Vicki to his cocktail parties. Her constant companion at these functions was a raven-haired Hungarian baroness who was rumoured to be yet another Nazi agent. Wheatley nicknamed her 'the Black Baroness', and used her as a model for a character in the fourth of his Gregory Sallust spy thrillers, which bore this soubriquet as a title. He also asked two other socialites, Charlie Birkin and Captain Bunny Tattersall, to keep an eye on the two suspect Hungarian ladies. Bunny, who had been 'Man about Town' for the *Daily Mail* and was now in the Inniskilling Dragoons, was particularly useful, for he knew everyone and went everywhere.

In December 1939 Vicki herself threw a party. Among the guests was the Turkish ambassador, who told Wheatley during the course of the evening that, in his opinion, Hitler would subjugate the French in the spring and then invade Britain. Wheatley countered his pessimism by declaring that the king and the government would merely retire to Canada with the

Navy, and continue the war from the outposts of the Empire. At the same time, he said, the Americans would come to the rescue. And with Russia waiting in the wings, he did not see how Hitler could possibly emerge victorious! This must have given the ambassador food for thought. Among the milling guests at that party were several members of MI6. Apart from Dennis and Joan Wheatley there was Bill Younger and his sister Diana, Friedl Gaertner, Bunny Tattersall, Knight himself, Charlie Birkin and several others. With such a high head-count of case officers, agents and contacts, there is little doubt that the mysterious Vicki was well watched – and that Wheatley was still collecting some remarkably good material.

In addition to Gregory Sallust, Wheatley created Roger Brook, a historical spy. In *The Launching of Roger Brook*, first published in the UK in 1947, the sixteen-year-old Brook runs away from the Royal Navy, becomes a spy in France and then a confidant of Napoleon, enjoying, en route, many romantic adventures. Brook is most likely to have been based on the French agent, Karl Schulmeister, who was Chief of Intelligence to the Austrian Marshal Mack.

Wheatley was lucky in his friendships: Gordon-Toombe, Hill and Knight, as well as Crowley, were wonderful sources of material. Their anecdotes, plus his careful research, the exploitation of sex and a cynical sense of humour, gave his fiction a strong identity. But it was to Wheatley's lasting regret that he never became an officially paid-up agent of British Intelligence.

Wheatley's fiction was highly coloured to say the least, and inevitably he wildly exaggerated the experiences he gained through Knight and others. This is a great pity, because he had access to fascinating material which, used with greater subtlety, could have enabled him to produce some major works of fiction.

CHAPTER ELEVEN

HOWARD HUNT:
THE SPY WHO KNEW TOO MUCH

Until Pearl Harbor, the United States had placed its security in the hands of a number of military Intelligence agencies, as well as the FBI. In 1942, President Roosevelt ordered the creation of the Office of Strategic Services – an amateurish organization under the tutelage of MI6. By the end of the war, the OSS had a healthy budget and mounting credibility based on hard-won experien *.*

In 1945, President Truman disbanded the organization, replacing it with the Central Intelligence Group, later renamed the Central Intelligence Agency. Its defined role was to collect and evaluate intelligence, as well as performing other 'duties and functions' which would be directed by the National Security Council.

The worsening of relations with the USSR and the coming of the Cold War really brought the CIA into its own as a powerful and often ruthless institution. In the struggle against Communism, no covert action was ruled out, practically anything went – including bribery, blackmail, assassination and guerrilla warfare. Humiliation struck with the Bay of Pigs fiasco in April 1961, and the head of the agency, Allen Dulles, resigned. The CIA's involvement in the Vietnam War further damaged its image. The CIA's operations were to come increasingly under attack in the succeeding years. In February 1973, following the Watergate scandal, Richard Helms, who had been appointed Director of the agency by President Johnson in 1966, was sacked by President Nixon.

'This fellow Hunt. He knows too damn much. Hunt will uncover a lot of things.'

Ex-President Richard Nixon

Howard Hunt was born on 9 October 1918, in Hamburg, a suburb of Buffalo to the west of New York. His father was a lawyer who later became a judge, and Hunt was brought up in a good middle-class home. His parents, Everette and Ethel Jean Hunt, lived in both Florida and New York, as Everette ran two law practices, devoting the winter to Florida and the rest of the year to New York. As a result of this Hunt's education suffered. He was slightly dyslexic and not a strong child, and was encouraged to work hard to keep up with his class-mates both in academic subjects and in sport. He was given private tutoring, and his father taught him to box, to fish and to shoot. An only child, Hunt was frequently left to his own devices and to the care of tutors and nannies, while his increasingly affluent parents played bridge and golf and spent long weekends in Havana, from which, during prohibition days, they returned with contraband supplies of liquor. Then came the 1929 Wall Street Crash, and the family's fortunes plunged.

Realizing that his practice in Florida had collapsed, Everette moved his family back north in the Buick convertible that was to be their principal means of transport throughout the Depression. Although heavily in debt, Everette managed to avoid being declared bankrupt, scrupulously applying himself to what remained of his law practice in Buffalo. The situation improved when one of his clients, Jacob Wurlitzer – the maker of the famous organ and, later, developer of the jukebox – asked him to re-orientate his company, as there was currently little demand for his expensive products. Meanwhile, despite his academic problems, Howard was showing promise as a musician and, in particular, as a trumpeter. In senior high school he and a group of friends formed a dance orchestra and, seeking a modest income, Hunt also ran a trap line along Eighteen Mile Creek, catching muskrats in winter, skinning, stretching and salting

205

their hides for eventual shipment to Sears. This entrepreneurial bent was symbolic of his future activities.

Eventually, Hunt conquered his academic problems and won a Regents scholarship, which would take him to any college or university within New York State. He elected to go to Brown University, where he quickly adapted to Ivy League style, and later travelled to Europe. In February 1941 he joined the United States Naval Academy as a midshipman. He was assigned to destroyers in the Atlantic, and eventually became assistant first lieutenant on the destroyer *Mayo*, whose job it was to protect British convoys from U-boats.

Injured by a deck fall, Hunt underwent a long convalescence and took an honourable medical discharge, which gave him the time to write his first novel, *East of Farewell*, published in 1942. He sent the manuscript to the publishing house Knopf, who accepted this fictionalized account of convoy duty in the North Atlantic. The book was a critical, although not a commercial, success, and as a result Hunt was hired by Louis de Rochemont to write *The March of Time*, in addition to composing naval training films. He then became South Pacific war correspondent for *Life* magazine, and learned to fly both land and sea-planes on his various missions. In 1943 he wrote *Limit of Darkness*, another fictionalized account, this time of life at Henderson Field on Guadalcanal, which was published by Random House in 1944.

In spite of this success, Hunt was restless; he did not want to be a civilian safe in the United States while the war raged abroad, so he made an appointment at the recruiting offices of the Royal Canadian Air Force at the Waldorf Astoria, where he was considered as a possible combatant, particularly as he had already mastered navigation. It was suggested that he might become a bombardier-navigator, but when he returned the next Monday morning to fill in the final forms, he was alarmed to see the furniture being moved out of the RCAF offices. The recruiting officer had disappeared; a secretary told him that a bilateral treaty had just been signed between the United States and Canada, whereby neither country would accept each other's nationals in their armed services. Not to be deterred, Hunt enlisted in the USAF, where he served and was awarded a second commission. While there, he volunteered for the Office of Strategic Services, and his long association with the US Secret Services had begun.

Hunt's initiation into the world of the clandestine was bizarre indeed. He was told to rendezvous near the old Christian Heurich brewery in Washington where, with eleven other officers, he was put aboard a personnel carrier and taken to a small white farmhouse. This innocent-looking building turned out to be an evaluation centre. On arrival, each officer was given a room and a good lunch; later in the afternoon, they were told that over the next week they would be set searching tests to determine their suitability for unorthodox warfare. They were also informed that one of their number was a planted OSS officer, who would closely observe their behaviour throughout. Each officer had been given an alias, which they were cautioned not to reveal at any cost. Hunt's alias was 'William', his grandfather's Christian name.

After dinner, the officers were taken to the basement of the farmhouse, where the mock-up of a hotel bedroom had been created. Lying on the bed were a number of items, including a railway ticket between Vienna and Belgrade. There was also money in different denominations, keys, a torn-up address book, clothing and an overturned chair – all of which gave the impression of a swift and unexpected departure. The nervous company were then told that each of them would be allowed to examine the room and its contents for three minutes, after which they were to retire elsewhere and write down their findings from the circumstantial evidence they had observed. Hunt's version suggested that a possible foreign agent, travelling from Belgrade to Vienna, had found sanctuary in a hotel room. Relaxing for a moment, he had decided to empty his pockets. Then, interrupted by an ominous sound at the window, he had made his getaway. Hunt realized that there were a number of inconsistencies in his story, but felt the scenario was the best he could invent in such a short time.

When the officers' perceptions had been perused by the staff, they were told, somewhat disappointingly, that there was no satisfactory answer, and that the scene had been made deliberately inconsistent so as to confuse. The real object of the exercise was to test their powers of observation, and to see how many of the items on the bed could be ingeniously woven into their conclusions. The trainees then underwent a variety of initiative tests, including a serious debate which was suddenly sprung on them after an alcoholic binge. Hunt managed to sound sober enough to impress his superiors, and was later told by OSS head General Donovan that, subject to intensive training, he had been accepted for duty in the OSS – particularly as he had guessed who the 'dummy' trainee officer was.

Hunt was sent almost immediately to his first centre of operations – China. First he went into intensive training on Catalina Island, off the West Coast – a training that included unarmed combat, knife and bayonet fighting, rapid fire with hand-guns, lock-picking, cryptography, Morse code, mountain climbing, demolition, the operation of Japanese mortars, the use of limpet mines and other explosives, and poison and survival techniques. Survival testing was tougher than expected. The training they had received for this aspect of the course, largely involving the use of archery and the preparation of animal snares, proved inadequate. They had been told that large abalones – a kind of shellfish, also known as 'sea-ears' – could be found below the low-tide mark on the rocks just off the beach, and that goats ran conveniently wild over the entire island. With this diet, the participants were assured, they should be able to keep well above the weight-loss limit, which was ten pounds. But on arrival they found a strange absence of goats, and although one marine raider managed to capture one, two instructors then kidnapped the wretched animal. Disconsolately, the trainees waded out to the rocks, prised off the abalone, and baked them over a camp fire. Although the shellfish turned out to be almost too tough to eat, they somehow survived two days of this diet, huddled round their rain-lashed camp fire, without losing more than five pounds of body weight.

In the next exercise, the men were issued civilian clothing, divided into teams, and ordered to enter Mexico with a suitcase radio and transmit a coded message back to headquarters. Each was given a five-dollar bill, and no identification or documents of any kind. Hunt's team found no difficulty in getting into Mexico, or in sending the message back from their grubby hotel room in Tijuana. The real problem was how to return to the States without papers. After considerable thought, they each placed reverse-charge phone calls to several friends in the States, asking them to cable ten dollars to the alias they had registered under at the hotel. Although some of Hunt's friends were less helpful than others, he, like his colleagues, managed to round up enough dollars to cross the border. The remaining problem was how to return with the radio, but in the end this proved of little hindrance as the customs officers, apparently wise to the game, waved them through.

After parachute training in China, Hunt worked on a number of operations against the Japanese, and then, following Hiroshima, volunteered to enter Nanking in east-central China to save the lives of Allied prisoners of war. Returning to America and to Hollywood, he began writing screenplays for which, unfortunately, there was little market. Frustrated, he returned to New York, where his luck changed when he wrote *Bimini Run*, published in 1948. Set in the Caribbean, it was his most successful thriller to date, and the film rights were bought by Warner Bros.

Hunt was now able to live well on the proceeds, playing tennis, squash and golf at country clubs, shooting pheasant in the autumn and ski-ing in winter on the slopes of Vermont. In the spring of 1948 he felt the desire to return to Europe and, through his father, met Paul Hoffman, who had been appointed by President Truman to head the European recovery programme. Hoffman agreed to give Hunt a post on the staff of the European administrator of the programme in Paris. It was there that he fell in love with Dorothy de Goutière, one of Ambassador Averell Harriman's secretaries. An American citizen, she had spent the war years working in Switzerland for the Treasury Department's hidden assets division, whose job it was to search for concealed Nazi assets in Europe and elsewhere. At the end of the war Dorothy had gone to Shanghai to open up the Treasury office there. She had been a technical adviser on a Dick Powell film called *To the Ends of the Earth*, the story of the Treasury's involvement in the international narcotics traffic. She had then resigned from the Treasury to marry the Marquis Peter de Goutière, a civilian pilot for the China National Airways Corporation. She was now in the middle of divorce proceedings.

Meanwhile, Hunt was still writing, and his latest novel, *Stranger in Town*, published in 1948, had won him a Guggenheim Fellowship and was selling well in paperback. He returned to Hollywood, where his increasing stature as a thriller-writer made him far more acceptable to the movie moguls, and at last his screenplays were turned into films – unmemorable as they were. He now proposed to Dorothy and she accepted, but his parents were not enthusiastic about the marriage – on a variety of grounds. They did not know her, she was a divorcee and, worse still, she was a Catholic. Although he was certain his parents would eventually accept her, the friction continued, and they were married in Millbrook, New York, rather than Albany, where his family were then living.

The Hunts were honeymooning in Sea Island, Georgia, when a telegram arrived, instructing Howard to report to CIA headquarters in Washington DC. There he found himself commissioned to work for the Office of Policy Coordination, the US government's new clandestine action arm. In Europe its main efforts were geared towards destroying Communist influence in labour organizations, in the Press and amongst youth and student movements. The electoral campaigns of high level pro-West politicians were also aided by OPC funding, as was Radio Free Europe.

Hunt was posted to Mexico to continue the fight against Communism. The couple's first child was born in Mexico City, and in the autumn of 1952, they had a second child. Hunt continued writing thrillers, and his manuscripts were regularly cleared by the State Department and by the CIA. About this time he was told he must have a regular polygraph test, using the standard lie-detection device. This was aimed at discovering operatives' behaviour in the realms of sex, money and foreign contacts. Failure to pass the test meant immediate dismissal from the CIA.

An incident concerning the CIA's habit of bugging the Communist embassies in Mexico City gave Hunt plenty of experience for the future burglary of Watergate. The Guatemalan embassy in Mexico City was in an apartment building only a couple of blocks away from the American embassy itself, and Hunt had a distinct view from his CIA offices of the front window of the third floor. Having mounted twenty-four hour surveillance on the more significant embassy officers, he fixed a date for what he called 'surreptitious entry', with the help of a CIA safe-cracking team. The ambassador's office was bugged up to a CIA listening post that had been rented on the floor above, the telephone was tapped and a plan of the offices was drawn up, together with a description of the safe and a putty imprint of its keyhole. Hunt helped to recruit the embassy's cleaning woman, who came up trumps with a key to one of the embassy's back doors, which was quickly duplicated.

The break-in was to be on a Friday night. As each member of staff left the embassy, he or she was followed home and kept under close surveillance. With their various bugging devices, the team would know when all the staff had finally departed. At 11 p.m. all was ready. A telephone call was put through to the embassy; it rang unanswered. This was the signal to go in. The entry team set off first, and Hunt, still in the US embassy offices, listened to their movements through the bugs. The team then covered the windows with opaque black muslin to eliminate the chance of flashlights being seen outside, and set to work on the safe. In the basement, the night-watchman was indulging in cards and tequila – generously orchestrated by his new friend, an agent who had made his acquaintance a month earlier.

The entry team then made a duplicate safe key, and before

opening the safe, took the precaution of placing an amplifying listening device to the keyhole in case they could detect the ticking of a time lock or, worse still, some kind of booby-trap bomb. Directly the safe door was opened, a photograph was taken of the contents and instantly developed. This meant that everything in the safe could be replaced in its original position, after the team had set up a camera specially adapted for document-photography. Floodlights were plugged into the embassy's electrical system, and the entire contents of the safe were photographed. Their task completed, the marauders put everything back, cleaned up and withdrew, removing the blackout drapes as they went.

The operation was quick and efficient, and by dawn the entry team had flown to Dallas, where an identity change was effected before they returned to Washington. The result of their night's work was then examined by various departments of the CIA. Lists of Mexicans whom the Guatemalan embassy had 'subverted', as well as the names of important Mexicans on their target lists, were sent to the CIA station in Mexico City. There were also the ambassador's notes detailing efforts to acquire arms and munitions in Mexico, a description of the ambassador's Soviet embassy contact, and profiles of senior officials in the American embassy that he had been analysing.

Hunt's next assignment was at Headquarters: a desk job on Balkan affairs. He knew the then Chief of Station in Athens, who was close to the royal family and had an excellent working relationship with the head of Greek intelligence. CIA agents regularly crossed into Bulgaria from the northern borders of Greece, and air operations were mounted from a Greek airfield into all Balkan countries with the exception of Yugoslavia and Albania. All operations into Albania were jointly run by the CIA and MI6, because it was considered that the British had more experience of the country. The Albanian agents, largely drawn from the exiled King Zog's bodyguard, were trained in West Germany and sent in by air from Bari, on the Adriatic Coast of Italy. But all was not well, and there were mounting suspicions at the constant loss of aircraft. On one occasion, when an Albanian team signalled for the pick-up of a supposedly injured member, the decision was taken to combine this difficult mission with a leaflet drop. The designated area was in a valley between two parallel ranges of low mountains. As the C–47 made its approach, flying only fifty to sixty feet above the ground, with its skyhook trailing, the pick-up was nowhere to be seen. Suddenly, a volley of fire assaulted the C–47 from each side of the mountains. Despite being hit, the plane escaped, eventually crash-landing at Bari, the impact causing the release of thousands of leaflets originally destined for Albanian patriots.

In 1953 Allen Dulles had become Director of the CIA, and it was he who sent Hunt to Guatemala to help overthrow the Communist regime. Hunt was upgraded to head of the projects propaganda and political action staff, and was told that the scheme had priority above all undercover actions at present being mounted. The Guatemala project was set up as a semi-autonomous unit within the Western hemisphere division of the agency, with its own funds and communications centre, and a chain of command that was able to operate without the customary attention of the enormous advisory staffs within the CIA hierarchy. One of Hunt's aims was to imitate the success of the CIA operator, Kim Roosevelt, who had achieved a virtually bloodless overthrow of the Iranian premier, Mohammed Mossadegh, by psychologically preparing the government and population, resorting to a sudden display of force only at the very end of the operation.

After apparently having warned the civilian population of Guatemala City, US planes were deployed in low-level strafing runs, dropping harmless smoke bombs. Using a powerful transmitter in neighbouring Honduras, where a small group of anti-government, pro-American Castillo Armas guerrillas were being trained, they interrupted Guatemalan national radio and broadcast propaganda designed to sever the population from its military government. Unfortunately, during the course of the operation, a British ship which was innocently unloading at Puerto Barrios was taken for a Czech freighter loaded with arms for Guatemala. It was bombed and sunk. Invading overland, the troops of Castillo Armas then seized control of Guatemala City and captured the political leader, Arbenz, and his followers. Amongst them was Ernesto 'Che' Guevara, who received political asylum in Mexico, where he later joined Fidel Castro and his partisans.

In the summer of 1956, Hunt had become chief of station at Montevideo, the capital of Uruguay. Dulles who had 'retired' after the Bay of Pigs episode, was succeeded by Richard Helms at the end of 1961. It was now proposed that Hunt should become deputy chief of station in Madrid. He was fluent in Spanish and had always wanted to live in Spain, but had not counted on a clash with Robert Woodward, the American ambassador in Spain, who had already disapproved of Hunt's aggressive attitude in Montevideo. As was his right, Woodward refused to accept him, and Hunt disconsolately withdrew. He was cheered, however, by an invitation to more skulduggery during the summer of 1964, when both the Republican and Democratic parties had established their candidates for the presidency. Hunt claims that he received 'confidential orders' from Stanley Gaines of the division executive offices to 'activate outside personnel', in order to discover information held in the headquarters of the Republican candidate, Barry Goldwater. Hunt insists that he was told that President Johnson himself was interested in finding out more about Goldwater's plans. As a result, Press material, position papers and advance speaking schedules were regularly picked up from Goldwater's headquarters by CIA personnel on some pretext or other, and taken to the White House. There, Hunt maintains, Chester Cooper, the CIA officer attached to the White House staff, received the material. Ironically, Hunt claims to be a Goldwater supporter, and justifies having allowed his subordinates to mount this domestic-political mission, seeing himself 'not as a partisan political appointee but rather as a career officer of the CIA whose professionalism required that he respond to the orders of whatever administration might be in power. This was my first exposure to White House use of agency personnel against a "domestic army", and I found it disturbing.' Even after he retired from the CIA in 1970, Hunt says, he remained predisposed 'by long professional service to accept without question orders which I believed to emanate from the White House'.

In the autumn of 1964, Victor Weybright, editor-in-chief of the New American Library, suggested to Hunt that he should write an American counterpart to the James Bond series, which his firm also published. Hunt submitted the idea to Helms, who felt that the CIA could well benefit from a popular all-American hero who would give them the cleaned-up image of the intrepid lionheart who always serves the nation's interest. Helms himself liked Ian Fleming's novels because of their totally fantastic plots, feeling that they bore the same relationship to the world of espionage as Western movies do to the Old West. Helms also enjoyed Hunt's novels, which he was still producing in quantity. Helms was not alone in stimulating writers to polish up the CIA image; Allen Dulles had encouraged writers by giving them ideas for plots, because he believed that they could help build public support for an organization that was not allowed to publicize its achievements.

Like many British Intelligence officers, Helms detested John le Carré's *The Spy Who Came in from the Cold*, which he saw as cynical and bitter. Like many others, he also feared le Carré's themes of betrayal, which attacked the very bedrock of the trust he believed was essential to Intelligence work. Le Carré's 'Circus' both deceived and sacrificed its agents, whereas, in Helms' somewhat naïve – or idealized – view, the CIA looked after its own. Helms told Hunt that he was to clear each manuscript with his deputy, Tom Karamessines.

When I asked Hunt if the Peter Ward series had been based on his own CIA experiences, he replied that he did not think that the agency would like him to be specific as to which books utilized actual experiences: 'I dealt more with the methodology of espionage than I *did* with actual cases.' In his opinion, his hero, Ward, is very different from Fleming's Bond. Initially he had never cared for the Bond books, because he felt that they

215

were written by 'a poseur, by a well intentioned amateur and . . . my impression was that he was a sort of gofer or bag carrier for the then wartime director of Naval Intelligence.' Hunt, as a result of researching the Ultra series, believed that Fleming was more involved with the Enigma and Ultra traffic – code-breaking during the Second World War – than with actual operations.

> Bond's adventures were, of course, preposterous. There was nothing in them really that was measurable in the experience of most Western Intelligence agencies or agents, and he relied very heavily on sex and *double entendre* such as naming a character 'Pussy Galore'. They were tongue-in-cheek, they were pure entertainment, and by contrast in the Ward series I tried to stay very strictly with reality.

Hunt claims that he wanted to write about plausible operations, using the methodology of espionage, although he did create some technical aids which did not then – at least, to his knowledge – exist. Fleming had said that in each of his books it was his policy to give his audience only one believable incident or situation, which he would then exploit. Hunt quoted as examples the stealing of gold from Fort Knox, and sealing off a portion of metropolitan London. Hunt saw all this as good fun, but added that his own books were not intended as 'fun', because he viewed the espionage business as a life and death struggle, as 'nothing to be flip about'.

But Hunt was frank about the comparative failure of the Ward series: he did not imagine that Fleming or any other fiction writer ever viewed the Peter Ward series as a threat. When it emerged, Bond was at his peak, but there seemed little enthusiasm for an American counterpart. His sales were mediocre, but Hunt felt that the reason lay in the fact that in 1972 there was considerable media distaste for covert operations, 'mainly as a result of the hearings that were held in America that emasculated the Central Intelligence Agency and held it up to ridicule'. The Senate and the House Investigation Committee, he believed, had very thoroughly sullied the name of the CIA, thereby discrediting it and playing into the Soviets' hands.

And that feeling was further compounded by the Watergate episode in which . . . very much in the old McCarthyite technique, allusions were made to some unnamed role that the CIA might have had in Watergate, and the fact that a couple of us involved, that is, Jim McCord and myself, had been with the CIA was enough to give the agency a bad name. And that was, as we say, a bad rap because it just never happened.

Hunt also feels that Ward could do little towards improving the image of the CIA, partly because of the advent of the spy fiction anti-hero. With the Vietnam war controversy then raging in America, the anti-war lobby had considerable support from Great Britain and Europe. Because of this, any writer naive enough to promote an American hero who was an antagonist, was viewed with distaste.

Hunt's relationship with Richard Helms and his deputy was good. Only one problem arose during the writing of the Peter Ward series – a problem connected with the machinations of an African plot which Hunt had developed. Hunt maintains, though, that there was never any real contention; Karamessines simply suggested he leave out a number of details, 'which I very happily did'. Karamessines and Hunt had known each other since Hunt had been on the Balkan side of the agency, while he was chief of station in Athens. Later on, when Hunt had been chief of station 'in another part of the world' and Karamessines was in Vienna, Hunt undertook 'some very rapid work for him in response to an urgent and semi-private request he sent me to facilitate an operation that he had on-going in Central Europe'.

After Watergate, Helms was quick to put as much distance as possible between himself and the 'notorious' Howard Hunt. Immediately before that episode, they had been on as friendly terms as ever, lunching together about once a month at their clubs. Hunt asserted that he had been a confidant, and that

Helms had revealed to him that he was going to be made Deputy Director of the CIA before he told anybody else, as well as entrusting him with the details of his divorce; 'So until Helms sought a Watergate repudiation I had always felt that he was a very reliable and fine friend.'

Hunt clearly much admired Helms as an individual: he went on to tell me that he was a superb Director of the CIA. He was anxious to follow Helms' methods and almost hero-worshipped him, encouraging personal friendship. He recounts in *The Hargrave Deception*, published in 1980:

> I can remember picking him up to go off somewhere for a drink and a snack at five, and his desk would always be clean. That was a great difference from the motivation – or the *modus vivendi*, I really should say – of too many people in the CIA, who felt that they gained brownie points by staying late at night and having their desks littered with files, folders and cables and memos to sign and initial.

Following Helms' work practices, unless he happened to have a late duty period, Hunt left the agency as soon after five as he could manage, during the few years that he was in Washington. He also had a heavy writing schedule and a growing family: 'Having completed my work for the day at the agency, although we were always on call, I felt that it was time for me to head for home and rid myself of international espionage concerns.'

In all, eight paperbacks were published about Peter Ward's adventures, under the pen name of David St John. But no sooner had the first book come out than the agency librarian, Walter Pforzheimer, pointed out to Hunt that the Library of Congress copyright card gave his real name in addition to the pen name. So it was decided to send Hunt abroad, at least for a while, in case any Congressmen started asking questions. He resigned from the CIA, and was rehired as a contract agent responsible only to Karamessines. A position was found for him in Madrid, and in 1965 the Hunt family sold their house and sailed for Spain on a Spanish merchant liner.

It was put to me that because my identity had been inadvertently revealed the agency did not want to confess that the series had been in a sense agency-inspired. Helms was always very well plugged-in on Capitol Hill, and although I couldn't see any particular problem for myself I thought that Helms might have received some indication that certain people in Congress were going to make an issue out of the fact that an active duty officer was writing a series about CIA figures and actually using the three initials.

Hunt was not destined to remain in Europe for long. Before his Spanish job ended, he asked for a transfer back to Washington because his son needed medical treatment that could not be had in Madrid. The accommodating Helms agreed, giving him the job of head of the covert-action staff in the DDP's Western European division. Hunt was not happy here either, largely owing to the fact that his right-wing politics were out of line with those of the German Social Democrats.

By 1970 Hunt was in financial distress, having for three years paid for the private hospitalization of his eldest daughter who had been seriously injured in a car accident. Accordingly, he retired from the CIA in search of private employment, and through the agency out-placement service was hired by a prominent Washington public relations firm as its Creative Vice President. The firm was eventually sold and at this point Hunt renewed his friendship with Charles W. (Chuck) Colson, a fellow graduate of Brown University, whose White House connections as counsel to the President were impressive. During the autumn of 1968 Hunt had become increasingly aware that Colson was involved in the Nixon presidential campaign. He therefore thought it appropriate to explain to Colson the role he had played in the Bay of Pigs episode, and Nixon's special interest in the project.

Colson and Hunt often lunched together, finding each other politically compatible as well as sharing a common interest in intrigue. In June 1971, Colson offered Hunt a job as a consultant to the White House. He was asked to operate a campaign aimed at discrediting Daniel Ellsberg, the former government employee who had leaked the Pentagon Papers, the Defense Department documents on US involvement in Southeast Asia, to the *New York Times*. Hunt's aim was to turn the embarrassment around, so that Nixon could have a public relations triumph. In *The Man Who Kept the Secrets: Richard Helms and the CIA*, Thomas Powers writes: 'Years before, Paul Lineberger, an expert in psychological warfare, had praised Hunt as having one of the two great "black minds" in the CIA.' John D. Ehrlichman, assistant to the President, was the first to approve Colson's plan, after a meeting with Hunt on 7 July 1971, and that afternoon he contacted General Robert E. Cushman, Deputy Director of Central Intelligence, to ask for the CIA's help. Ehrlichman told him: 'Hunt may be contacting you sometime in the future for some assistance. I wanted you to know that he was in fact doing some things for the President. He is a longtime acquaintance with the people here. You should consider he has pretty much *carte blanche*.'

When Hunt began work at the White House in July 1971, it was not just the Ellsberg project that he was involved in. There was also a plan to discredit Senator Edward Kennedy with new information about the Chappaquiddick scandal, and a more general campaign to smear the Kennedys by implicating the USA in the murder of Diem, Prime Minister of South Vietnam, in 1963.

During the summer and autumn of 1971, Hunt needed the CIA's help in all these scurrilous operations. On 22 July he saw General Cushman at the CIA and asked for special equipment for a 'sensitive' interview. Cushman agreed to the request. The next day an officer from the CIA's technical services division brought Hunt a speech-altering device and identity papers at a safe house in Washington. On 28 July, Hunt proposed to Colson that the CIA should be asked to create a psychological profile .of Ellsberg who was reputed, on the Washington grapevine, to be unstable. Colson contacted David R. Young, a White House aide who was working with the leak-plugging specialists, the Special Investigations Unit, known as 'plumbers'. Young then approached the next in the chain of command – Howard Osborn, at the CIA. Osborn went to Helms, and Helms reluctantly agreed to Hunt's demands. The first attempt at a profile of Ellsberg was too vague and unsubstantial to satisfy Ehrlichman and the plumbers, so on 13 August 1971 Helms put himself on the line by personally asking for a leak hunt.

Hunt, meanwhile, was becoming more ambitious. On 18 August he asked the CIA to lend him his former agency secretary who was at that time working in Paris. Two days later he requested a tape-recorder and some alias business cards, and then a 'back-stopped' telephone number – i.e. one which would always be answered – in New York with matching driver's licence and credit cards. On 25 August he asked for a disguise kit and identification papers for Gordon Liddy.

Hunt's multitudinous requests finally began to worry grass-roots officers in the CIA. They reported their concern to their superiors, and eventually Cushman's executive assistant, Karl Wagner, gave instructions to refuse any further Hunt requests. He then sent Cushman a memo protesting about the involvement of the unknown Liddy and about Hunt's constant requests, raising the question of the material's use in domestic clandestine activity. Cushman called Ehrlichman, who agreed to call a halt on all this.

In August Hunt organized the burglary of the Los Angeles office of Daniel Ellsberg's psychiatrist, Dr Lewis Fielding. One of the Cubans used in the break-in was Eugenio Martinez, a veteran of much clandestine CIA activity. Martinez was experienced enough to realize that it was advisable for some operators to move secretly inside the CIA – in other words, without authorization from their case officers. Eventually, however, Martinez began to talk. As the Watergate scandal blew, Helms, although suspecting a great deal, stayed within his

221

own guidelines: 'Stay cool, volunteer nothing, because it will only be used to involve us. Just stay away from the whole damn thing.' Later, during the Watergate hearings, Hunt was reminded of one of Eric Ambler's novels, *Judgement of Deltchev*. One passage, he felt, had singular relevance to his sufferings at that time: 'His trial, therefore, is no formality, but a ceremony of preparation and precaution. He must be discredited and destroyed as a man so that he may safely be dealt with as a criminal.'

Hunt's version of events was that, after retiring from the CIA, he had been employed 'by a firm whose officials maintained a relationship with the CIA'. Some months after joining the firm, he had been approached by Charles W. Colson, special counsel to the President, to become a consultant to the President's executive office. Colson told him that the White House needed the kind of Intelligence background that he possessed. That, he argued, was the basic reason for his employment, and he understood at the time that his appointment was approved by John D. Ehrlichman and H. R. Haldeman, both assistants to the President. Hunt maintains that from the time he began working at the White House until 17 June 1972, the day of the second Watergate entry, he had been engaged in essentially the same kind of work as he had performed for the CIA. He had, he says, become a member of the Special Investigations Unit – the 'plumbers' – which the President had created to undertake specific national security tasks for which he considered the traditional investigative agencies to be inadequate. In this capacity, Hunt states, he was involved in tracing leaks of highly classified information. These investigations led to an entry by the plumbers into the office of Dr Lewis Fielding, Daniel Ellsberg's psychiatrist – an entry authorized, on his own admission, by Egil Krogh, deputy to John Ehrlichman. The action was considered necessary because of the belief that Ellsberg or his associates were providing classified information to the Soviet Union. The operation was carried out with Hunt's assistance, under the direction of G. Gordon Liddy, a lawyer, former FBI agent and member of the plumbers' unit.

The Fielding entry occurred in September 1971. In late November, Hunt was told by Gordon Liddy that Attorney-General John N. Mitchell proposed the establishment of a large-scale Intelligence and counter-Intelligence programme, with Liddy as its chief. Liddy and Hunt designed a budget suited to the kind of activities to be carried out in the programme, which came to be known as 'Gemstone'. It was Hunt's understanding – or so he maintains – that the programme had been approved by Jeb Stuart Magruder, a former White House aide, and John W. Dean III, counsel to the President. Later, he claims to have learned that Charles W. Colson had approved it too. According to Hunt's court testimonies, in April 1972 Liddy told him that they were to undertake the Watergate operation as part of the Gemstone programme. He told Hunt that he had information – the source of which Hunt understood to be a government agency – that the Cuban government was supplying funds to the Democratic Party campaign. To investigate this report, a surreptitious entry of Democratic national headquarters at the Watergate office building was made on 27 May 1972, followed by a second entry in the June.

Fifteen years after Watergate, national disgrace and a prison sentence, Hunt regards his thriller-writing as rather more than entertainment. He feels that the critics who have charged him with offering a political view of espionage are right, and that this was partly his intention. In explanation, he declares that he committed his adult life, starting with his involvement in the Second World War, to loyally serving his country:

I took the point of view that the United States wore the white hat in world affairs and the Soviet Union and its allies and surrogates wore the black hats, and, of course, this was offensive to large sections of the media and to reviewers – most of whom were quite liberal by bent. This served me poorly during the height of the Watergate trauma, when I was often referred to as a fanatical right-wing writer.

223

Hunt's best-received Intelligence thriller was *The Berlin Ending*, which he also regards as his most important work. The book appeared at a bad time for him – just after the beginning of the Watergate débâcle – and as a result it received considerable publicity. Hunt regrets this, as he feels that the book's particular significance lies in the fact that, for the first time, to his knowledge, in espionage literature, the existence of the 'agent of influence' is revealed – one who, by virtue of substantial public position, is able to influence events in his country for the benefit of a foreign power. He had come upon this phenomenon late in his CIA career, and claims to have made a special point of searching for individuals around the world who might be 'agents of influence' and who were working for Soviet Intelligence. He says he found a sizeable number. Some of these were translated into the fictional characters who appear in *The Berlin Ending*. The book was cleared by the CIA, as 'those in charge of the agency at that time clearly believed that there was nothing wrong with revealing the existence of agents of influence . . . and I certainly didn't, because I thought it was something people should be aware of.' But Hunt viewed the world through suspicious eyes: 'With the veil of innocence peeled away from your vision you can start to pick out groups of people, not only in the United States, but also abroad, who are motivated always to support the Soviet Union in their every endeavour, and that is a rather sickening experience to go through.'

He is bitter about not having been allowed to write during his prison sentence. He acidly points out that, whereas every black activist group was provided with typewriters and typing materials, he was not even allowed a notebook. He did, however, manage to keep a clandestine diary, but could not find a publisher after his release from prison. He was moved frequently from one prison to another, scoring a grand total of thirteen in all. To make matters worse, his wife had been killed in a plane crash just as the hearings began, and he deeply felt the trauma of her death.

Hunt did, however, manage to turn one of his Watergate experiences into fiction. In *The Hargrave Deception* the protagonist recalls in flashback an appearance before a congressional committee and being held in contempt of Congress. Hunt had gone through a very similar experience, although he had not been jailed for contempt. But he had lied to congressional bodies and investigators,

> feeling that that was in the best interest of the country for me to do and not out of a narrow sense of self-preservation. When other people sort of defected and went over to the side of our prosecutor, then my lies became apparent and I was threatened with prosecution for perjury, which was the last thing that I wanted at that juncture of my life.

Hunt's favourite among writers who worked as secret agents is Daniel Defoe. He has little time for the subtle machinations of Somerset Maugham's Ashenden, but his real contempt is reserved for Graham Greene and John le Carré, whom he regards as continually 'trashing' the United States as often as they can. He enjoys Len Deighton, seeing him as 'one of the few British writers in the field who sees the East/West issues in the same terms as I do' – a doubtful accolade for Deighton, perhaps.

Hunt believes that the basic difference between le Carré's Smiley and his own CIA hero lies in the fact that Smiley was a counter-espionage officer: 'He is a man who is a special detective called in after the damage is done. I don't recall any situation in which Smiley ever took or proposed any operations either to gain positive Intelligence or to activate a covert operation in any political field.' Peter Ward is never asked to be 'a damage repair specialist'; his job is to make expeditions into foreign countries to deal with anti-American operations. Hunt believes that le Carré postulates a moral equivalence between the Western nations and the Soviet Union, and that he has a perfect loathing for the CIA. He feels that it was very much for the best that le Carré did not stay on with British Intelligence, detesting MI6 as he did, for he might have been a ready and easy target for Soviet recruitment. Hunt complains about le Carré's perpetual themes of betrayal. Helms believed – and Hunt agrees with him – that espionage is based on trust: that is why 'the CIA has become . . . the leading Western Intelligence apparatus.' Hunt claims to have had a long and good working relationship with British Intelligence, but he feels that 'at least budgetarily, they had become so debilitated and directionless in terms of who the enemy was, that they turned to us necessarily to mount any operation that required more than a few pounds.' It was for this very reason, he believes, that MI6 operations were often turned over to him and that was 'a very poor reason for the transfer of operational responsibility'.

Hunt was fascinated by Chapman Pincher's book, *Their Trade is Treachery*: he feels that MI6 lacks a sense of purpose, and that there is still too much of the 'old school tie' influence:

> You have to know who the enemy is before you can really devise any sort of strategy to either outwit or overcome him, and I felt definitely, at least when I was working in the Western hemisphere, that MI6's brief was for economic Intelligence rather than for positive ops against the Soviet target, or even counter-espionage ops. Everything seemed to be subordinate, within the British station, to the quest for economic Intelligence, and I suppose this is understandable in terms of Britain's lost markets at a time when the Empire was radically shrinking.

Hunt also considers that most of British Intelligence's efforts within the last decade have been devoted to routing out spies and traitors, and indulging in post mortems.

Because of Hunt's public disgrace over Watergate and because he wrote about his experiences in his autobiography, many people think of him as a one-book man – a fact that has made him particularly bitter:

> The public reception to me as a writer as opposed to a Watergate figure – fairly seedy, I suppose – is very slim, and in fact, during some of the publicity, interviewers were astonished to find that I had ever written a book. They

226

regarded me much as one might regard a monkey, who, through repeated random punchings on a typewriter, has produced something as cohesive as the *Iliad*. Though, I suppose, that I could write at all was astonishing to this younger generation of journalists, who have been schooled to regard all the Watergate people as perhaps worse than Charles Manson. So that is one difficulty I have with the media.

Hunt has been thoroughly disillusioned by the CIA loyalty and trust he has written about so much. He had always assumed that the CIA stuck by their own, but his own cover, successfully maintained for many years by the agency, was revealed and broken almost instantly, when it became expedient for them to do so. The CIA did not seem to hesitate for a moment about blowing Hunt's cover, not only to the Department of Justice, but also to the world media; they made it quite clear to all that the individual involved in the Watergate break-in was also a former CIA officer. Hunt is very bitter about the agency's 'betrayal'. He added that Helms' postulation that in the CIA agents stood by each other 'went out of the window somewhere along the line', and that the agency was very little help to him when he was tried and imprisoned.

As to trust, Hunt feels that this is more important between agent-handler and agent than between the American agent and his superior. Good work can be achieved with a foreign agent who is working for a CIA operative, even if that person does not have the total trust of his superiors. In the Intelligence field, internal popularity is not a vital factor. Indeed, in this particular episode some of the figures most popular with the agency were the least competent, because, Hunt felt, a good portion of their time and energy was occupied with socializing and entertaining. Regarding the problem caused by the publication of espionage non-fiction in the UK, Hunt considers that because of the D notice procedure MI5 is better at concealing their embarrassments than the CIA: 'Of course, they become very hostile to a chap like Chapman Pincher who, as far as I can see, has done an outstanding job in helping reshape modern British Intelligence.'

Hunt is currently engaged in another fantasy, a musical drama about Claus von Bülow who was tried and acquitted for the attempted murder of his wife, the rich and beautiful Sonny von Bülow. Called *Beautiful People*, the musical is based on the von Bülow trial, and Hunt is currently writing the book. Hunt told the US showbusiness magazine *Playbill* in November 1985: 'The von Bülow trial is a classic drama. It has all the elements used frequently in Shakespeare. I've taken the basic story – the parvenu, the wealthy wife, the aspiring mistress, the rejected children – and manoeuvred them as I see fit. Some of the characters are not beautiful people, but have spent their lives trying to be.' Hunt has introduced a psychic – 'to advance the story'.

In 1986, Hunt and his second wife, Laura, and their two children, aged six and two, moved to Mexico, so that he would pursue a rather more sheltered writing career. He is firm in his resolution to avoid notoriety: 'I don't really want to go on television any more and talk about different aspects of espionage. I don't want to respond to the media on the subject.'

Howard Hunt's writing flowered in tandem with his Intelligence work. He has always advocated the committed CIA view of serving the country with undivided loyalty. His fictional CIA agents were the hard-riding cowboy good guys, alert at all times to the subversive malevolence of the Soviet baddies. After Watergate, however, the American public and the CIA itself were forced to reappraise this notion. Though Hunt himself may be embittered by having been 'let down' by the agency, his role as fall-guy had already been scripted. Today, his writing still reflects the machinations of the American agent-hero. But his life is changing and perhaps with this a new style of writing will develop. He certainly has some fascinating material to draw on.

CHAPTER TWELVE

JOHN LE CARRÉ:
THE NATURAL SPY

When David Cornwell joined MI5, in the late fifties, the Director-General, Sir Roger Hollis, was under suspicion of espionage. Although Cornwell did not know this at the time, he could see how much hatred and mutual suspicion there was amongst senior officers. MI6 was wrestling with the problems of Kim Philby, while one of their best field officers, George Blake, was about to be sentenced to forty-two years' imprisonment for spying for the Russians. At the same time, Anthony Blunt, basking in the warmth of an unofficial amnesty, was enjoying a Knighthood, as well as a distinguished position as Keeper of the Queen's Pictures.

'It is arguable that Kim Philby, spiteful, vain and murderous as he was, was the spy and catalyst whom the Establishment deserved. Philby is a creature of the post-war depression, of the swift snuffing out of the Socialist flame, of the thousand-year sleep of Eden and Macmillan.'
From le Carré's introduction to Bruce Page, David Leitch and Philip Knightley's *Philby: The Spy Who Betrayed a Generation*

David Cornwell, or as he is better known, John le Carré, suggests that the state of the Secret Service may be taken as a measure of the nation's moral health. His traitor Bill Haydon, unmasked in *Tinker, Tailor, Soldier, Spy*, is a case in point: he becomes treacherous because all the moral forces he has been educated to respect and to admire have disappeared, or have themselves been betrayed. The Empire has long since faded

229

away and, given the choice between subservience to the United States and adherence to Moscow, Haydon chooses the regime that he hopes will at least allow him some independence.

Cornwell is strongly of the opinion that it would be a great mistake to assume that the thirties school of ideological spies has been flushed out. He is certain that, since the war, the greatest damage to Britain has been done not by the traitors, but by the decision-making elite, who, because they have traditionally been drawn from a very small segment of British society, have approached the country's problems from the perspective of that same privileged coterie. Cornwell believes that where power derives from a one-class, one-group elite, the guiding control will be the most powerful personality. Today, he feels, although the power of this elite has waned to some extent, and the reins are now in the hands of the middle classes, a further breaking-up of the old regime and an injection of new blood would produce far greater effectiveness.

David John Moore Cornwell was born on 19 October 1931 in Poole, a small coastal town in Dorset. He had a strange, unsettled childhood in which his manipulative father, Ronnie, tried unsuccessfully to dominate him. Le Carré's spy stories have been heavily influenced by two factors: living under the shadow of his confidence-trickster of a father, and his own involvement in the Secret Services. Of the two, it was the former that made the greater impression. Ronnie was an extraordinary figure, as Cornwell told Miriam Gross in 1980 in an interview for *The Observer*:

> A Micawber character who always managed to spend twice as much as he earned – or twice as much as he obtained. He was a fantasist, perhaps a schizophrenic. He liked using several names. A lot of people found him magical; as a boy, I suppose I did too. So we found ourselves, my brother and I, often living in the style of millionaire paupers.

When Cornwell was five, his father was imprisoned for fraud, and not long afterwards his mother, Olive, left home. She did not contact him again until he was in his twenties. It soon became clear to David and his brother that, contrary to what they had been led to believe, their father had no money. The lives they led were a financial lie, and unpaid bills and unpaid household wages were to become routine. Ronnie's past was a network of evasion, and he had fantasized to the extent that he had come to believe his own lies. He was also an energetic womanizer, and there were many love affairs to hide, as well as financial demands from his lovers, which were a further drain on the family's slender resources. To maintain the bogus image of belonging to the gentry – essential in Ronnie Cornwell's scheme of things – the boys had to go to private schools. So their grandparents paid for them to attend St Andrew's Preparatory School at Pangbourne in the Thames Valley; but when they later went to public school, they were dependent on their father's fluctuating income. As a result, Cornwell and his brother felt as alien in educated middle-class society as if they were spies, deeply conscious that their background was the shifting sands of their father's aspirations.

Like Graham Greene, Cornwell endured an isolated childhood in 'enemy territory' – an upbringing that literally schooled him to become a spy, both as an agent and as a writer. In similar vein to Graham Greene, he recalled, on *The South Bank Show* in March 1983: 'I, from very early, lived a secret life, an inward life, became extremely secretive, and began to think that I was, so to speak, born into occupied territory, because the catastrophies in our family were so great and there were so many things that I couldn't reveal that I seemed to go about in disguise.' He desperately wanted to belong to the real world, but to do this he knew it was essential to protect his background from exposure.

Many of Cornwell's feelings of isolation went into the character of a similar outsider, Bill Roach, a pupil at Thursgood's Preparatory School in *Tinker, Tailor, Soldier, Spy*, published in 1974. Roach is recognized by ex-spy turned teacher, Jim Prideaux, as having all the potential of a good agent, and Prideaux actually uses Roach to spy for him at school. Here, Roach exposes much of Cornwell's own predicament and his attendant feelings in his first meeting with Prideaux:

'What are you good at, Bill?'

'I don't know, sir,' said Roach woodenly.

'Got to be good at something, surely? Everyone is. How about football? You good at football, Bill?'

'No, sir.'

'You a swot, then?' Jim asked carelessly as he lowered himself with a short grunt onto the bed and took a pull from the beaker. 'You don't look a swot, I must say,' he added politely, 'although you're a loner.'

'I don't know,' Roach repeated, and moved himself half a pace towards the open door.

'What's your best thing, then?' He took another long sip. 'Must be good at something, Bill. Everyone is. My best thing was ducks and drakes. Cheers.'

Now this was an unfortunate question to ask of Roach just then, for it occupied most of his waking hours. Indeed, he had recently come to doubt whether he had any purpose on earth at all. In work and play he considered himself seriously inadequate. Even the daily routine of the school, such as making his bed and tidying his clothes, seemed to be beyond his reach . . . He blamed himself for the break-up of his parents' marriage, which he should have seen coming and taken steps to prevent. He even wondered whether he was directly responsible, whether for instance he was abnormally wicked or divisive or slothful and that his bad character had wrought the rift . . . Therefore, this chance question levelled at him in the cramped caravan by a creature at least halfway to divinity, a fellow solitary at that, brought him suddenly very near disaster. He felt the heat charging to his face. He watched his spectacles mist over, and his caravan began to dissolve into a sea of grief . . .

'You're a good watcher, anyway. I'll tell you that for nothing, old boy. Us singles always are. No one to rely on, what? No one else spotted me. Best watcher in the unit, Bill Roach is, I'll bet. Long as he's got his specs on, what?'

'Yes,' Roach agreed gratefully, 'I am.'

Cornwell's first attempt at writing was made at St Andrew's: he wrote a story about a brave veteran race-horse, ridden to victory by a villainous jockey who loaded his whip with buckshot. He persuaded the school secretary to type the piece for him, but when the headmaster discovered what was happening he was strangely angry, informing Cornwell that if he wished to write trash he could type it at his own expense. St Andrew's gave Cornwell his first consistent period of schooling, and he regarded it as an essential part of his development. Up until then the family had moved from place to place, the boys frequently changing schools. Partly as a consequence of this itinerant life, Cornwell had developed a shrewd aproach to personal comfort. He would look out for the best bed in the dormitory, the most susceptible female members of staff, the most satisfactory way of creating a good relationship with the cook. Regarding himself as a soldier in enemy country, he knew the only way to survive was to develop a plan.

Meanwhile, the problems in Ronnie's life continued to proliferate. He ran dozens of companies which had no capital whatsoever; his bankruptcies were to span fifty years, but he never learned from experience. He had three wives, dozens of mistresses and many understanding friends, who were often hypnotized into becoming his victims. He looked like a bishop, and his front of pious respectability was ideal for a conman, as was his lifestyle: he had a flat in Chelsea, offices in Jermyn Street, handsome cars, tailor-made suits and handmade shoes. He signed for everything, as he never had any ready cash, but he was capable of great generosity – although, of course, his funds really belonged to banks and finance houses. Like a very young child, he had no idea of the concept of money. His face, even towards the end of his life, was completely unlined.

Throughout Cornwell's childhood and well into his teens, Ronnie spied on him. He searched his room, opened his post and listened to telephone calls on the extension, trying to make his children the prisoners of his own closed, manipulative world. Cornwell responded by spying on his father. He would search among his private papers, go through the pockets of his cashmere suits and camel-hair coats, examine his diaries. He learned to move quietly, having observed that his father never made any sound. He became a double agent within his own home: he spied for his father as well as on him. Ronnie had surrounded himself with the whole paraphernalia of the Intelligence world. He had safe houses, a string of contacts that needed regular servicing, slush funds, clandestine transport and couriers, and he used cover stories, false names and false identities. He was also highly resistant to interrogation. The couriers were often his children – of which he had four – who would regularly and obediently tell his many creditors that 'the cheque was in the post'. Yet Ronnie disciplined his offspring with erratic intensity: 'To see us right, as he had it. To elevate us to some quality of life which he felt had eluded him.' But why did Ronnie harbour these feelings of deprivation? He was the son of respectable, wealthy parents and had never known hardship, 'yet he clung to the notion of his disadvantage so doggedly that the very reason for his way of life was a lie even to himself'.

After leaving St Andrew's, Cornwell went on to Sherborne School in Dorset, while his brother went to Radley. Cornwell was miserably unhappy at Sherborne, for, bereft of staff and amenities because of the war, the school had fallen back on rule by the rod. Athleticism was seen to be the highest form of achievement. In an atmosphere of bigotry, the luckless pupils were taught that their future careers could only lie in the service of the Empire. Even at thirteen, Cornwell was horrified at the arrogance of such an assumption, and he began to find each schoolday more intolerable than the last. Finally, at sixteen, he defected, refusing to return to this Establishment hot-house. After some persuasion, Ronnie agreed to his son going to the University of Berne in Switzerland. At least it would be socially acceptable, Ronnie must have mused. Looking back, Cornwell realizes that his flight to Switzerland in 1948 was almost that of a political refugee. He remained in Berne for a year, spending most of his time learning German as well as the local Swiss dialect, and trying to manage on very little money indeed. While there, he visited Berlin, and post-war Germany made a vivid impression on him as he surveyed the ruins of Hitler's ideals.

The following year, Cornwell was conscripted for national service, and served his term with the British Army of Occupation in Austria. Because of his good command of the German language he was posted to Intelligence, where he was involved in interrogating and checking the security risks of displaced people in refugee camps. This gave him his first experience of the victims of conflict, and was similar to the work that his future Secret Service boss, John Bingham, was then undertaking. Two years later, his military service completed, Cornwell returned to England and, despite his lack of qualifications, managed to squeeze into Lincoln College, Oxford, to read modern languages.

In 1953, however, his second year at university was terminated by his father's major bankruptcy: he was forced to make an ignominious departure from Lincoln, hopelessly in debt. For a year he was obliged to teach at Millfield, the public school, until Ronnie scraped up enough money to return him to Oxford. During his Millfield experience, Cornwell met another solitary, another victim in the making. On his first night as duty master, he was sitting before the great Victorian fireplace in the common room waiting for the boys to be put to bed, when a prefect rushed in with the information that one of the younger boys was trying to commit suicide. Dashing to the stairwell in considerable agitation, Cornwell looked up to see a small fat boy with glasses, clawing at the bannisters and looking as if he meant business. The long drop would certainly have killed him if he had fallen, but by the time Cornwell reached the top of the stairs, another boy had come to the rescue. The would-be suicide finally admitted that, as he was not very good at making his bed or arranging his day or finding the right books for the right lessons, he did not think he was fit to be at the school – or fit to live at all, in fact. His predicament struck a sonorous bell in Cornwell's own psyche, and was to help shape the character of Bill Roach in *Tinker, Tailor, Soldier, Spy.*

On Cornwell's return to Lincoln College, his senior tutor, Vivian Green (who was the former chaplain of Sherborne and

235

one of the few friends he had made) allowed him to pay the rest of his fees at a later date. Cornwell rewarded his tutor by graduating with First Class Honours, in 1956. While at Oxford, he married Alison Ann Veronica Sharp, the daughter of a high-ranking Royal Air Force officer. (Ann is the name of George Smiley's wife, but Cornwell insists that there is no resemblance.)

Cornwell took a very unexpected step after leaving Oxford. As he put it on *The South Bank Show* in March 1983: 'In the best Pavlovian way, I was fascinated by the things that had persecuted me. Inevitably I accepted their culture, or wished to study it at Eton.' He found his period at Eton, where he taught modern languages, totally absorbing. He had never had any experience of the British ruling class before, and he admits that it 'probably coloured my later writing more than any other experience'. He did not take to his pupils, condemning them not only for the way they spoke and behaved, but also for their prejudices which were even more rigid than those he had encountered at Sherborne. Old Etonians always became very involved politically, and at the time Cornwell was at Eton there were over a dozen in the Cabinet. He was teaching there during the Suez crisis, which spurred him and some other young masters to write a letter to *The Times* dissociating themselves from the actions of the old Etonians in the Cabinet. The reaction was flattering indeed: Anthony Eden was so angry at this rebellion that he sent down Lord John Hope, a minister at the Foreign Office, to explain to the wayward Eton masters the reasons why the Suez offensive was undertaken.

Although Cornwell has always remained highly critical of the upper classes, he admits that in some ways Eton surprised him. In 1974 he told Michael Dean, a journalist on the *Listener*: 'At its best it is enlightened, adaptable, fluent and curiously democratic.' But, he added cuttingly, 'Eton gave me familiarity with crime, as well as an instinct for hypocrisy. And both of them, in different ways, are not absolutely unknown in diplomacy.' After he left Eton in 1958, Cornwell became a freelance illustrator for a brief period. He was a good caricaturist, and was extremely accomplished at drawing birds. He illustrated

Maxwell Knight's *Talking Birds*, which was published in 1961.

Knight, the veteran head of MI5's counter-subversion department, was now nearing retirement. He immediately spotted Cornwell's talents, and was able to convince him that working for MI5 would be an interesting proposition. He recognized in Cornwell all the powers of observation of the loner – the very skills that Cornwell had seen in himself, and in the sadly confused boy at the prep school. And not only could he watch, but he was also sophisticated and intelligent enough to mix with more or less any level of society – Ronnie had seen to that. He told Melvyn Bragg on *The South Bank Show* in March 1983:

> I wasn't Mata Hari, and I wasn't Himmler's aunt, but it would be stupid of me to pretend that I was not, like Somerset Maugham, Graham Greene and lots of other writers, for a time engaged in that work. It would be terribly disappointing for the livelier fantasies of people who have written about me in that capacity, if they knew how boring my life had been. And how humdrum is the world of Intelligence in many ways. I've always tried to deny it and keep away from the subject, and I intend to go on doing so.

Watchfulness, Cornwell thinks, is the keynote. Curiosity comes into it too. He remembers that it was L. P. Hartley who said: 'Don't leave me alone in your study, for I'm certain to read your letters.' Cornwell feels that he would not have gone that far. But he knows that the part of the writer's mind that watches and records is the same part that operates in the Intelligence world, the part that Graham Greene refers to as 'the chip of ice in every writer's heart'. Just as a great deal of insight and imagination goes into espionage work, so is it with writing. Cornwell realized early on that the components of a good spy are mental flexibility, invention, agility and plausibility – in his case highly developed, because of his relationship with his father. And in the making of fictitious plots, exactly the same components are required. He feels that he has been in 'Intelligence' all his life, because of his early home circumstances, because of his school experiences, even because of Eton, but largely because of Ronnie. When he was actually being recruited himself, he looked back on his childhood as a natural training ground. Continually moving house and changing schools, he had begun to dream of the secret centre to the world which, if he ever reached it, would reveal the purpose behind the mad round that formed his childhood. 'Seems to live in a world of his own', Cornwell's school reports had stated disapprovingly, but he knew that it was a better world than theirs. When he was seven, Cornwell had read a piece by G. A. Henty called *Oscar Danby VC*, which concerned a brave boy scout. The story filled him with a strong desire to die before a German firing squad. Weeks later he was telling people that his father was in the Secret Service. He added that his father was being trained and that he would soon be parachuted into Germany. Whether the seven-year-old Cornwell was being intuitive about Ronnie is hard to say, but it was certainly an appropriate fantasy.

When Cornwell was recruited by Knight, he had the highest expectations. He was married at the time, and he supposes he must have passed for mature. In spite of his strong sense of his own potential, he could not decide which path he should take to achieve it. He was vaguely left-wing, but reserved about his politics. One thing he was sure about was that he wanted to delve into his country's subconscious, to discover its secret wishes, fears, and intentions, just as he used to search his father's drawers and cupboards in search of clues to *his* secret lives. In an interview for *The Sunday Times* in March 1986, he said: 'I wanted sacrifice. Mine. I wished to have my scattered identities and talents gathered up and used. It was a tough bill for an overstretched employer with other things on his mind to fill.' Cornwell liked the image of the outwardly dull civil servant – 'while at the time, I was somebody terribly exciting'. He is still surprised that Fleet Street's so-called Intelligence experts do not understand that one of the main reasons behind the desire to be recruited into the Secret Services is the lure of secrecy itself, 'as a means of outgunning people we would otherwise be scared of;

of feeling superior to life rather than engaging in it; as a place of escape, attracting not the strong in search of danger but us timid fellows, who couldn't cope with reality for one calendar day without the structures of conspiracy to get us by.' This is as true of the other writers discussed in this book as it is of Cornwell.

But once inside MI5 – and later MI6 – all romance vanished, and he found 'a bunch of people all asking each other where the secret world had gone'. Cornwell entered the Intelligence community at a time when it was tortured by self-doubt and self-delusion. He soon picked up the vibrations of continual suspicion amongst his colleagues, and those in the know mysteriously hinted that it was only a matter of time until Anthony Blunt was exposed as a traitor. Cornwell himself never believed that Roger Hollis was a spy; rather, that 'he was probably a bit of a fumbler . . . the unfulfilled fiction-writers of his court attempted to dignify their collective incompetence by calling him a traitor, and used a gullible Press to help them do it. Successful novelists may be bad news for the secret world, but they are not half as dangerous as the failed ones.'

Cornwell freely admits that the Intelligence world that he calls 'the Circus' (his fictitious special department of the British Intelligence Service) in his Smiley trilogy has no existence in reality. But now even the tawdry MI5 world that Cornwell himself inhabited no longer exists.

The warrens of cabbagey passages with their fish-eye mirrors and rickety lifts that did not stop at certain floors, their half-landings, false doors and grizzled janitors who peered at you like friendly hangmen, have been replaced by a glass and concrete box in South London, just a stone's throw from the spot where, a decade earlier, I had set my crumbling Intelligence department.

The fact that some, perhaps a high proportion, of MI5 and MI6 personnel were homosexuals, was irrelevant to Cornwell's theories about treachery. In his opinion the elite, class-based brotherhood that dominated the British Secret Services was a far greater menace.

In 1960, David Cornwell left MI5 for MI6. A front cover was established for him, first as a second secretary at the British embassy in Bonn, and later consul in Hamburg. Before leaving for Germany, former Intelligence sources relate, Cornwell was put through an intensive course at an Intelligence training camp in England. There he was taught everything from silent boat landings to the most sophisticated new codes and micro-photography. It was probably from this course that he gathered material for Sarratt – the site in Hertfordshire and alternative name for the nursery where new Circus recruits were trained and agents briefed. Once in Germany, Cornwell found that he disliked intensely the social round of diplomatic life, but he considered that being very much at the centre of things was an important compensating factor. The period was one of hectic activity and tension, with a number of crises dominating his professional life – the Berlin Wall, the Bay of Pigs incident and the end of the Adenauer government. His duties in Bonn involved reporting back on the political situation in West Germany, as well as accompanying high-level West German delegations on visits to London. Both these responsibilities took him into private meetings with British Cabinet leaders and officials, giving him a detailed insight into the British political structure that was later to serve him well when he was creating the intricate machinations of the Circus.

When the Berlin Wall was erected, Cornwell was asked by MI6 to report back on every development, and to undertake the dangerous mission of assisting valued East German contacts to escape from the Soviet section. Conscious of the rich vein of material that his new job opened up, he began to write in his spare time. His first two novels, *Call for the Dead* (1961) and *A Murder of Quality* (1962), introduced the ageing British agent, George Smiley. Cornwell admits that he has a strange relationship with Smiley, who is portrayed as being about Ronnie's age, and he concedes that in Smiley he has inadvertently assembled something of a substitute father.

The thriller-writer most in vogue in England towards the end of the fifties was, of course, Ian Fleming. Each new James Bond adventure – one came out every year – was eagerly lapped up. There was considerable public anxiety at this time over a possible Third World War, and Bond, in his persistent fight against Communism, seemed the ideal antidote. Britain could still be great, was Fleming's message, but Cornwell, with his first-hand knowledge of upper-class intrigue, saw Britain in desolation. *Call for the Dead* was, in some ways, a reaction to Bond's fantasy machismo. Cornwell hated Bond, calling him 'the ultimate prostitute' and the 'ideal defector', but in an interview for *The Listener* in September 1974 he rejected the suggestion that *Call for the Dead* was an anti-Bond novel:

> That was nonsense. I'm not nearly clever enough to have done that at the time, and I wrote about the things that I knew of, the tensions in Berlin which I witnessed: institutional behaviour, British nostalgia for power, perhaps, and I imported from my experience of the Foreign Service, a great deal of the way paper is moved around and the dinginess of decisions sometimes.

Smiley is as far a cry from Bond as is Len Deighton's Harry Palmer. Described by his wife in *Call for the Dead* as 'breathtakingly ordinary', Smiley is certainly hardly glamorous: 'Short, fat and of a quiet disposition, he appeared to spend a lot of money on really bad clothes, which hung about his squat frame like a skin on a shrunken toad.' Smiley's chief ambition is to devote his life to the study of the obscurities of seventeenth-century German literature. He is recruited at a panel of the 'Overseas Committee for Academic Research', to which he has been sent by his tutor. This was very much in line with the policy of some real-life tutors at Oxford and Cambridge who, between the wars, selected what they thought were potential spies from the universities.

At the end of the Second World War, Smiley leaves intelligence work so that he can devote himself to his wife and to academic research in Oxford. He is recalled to the Intelligence world in 1947. Cornwell's fictitious subjects have many links with reality. In *Call for the Dead*, for instance, the reason behind Smiley's return to Intelligence work is said to be that 'the revelations of a young cipher-clerk in Ottawa had created a new demand for men of Smiley's experience.' The cipher-clerk in reality was Igor Gouzenko, who defected to the West in September 1943 and who revealed information about Soviet penetration of British Intelligence organizations. Later on in the novel, there are references to the atom spy Klaus Fuchs and Donald Maclean.

One question we must ask is: how much of Cornwell is there in Smiley? In *Call for the Dead*, when Smiley's wife, Ann, leaves him, Cornwell writes: 'And so Smiley, without school, parents, regiment or trade, without wealth or poverty, travelled without labels in the guard's van of the social express, and soon became lost luggage, destined, when the divorce had come and gone, to remain unclaimed on the dusty shelf of yesterday's news.' Smiley leaves his 'unimpressive school' for his 'unimpressive Oxford College'; he, like Cornwell, is fluent in the German language; both were members of the Secret Service. Like Cornwell, Smiley commits himself to the Establishment cause. But it is in his political views that Smiley most clearly resembles Cornwell, as he explained to *The Observer* in February 1980:

[Smiley's] engagement against Communism is really an intellectual one. I think he stands where I stand; he feels that to pit yourself against any 'ism' is to strike a posture which is itself ideological, and therefore offensive in terms of practical decency. In practice almost any political ideology invites you to set aside your humanitarian instincts.

It was Cornwell's third novel, *The Spy Who Came in from the Cold*, published in 1963, that brought him to the public's attention, enabling him to leave the Foreign Service and become a full-time writer. He wrote *Spy* with far more passion than he had put into his previous two books. Strain in his personal life, largely caused by Ronnie's nefarious activities, had triggered off a rare quality in his writing. He was also confronted with political pressures, and a continual flow of embassy telegrams warning that the world was on the brink of another war. Cornwell admits that *Spy* is a very bitter book, and a far cry from anything Fleming ever wrote: 'I mean the world had been aware from its newspapers of this great grey army of cold warriors, of defectors, of spies, frontier crossers. And what had literature produced? This candy-floss image of a macho man, an Etonian who really seemed not to have a moral doubt in his head.'

By contrast, the plot of *Spy* is deeply concerned with the morality of spying. In this passage the central character, Alec Leamas, is driving towards Berlin in an attempt to escape from his enemies. His girlfriend, who is also enmeshed in the espionage conflict, attacks him about the ethics of the business:

'This is a war,' Leamas replied. 'It's graphic and unpleasant because it's fought on a tiny scale, at close range; fought with a wastage of innocent life sometimes, I admit. But it's nothing, nothing at all besides other wars – the last or the next.'

'Oh, God,' said Liz softly. 'You don't understand. You don't want to. You're trying to persuade yourself. It's far more terrible, what they are doing; to find the humanity in people, in me and whoever else they use, to turn it like a weapon in their hands, and use it to hurt and kill . . .'

'Oh, Liz,' said Leamas desperately, 'for God's sake believe me. I hate it all; I'm tired. But it's the world, it's mankind that's gone mad. We're a tiny price to pay . . . but everywhere's the same, people cheated and misled, whole lives thrown away, people shot and in prison, whole groups and classes of men written off for nothing.'

Once again, the influence of Ronnie was abroad. It was he who cheated and misled and would have thrown his family's lives away for the sake of his own false image – or even theirs.

Cornwell wrote his first three books knowing that he could no longer conform to the Foreign Service, just as, earlier, he had no longer been able to conform to Eton. By writing in his spare time, he was at least asserting his freedom and seeking after identity. *Call for the Dead* was written in notebooks while he commuted from Great Missenden to the Foreign Office in London. *A Murder of Quality* was written in Bonn, just after his first posting. *The Spy Who Came in from the Cold*, inspired by the building of the Berlin Wall, was written with great speed. All three books were composed during Cornwell's early-morning journeys to work, so by the time he had completed *Spy* he knew at least that writing was an occupation that he could fit into his everyday life. Cornwell sees *Spy* as a very romantic story in which two people fall in love, with one having to betray the other in the end. The conclusion is bleak and institutional. The success of *Spy* put him strongly in the mould of the thriller-writer, but this did not deter him. In some ways it assured him that it was the kind of writing he did best, although he did not see himself as essentially a writer of spy stories.

The choice of the pseudonym John le Carré seems to remain a mystery, even to Cornwell himself. When Victor Gollancz had taken the decision to publish *Call for the Dead*, Cornwell asked him for advice on the subject. His job in the diplomatic service made using his own name quite out of the question; Gollancz suggested something butch and cryptic such as Chuck Smith, but Cornwell wanted something more up-market. He thought that to break up a name and give it a slightly foreign sound would make people remember it. He admits to having spun so many fantasies as to how the name was created that he can no longer remember what he said in the first place. When, later, he was working the celebrity circuit in America, he invented the fiction that he had been riding on a bus to the Foreign Office when he saw the name le Carré above a shoe shop. 'But that was simply because I couldn't convince anybody it came from nowhere.'

His father, of course, provided some of Cornwell's truly unique material. But there was to be a long history of interference and deception before he was able to exorcise Ronnie's personality in this way. It was Ronnie, who, in an attempt to oppose Cornwell's original recruitment by Maxwell Knight, had torn open the suspicious-looking envelope purporting to emanate from a department of the Foreign Office that did not in fact exist. And it was Ronnie who telephoned a contact in Whitehall to find out who was trying to recruit his son. When Cornwell was asked to the Travellers' Club for an initial interview over lunch, Ronnie would have gone there to warn the MI5 officers off, had not Cornwell stood firm. 'Twenty years later,' says Cornwell, 'when I gave a television interview about my life without mentioning him as its architect, he first threatened to sue me, then went to my accountant and, as a gesture of compromise, demanded £10,000 in compensation.' No wonder Cornwell writes so well about manipulation.

David Cornwell tried to write about Ronnie many times, but always with unsatisfactory and painful results. He was too much a part of his father to see him in any real perspective, and he felt that, when he wrote about Ronnie, he employed the self-conscious tone of a Gosse or an Ackerley, hoping that the reader would see him as a tender soul being crushed by a tyrant. But in reality Cornwell remained uncrushed and in bitter combat for his own identity, which his father was always trying to take from him – 'if anybody was going to do the tyrannizing in those days, I was.' But he now feels he was mistaken in making efforts in his early drafts of books about Ronnie to separate his relationship with his father from his involvement in the world of Intelligence. Not only, he says, did he omit the links between the two, but he neglected the possibility that his own struggle with Communism might, at least in part, be the continuation of the secret war with his father.

Even after Ronnie's death Cornwell was to write many more books before he could see him in any objective light at all. Over a period of twenty-five years, each time he finished a novel he would continue to revise the pages about Ronnie, pages that always failed to crystallize. Then he would push them aside, taking refuge in proxy father-figures such as Smiley – who was, significantly, parentless – bogging them down with his unfocused broodings about love and loyalty. The big book, he thought, the book about Ronnie, would be the one he would never write, and all the others would be satellites, circling round a missing centre.

Nevertheless, Cornwell knew he was stalking Ronnie, even if he could never successfully focus him in his sights. In *The Naïve and Sentimental Lover*, published in 1971, he gave his central character a pale Ronnie for a father, an indolent and feckless publican.

> Cassidy's feelings about his father varied. He lived in a penthouse in Maida Vale, a property listed among the assets of the company and let to him rent-free in exchange for unspecified consultative services. From its many large windows, it seemed to Cassidy, he followed his son's progress through the world as once the eye of God had followed Cain across his desert. There was no hiding from him: his intelligence system was vast, and where it failed, intuition served him in its place. In bad times, Cassidy regarded him as undesirable and made elaborate plots to kill him. In good times he admired him very much, particularly for his flair. When younger, Cassidy had made copious researches about old Hugo, interviewing lapsed acquaintances in clubs and browsing through public records; but facts about him, like facts about God, were hard to come by.

Ronnie was still alive when the book was written, and although he never actually read it, he was tipped off by friends. As a result, he gave serious consideration to taking his son to court, but in the end decided against it.

Cornwell made a second attempt at portraying Ronnie in *The Honourable Schoolboy*, published in 1977, this time making him a dead newspaper magnate rather than a publican: 'The father, a flamboyant figure, fair-haired like the son, kept racehorses . . . Like the son he was never at peace; women and houses, changing them all the time; always roaring at someone, if not at his son then at someone across the street.' Cornwell tried for a third time in *The Little Drummer Girl*, published in 1983, but on this occasion he portrayed Ronnie in a more roundabout way. Charlie, the heroine, is given to telling tall stories about her father in order to dramatize herself. Yet many of the things that were untrue about Charlie's father were true about his own. Now that Ronnie was in his grave, Cornwell felt more able to spread himself. *The Little Drummer Girl* was Cornwell's first book not to involve Smiley, although some years before, particularly during Ronnie's lifetime, he had wanted to bring Smiley into every book. In banishing Smiley at this point, Cornwell was already subconsciously making space to write about his father.

Ronnie's death did not mean the passing of his influence on his son, who was overwhelmed at that time with conflicting intelligence about him, as tortuously confused deals, relationships and swindles began to come home to roost. One such concerned a lady from a European capital who, shortly before Ronnie's death, wrote Cornwell a number of letters, care of his publisher. In them she insisted that she and Cornwell had had a love affair on the Rome express. And these were not the letters of a lunatic: they were sensitive, pained and extremely credible in their detail. The lady accused Cornwell of missing a rendezvous, declaring that she had met various trains, in the hope that he would be on one of them. She even sent some photographs of herself sitting at a fireside reading and looking lonely. That Ronnie had been masquerading as his own son seemed to Cornwell too implausible to be true, but eventually he had to accept that this was exactly what his father had done. Predictably, Ronnie had been enchanted by his son's success as John le Carré, immediately claiming to be his literary mentor and – even more attractive to him – manager of his financial affairs. Unabashed by the fact that all this was patently untrue, he would frequently boast of negotiating Cornwell's film deals, and of how his beloved son would consult him on every facet of his literary career. Sometimes his fantasies would overlap into real life. On one occasion, Cornwell received puzzled letters from the chief of a West Berlin film studio, who was under the impression that he was going to make Cornwell's next film. But it was Ronnie who had toured the studio and then offered the deal – and it was Ronnie who had extorted suitable expenses. Yet, despite all this, so intense was Cornwell's relationship with his father that, rather than condemn him for his con-artistry, he merely wrote: 'We can forgive our parents almost anything if they are proud of us.'

Meanwhile, the unfortunate European lady persisted in her claims, sending Cornwell a regular supply of sadly accusing letters. With great restraint – for curiosity must have played its part – he did not answer them. But he was puzzled, for, given that, all over the world, his photograph was staring from the dust-jackets of his books, surely she would have identified the physical difference between Ronnie and his son by now? Then a new and disquieting thought crept into his mind. Could there be a third man, someone of his own age with similar features, who had taken over his identity? In the end, he was advised to send the lady a standard Law Lords' letter, (a form of legal document) stating that the nuisance must cease. It did – and he never heard from her again. Yet, if it was Ronnie who had begun the relationship with her – and he was sure that it was – what on earth had he said to her? Cornwell pondered this point in his 1986 interview with *The Sunday Times*:

> Did he regale her with the agonies of a writer's solitary life? I wondered. Did he describe to her my doubts and blocks and insecurities, my night thoughts as I spun my plots and conjured up my characters? And was there, in the imagined lands of our separate fantasies, some secret battleground where we were fighting out our rivalry? . . . I took refuge from my father in the world of spying. With Smiley as my imaginary companion, I set off to South East Asia to start work on *The Honourable Schoolboy*, though I should have guessed that Ronnie's ghost was already out there waiting for me.

In 1980, still obsessed with the idea of exorcising his father in a book, Cornwell was considering the possibility of dispatching a researcher in Ronnie's disastrous wake. He based *The Looking-Glass War*, published in 1965, on the special ability that Ronnie shared with other confidence-tricksters – the ability to deceive oneself, as a prerequisite to deceiving others. In his Intelligence experience, Cornwell had seen hitherto sane men succumb to the same kind of self-delusion. In Ronnie's case there was his quite insane ambition to become an MP. He should have realized – and, indeed, one part of him must have realized – that once he stood for election, the details of his past life would almost certainly be revealed. Yet he continued to stand as a prospective Liberal, manipulating his friends, as well as his family, into supporting him. Any doubters were immediately dismissed as 'cynics' – a word he reserved for his worst enemies, and to be compared to his other hates: 'airy-fairies' (intellectuals), 'flunkies' (civil servants) and 'twerps' (unbelievers).

When, in 1986, Cornwell was at last able to write objectively about his father in *The Perfect Spy*, his most literary work so far, he had finally realized that Ronnie was not unique, that the tangled home life from which he had fled was no more extraordinary than the attitudes and lives of many respected members of the Establishment. The only difference between them and Ronnie was that they deceived and lied in the name of service to the government. Cornwell felt that Ronnie's justification lay 'in the culpable obedience of his natural adversaries, to whom I myself, in an exaggerated rush away from him and towards respectability, had belonged'. Cornwell believed that *The Perfect Spy* could only work when the sins of the son were seen to be as great as the sins of the father, 'and when both were seen to be less than the sins of the collective that the two men had alternately deceived and served.'

The Intelligence world was considerably enraged by the poor image it was given in the Smiley trilogy. 'We are definitely not as our host here describes us,' declared Sir Maurice Oldfield when he lunched with Sir Alec Guinness at La Poule au Pot in Ebury Street in London – an event organized by Cornwell himself. Oldfield was yet another C, Director-General of MI6 from 1973 until 1978. The son of a Derbyshire farmer and the eldest of eleven children, he had originally been destined for an academic career, winning a scholarship to Manchester University. During the Second World War, he had served with the Military Intelligence Corps, where he was discovered to have a particular talent for espionage. On this occasion, Guinness was about to play George Smiley in the BBC television version of *Tinker, Tailor, Soldier, Spy*, and particularly wanted to meet a professional spy-master. During lunch, in a positive attempt to destroy Cornwell's image of dishonourable Establishment life, Oldfield stressed the high ethical standards of the Secret Service, clearly showing his disapproval of Cornwell. Sir Alec enjoyed the lunch, finding Oldfield outgoing, charming and amusing. They corresponded several times, and he wrote to Guinness after the television series: 'I still don't recognize myself.' Oldfield was also rumoured – erroneously – to be a model for Fleming's M.

Like John Bingham, Oldfield answered the physical description of George Smiley: 'Small, podgy and at best middle-aged, he was by appearance one of London's meek who do not inherit the earth. His legs are short, his gait anything but agile.' Oldfield had a similar flat-footed walk, and, like Smiley, he wore thick-lensed glasses. Either way, Oldfield did not seem to mind the comparison. Indeed, despite his abhorrence of the image Cornwell had given to MI5, he appeared quietly amused. Of course, the fact that he was officially retired when the question of the television series arose, must have had some bearing on his attitude.

When Oldfield died in March 1986, even the London *Times* contributed to the supposition that he was the model for Smiley; ITV's News at Ten actually claimed that Cornwell had stated it to be the case. This prompted an immediate denial from Cornwell, writing as le Carré in the *Times*:

I have never in my life made such a statement, least of all on the day of Sir Maurice's sad death . . . The truth, once and for all, is this. I never heard of Sir Maurice either by name or in any other way until long after the name and character of George Smiley were in print. I knew him, whether by reputation or personality, scarcely at all. Our social contact, such as it was, occurred after his retirement and amounted to a couple of lunches, over which he was inclined to rebuke me, albeit amiably, for what he regarded as the unflattering portrait I had given of his former service. At his request, I once produced Sir Alec Guinness for him, for the good reason that he had always been, in his modest way, one of Sir Alec's fans. Sir Maurice was tickled pink.

There are, nonetheless, other positive similarities between Smiley and Oldfield. Both came from grammar schools, both were south-east Asia specialists, both had a passion for history. However, here the similarities end.

Madeleine Bingham, now Lady Clanmorris, John Bingham's wife, shared Oldfield's disapproval of Cornwell's disparagement of the Secret Services. She wrote to Richard Deacon, Oldfield's biographer: 'As long as he was alive, we were led to believe that Sir Maurice Oldfield was the model for Smiley. Only when he was dead were we informed that this wasn't the case.' She wrote a book herself, based on the premise that her husband was the original model for Smiley: 'Clearly David never wanted to publicly admit that Jack was Smiley because Jack was working for MI5 right up until the end of the sixties. But when he retired I feel that David should have said who his model really was.' She felt that Cornwell had, in fact, caricatured her husband. Her book was banned from publication by MI5, but in fact it contains perfectly harmless information, which could in no way be condemned as a breach of security. Madeleine Bingham wrote: 'As far as the content of the book is concerned, it is simply the story of one Intelligence officer and his family, and the introduction was designed to defend the Intelligence

Services against the ludicrous attack of David Cornwell.'

There is a far more important reason why it is unlikely that either Oldfield or Bingham could have been the model for Smiley. Throughout the le Carré books there are significant references to other machinations, such as: 'The Optimates [the Apostles, an aesthetic club to which many of the Cambridge spies belonged] . . . an upper-class Christ Church Club, largely Old Etonians . . . a private selection tank for the Great base'. Substitute Trinity College, Cambridge, for Christ Church, Oxford, and the real derivations become clearer. All these signs point to Vivian Green – Cornwell's former chaplain at Sherborne and, later, senior tutor at Lincoln College – being the model for Smiley. Cornwell also tells us: 'Most of the English moles were recruited by Karla before the war and came from the higher bourgeoisie . . . and became secretly fanatic, much more fanatic than their working-class comrades.' And Green later told Richard Deacon: 'When David and his wife stayed with me last October, they bought a present of caviar and vodka with the card reading: "With love from Karla [head of 'Moscow Centre' in le Carré's novels]".' Cornwell confirmed that this episode had occurred.

Madeleine Bingham was not concerned solely about Cornwell's true model for Smiley; she also told me: 'Jack was always very angry about the way David portrayed Intelligence, and I have a letter he wrote to Jack in which in answer to his objections David wrote, "I write Westerns, and because I am plausible people take it to be the truth." ' When Cornwell was an agent-running officer, Bingham felt that he was unsympathetic, not caring or perceptive enough *vis-à-vis* his agents. He later made his criticisms of Cornwell apparent anonymously in an unpublished manuscript, in which he says: 'The belief encouraged by many spy writers that Intelligence officers consist of moles, morons, shits and homosexuals makes the Intelligence job no easier.' Madeleine is even more outspoken. In her opinion, 'David has denigrated the Secret Service institution and severely damaged the true character of loyalty that the service has always displayed. By denigrating Jack's job he has undermined our country and let us become the laughing stock of the Soviets.'

The Soviets are, in fact, reputed to have contacted Cornwell in Greece, after he had written *The Spy Who Came in from the Cold*. When he won the Somerset Maugham prize, he said, apparently, that he was unwilling to go to Russia because of this. However, another reason may have been the rule that Intelligence officers cannot go behind the Iron Curtain for five years after they have retired from the Secret Services. Cornwell believes that there is a great need to combat Communism, and he does not think that many British people are aware of the extent to which the British Secret Services are involved in this. He also feels that Smiley's world should be familiar to us all, for 'conspiracy alone is some kind of solace, to the reader or to the audience. People want to interpret their lives in terms of conspiracy. They know it is around them, they know that we live in an increasingly secretive society in many ways, where they're cut off from the decisions of power.' In *Tinker, Tailor, Soldier, Spy*, *The Honourable Schoolboy* and *Smiley's People* Cornwell develops a truly massive conspiracy for his readership. He considers that he leads them to a conclusion – and that is something that they do not normally find in office politics.

Cornwell has invented many of his own Intelligence terms. Only a few are real. A 'legend', meaning a false biography or a cover story, is KGB jargon; 'Mole' is also a KGB word, dragged out of obscurity; but the others emerged from his ever-fertile imagination. Cornwell believes there is an eerie and uneasy camaraderie between professional Intelligence officers on opposite sides; to give the reader the illusion of entering the secret world, he thought it essential to provide a mysterious jargon.

In his introduction to Page, Leitch and Knightley's *Philby: The Spy Who Betrayed a Generation*, Cornwell tells us that, in his opinion, Philby inherited a manipulative nature from his father, Sir John Philby, and from exaggerated ideas of his own worth. As Connie Sachs says of Bill Haydon, Philby grew up with the idea that he was born an Empire baby – to rule; and he was born in a world where 'all his toys were being taken away by history.'

Cornwell believes that this was a far more potent reason for Philby's betrayal than the fact that he was an ardent Marxist. His introduction to the book incurred the wrath of Graham Greene, who felt that Cornwell was being cheap at the expense of a man he had a liking for. He was also attacked by the historian Hugh Trevor-Roper, who claimed that Cornwell was in total ignorance of the period in which Philby purportedly became a Communist – the thirties. But Cornwell was unabashed, convinced that he was correct.

Blunt, feels Cornwell, is a rather different case. As a member of an elite homosexual group, he was already committed to secrets. Cornwell had been deeply angered by Blunt's television performance, in the interview in which he first confessed his treachery, at the time of his public exposure. He found it macarbe to hear a self-confessed Russian spy rather primly taking refuge in the Official Secrets Act. He also found Blunt patronizing, and 'his performance in *The Times* offices brought out practically all the social resentments that are still left in me.'

While working for MI5 in the fifties, Cornwell discovered that Graham Greene was in much disfavour – indeed, he was to come very close to following Compton Mackenzie to the Old Bailey. Bumping into MI5's lawyer in the Whitehall canteen one day, Cornwell saw a virgin copy of *Our Man in Havana* lying in front of him on the formica-topped table. Greene would have to be prosecuted, the lawyer said, because, as an ex-member of the Service, he had authentically portrayed the relationship between a head of station in a British embassy and his agent in the field. This was definitely not on, despite the fact that the lawyer thought highly of the book's literary merits. For some weeks after this conversation, Cornwell watched the newspapers with interest, waiting for news of Greene's arrest, but, to his relief, nothing happened. Twenty years later, Greene was to write *The Human Factor*. *Our Man in Havana* had depicted the Secret Service as fools, but in this latest work he saw them as murderers. In the foreword he went out of his way to state that he had not infringed the Official Secrets Act. A similar claim had been made in early editions of *Our Man in Havana*. Cornwell had this to say to *The Sunday Times* in 1986:

> Writers are a subversive crowd, nothing if not traitors. The better the writer, the greater the betrayal tends to appear, a thing the secret community has learned the hard way, for I hear it is no longer quite so keen to have us abroad. Nevertheless, Mackenzie ended his days with a knighthood. Greene will end his with the Order of Merit at least, and if there is any justice at all in the secret world of literary awards, a Nobel prize.

One day in the mid-sixties, Sir Roger Hollis made a bizarre appearance in Cornwell's life. Then a full-time writer, Cornwell was living in a house near Wells in Somerset, and working from a studio in the garden. Answering a knock on his front door, he found Hollis standing there on the doorstep. Hollis announced that he was collecting money for the nearby Cathedral School. He seemed to find solace, that day, sitting with Cornwell in his studio, drinking coffee and talking over old times. At one point he asked Cornwell if he could read his newspaper, and later they had some bread and cheese. Cornwell had the impression that Hollis had not seen a paper for some time. Then he left, only to return on three or four more occasions. Gradually conversation ran out, but by then they felt no need to speak. Cornwell sat upstairs writing, and Hollis, 'a touchingly ordinary man', sat downstairs. Cornwell discovered later that it was at exactly this time that Hollis was being interrogated by a Whitehall committee as to whether or not he had been a Russian spy. No doubt, when he visited Cornwell, he was savouring the freedom of the safe house.

David Cornwell is not interested in the political aspects of espionage, but in the minds of those who set themselves apart from ordinary society by joining a secret society which, they feel, gives them a moral dictate. In such circumstances, an agent can easily become a traitor and deceive those closest to him. Betrayal, he feels, will always be with us, for every generation has as great a capacity to produce traitors as to produce the disenchantment which is the breeding ground of betrayal. Cornwell was repeatedly told by his own Secret Service contacts that, once the thirties intake was flushed out, then undivided loyalty would reign. Cornwell does not agree: as long as he has been alive, the hopes of every British generation have come to nothing. He sees the aftermath of the Second World War as a 'dreary seesaw between failed socialism and failed capitalism . . . there is enough motive for any number of angry or despairing gestures.' He would not like, he says, to be a security officer in the year 2000, trying to maintain the status quo, with a new generation to contend with, the product of despairing schools in inner-city conurbations who have lived all their lives in substandard housing, with their parents permanently un-employed: 'What inward, angry, over-controlled little Bettaneys will be getting on their secret bikes by then?' As Cornwell sees it, the current climate of disillusionment and unemployment in Britain is set fair to become a breeding ground for traitors.

EPILOGUE:

LEN DEIGHTON:
THE UNASSUMING SPY

'All over the world people are personally opposing things they think are bad, but they do them anyway because a corporate decision can take the blame.'

Len Deighton, *An Expensive Place to Die*

Len Deighton never worked for the Secret Services, but he had one particular encounter that was to provide inspiration for his many novels about the world of espionage. Born in an Edgware Road workhouse – because the Queen Charlotte Hospital was too full – in 1929, Deighton was the son of the chauffeur in the household of Campbell Dodgson, Keeper of Prints and Drawings at the British Museum. His mother was the cook there. She also cooked for the ex-White Russian Fascist and fanatic, Anna Wolkoff. One night, at the behest of Maxwell Knight, Special Branch came to arrest Wolkoff. Deighton remembers a group of grey men arriving in unofficial cars. Wolkoff left quietly with her discreet retinue, and Deighton still vividly recalls the extraordinary feeling of emptiness after they had taken her away. He discovered much later that Wolkoff and Tyler Kent had been accused of stealing copies of correspondence between Roosevelt and Churchill (see pages 89, 176–7).

Deighton believes that writers have much in common with spies; he has deliberately adopted a mask of ordinariness so that he can watch without drawing attention to himself, and listen to conversations without people turning round to look at him. He lives with his fictitious spies all the time, plotting every detail of their lives. During writing periods, he rarely switches off and his

257

family find him passive, living out the world of whatever book he is working on. This kind of total involvement makes for very visual writing: Deighton not only leads his readers through every complex twist of the plot with compelling authenticity, but he can also take them through a room, a meal, a continent with such attention to detail that they feel they are there.

In his role of spy and writer, Deighton has adopted different guises throughout his life. He left school to become a railway clerk, before doing his National Service in the RAF. There he became a photographer, sharing a room with a bookie's runner, a circus artist and an Oxford undergraduate. He then went to the St Martin's School of Art in London on an ex-serviceman's grant, moving on to the Royal College of Art; next, he became an illustrator in New York. Then he returned to London, where he took the job of art director with an advertising agency – a situation that he did not enjoy. In 1960, dissatisifed with the rat race of advertising, Deighton went to the Dordogne and wrote a thriller. *The Ipcress File* was an instant success. The anonymous hero, eventually named Harry Palmer when the film was made, is involved in the rescue of a bio-chemist who has been kidnapped in the Lebanon en route to the Soviet Union. Palmer, a working-class boy from Burnley who enjoys cooking and girls, was a gritty antidote to James Bond, and the plot had an authenticity that no one had hitherto come across in the spy genre. Gone were the lush settings and fast cars of Bond. Instead, Deighton introduced the seaminess of East Berlin, the grubby trading of lives and the intricately manipulative mechanics of Cold War politics.

Since *The Ipcress File* was published in 1962, Deighton has written sixteen thrillers and three works of non-fiction. Publicly he has always been anonymous and self-effacing, although as a personality he has tremendous drive, wit and charm. His first spy stories contained a good deal of working-class morality, but now the tone is much more middle-class. His latest trilogy, *Game, Set and Match*, has as its central character Bernard Sampson, a flawed man who has sat for five years behind a desk in Whitehall before his bosses decide to reassign him to East

Berlin. Much of what happens in the trilogy is as Sampson sees it. Nothing and no one is wholly good or bad; everyone is ambiguous, and everyone is eventually betrayed. In Deighton's opinion, betrayal is serious only in marriage.

Deighton is not a natural technician, but he researches his books so thoroughly that he can exactly inform his readers about how to tap a telephone, crack a code or dive into a sunken submarine. When *An Expensive Place to Die* was published in 1967, Deighton faked some facsimiles of what purported to be top secret documents, which claimed to refer to correspondence between the White House and the then Prime Minister, Harold Wilson, concerning nuclear secrets. There are overtones of the Anna Wolkoff affair here. When Deighton's faked documents arrived in America, customs officials called in the FBI, and matters began to get out of hand. Later, some of the documents were discovered in a dustbin by a Slav with a sense of humour. Although he realized they were not authentic, he took them along to the United Nations office and offered them to a Russian official. When he asked a price of $100,000 for them, the Russian replied very seriously that he would have to apply to a higher authority for permission to pay. It was at this stage that the Slav sensibly withdrew from the market-place.

Deighton's books have always been best sellers, and he has generally collected excellent reviews. The distinguished detective story writer, essayist and critic, Julian Symons, regards him highly as a writer: 'There is something lyrical about his re-creation of the dangerous and transitory lives of agents . . . Writing of this quality . . . makes Deighton a kind of poet of the spy novel.' Like many before him, Deighton typifies the writer as spy and observer of mankind. Had he, like the others discussed here, been offered the chance of becoming a member of the Secret Services, he would have made a technically astute and highly imaginative operative.

Deighton might have enjoyed the intricacies of the Intelligence world, but many of his fellow writers were disappointed; for, as Maugham points out, 'Fact is a poor story-teller'.

BIBLIOGRAPHY

Adam Smith, Janet. *John Buchan* (Rupert Hart Davis, 1965)

Allain, Marie-Françoise. *The Other Man: Conversations with Graham Greene* (Bodley Head, 1983)

Allen, Peter. *The Cambridge Apostles: The Early Years* (Cambridge, 1979)

Allot, Kenneth and Farris, Miriam. *The Art of Graham Greene* (Hamish Hamilton, 1951)

Ambler, Eric. *To Catch a Spy* (Bodley Head, 1964)

Amis, Kingsley. *The James Bond Dossier* (Jonathan Cape, 1965)

Amory, Mark (ed.) *The Letters of Ann Fleming* (Collins Harvill, 1985)

Andrew, Christopher. *Secret Service* (Heinemann, 1985)

Atkins, John. *Graham Greene* (Calder & Boyars, 1957)

Atkins John. *The British Spy Novel* (John Calder, 1984)

Barley, Tony. *Taking Sides: The Fiction of John le Carré* (OUP, 1986)

Bingham, John. *Night's Black Agent* (Victor Gollancz, 1961)

Bingham, John. *A Fragment of Fear* (Victor Gollancz, 1965)

Bingham, John. *The Double Agent* (Victor Gollancz, 1966)

Bingham, John. *Vulture in the Sun* (Victor Gollancz, 1971)

Bingham, John. *Brock and the Defector* (Doubleday & Co., 1982)

Boyle, Andrew. *The Riddle of Erskine Childers* (Hutchinson, 1977)

Boyle, Andrew. *The Climate of Treason* (Hutchinson, 1979)

Brophy, John. *Somerset Maugham, Writers and their Work* series (Longmans Green, 1952)

Bryce, Ivar. *You Only Live Once: Memories of Ian Fleming* (Weidenfeld & Nicholson, 1975)

Buchan, John. *Greenmantle* (Blackwood, 1916)

Buchan, John. *Mr Standfast* (William Blackwood, 1919)

Buchan, John. *Memory Hold the Door* (Hodder & Stoughton, 1940)

Buchan, John. *The Thirty-Nine Steps* (William Blackwood, 1915)

Buchan, John. *The Power House* (William Blackwood, 1916)

Buchan, William. *John Buchan: A Memoir* (Buchan & Enright, 1982)

Calder, Robert Lorin. *W. Somerset Maugham and the Quest for Freedom* (Heinemann, 1972)

le Carré, John. *Call For The Dead* (Victor Gollancz, 1961)

le Carré, John. *A Murder of Quality* (Victor Gollancz, 1962)

le Carré, John. *The Spy Who Came In From The Cold* (Victor Gollancz, 1963)

le Carré, *The Looking Glass War* (William Heinemann, 1965)

le Carré, John. *The Naïve and Sentimental Lover* (Hodder & Stoughton, 1971)

le Carré, John. *Tinker Tailor, Soldier, Spy* (Hodder & Stoughton, 1974)

le Carré, John. *The Honourable Schoolboy* (Hodder & Stoughton, 1977)

le Carré, John. *Smiley's People* (Hodder & Stoughton, 1980)

le Carré, John. *The Little Drummer Girl* (Hodder & Stoughton, 1983)

le Carré, John. *A Perfect Spy* (Hodder & Stoughton, 1986)

Childers, Erskine. *The Riddle of the Sands* (Blackie, 1961)

Colby, William, and Forbath, Peter. *Honourable Men: My Life in the CIA* (Hutchinson, 1978)

Connolly, Cyril. *The Missing Diplomats* (Queen Anne Press, 1952)

Deacon, Richard. *A History of the British Secret Service* (Frederick Muller, 1969)

Deacon, Richard. *The Cambridge Apostles* (Robert Royce, 1985)

Deacon, Richard. *'C': A Biography of Sir Maurice Oldfield* (Macdonald, 1985)

Deighton, Len. *Spy Story* (Jonathan Cape, 1974)

Deighton, Len. *SS-GB* (Jonathan Cape, 1978)

Deighton, Len. *Goodbye Mickey Mouse* (Hutchinson, 1982)

Deighton, Len. *Berlin Game* (Hutchinson, 1983)

Deighton, Len. *Mexico Set* (Hutchinson, 1984)

Deighton, Len. *London Match* (Hutchinson, 1985)

Dobson, Christopher, and Payne, Ronald. *The Dictionary of Espionage* (Harrap, 1984)

Driberg, Tom. *Guy Burgess: A Portrait with Background* (Ebenezer Bayliss, 1956)

Driberg, Tom. *Ruling Passions* (Jonathan Cape, 1977)

Fitzherbert, Margaret. *The Man Who Was Greenmantle* (John Murray, 1983)

Fleming, Ian. *Casino Royale* (Cape, 1953)

BIBLIOGRAPHY

Fleming, Ian. *Live and Let Die* (Cape, 1954)

Fleming, Ian. *Moonraker* (Cape, 1955)

Fleming, Ian. *Diamonds are Forever* (Cape, 1956)

Fleming, Ian. *From Russia, With Love* (Cape, 1957)

Fleming, Ian. *Dr No* (1958)

Fleming, Ian. *Goldfinger* (Cape, 1959)

Fleming, Ian. *For Your Eyes Only* (Cape, 1960)

Fleming, Ian. *Thunderball* (based on a screen treatment by Kevin McClory, Jack Whittingham and Ian Fleming; Cape, 1961)

Fleming, Ian. *The Spy Who Loved Me* (with Vivienne Michel; Cape, 1962)

Fleming, Ian. *On Her Majesty's Secret Service* (Cape, 1963)

Fleming, Ian. *Thrilling Cities* (Cape, 1963)

Fleming, Ian. *You Only Live Twice* (Cape, 1964)

Fleming, Ian. *Octopussy and the Living Daylights* (Cape, 1965)

Fleming, Ian. *The Man With the Golden Gun* (Cape, 1965)

Greene, Graham. *The Man Within* (Heinemann, 1929)

Greene, Graham. *England Made Me* (Heinemann, 1935)

Greene, Graham. *Journey Without Maps* (Heinemann, 1936)

Greene, Graham. *Confidential Agent* (Heinemann, 1939)

Greene, Graham. *The Power and the Glory* (Heinemann, 1940)

Greene, Graham. *The Ministry of Fear* (Heinemann, 1943)

Greene, Graham. *Nineteen Stories* (Heinemann, 1947)

Greene, Graham. *The Heart of the Matter* (Heinemann, 1948)

Greene, Graham. *The Quiet American* (Heinemann, 1958)

Greene, Graham. *Our Man in Havana* (Heinemann, 1958)

Greene, Graham. *In Search of a Character* (Bodley Head, 1961)

Greene, Graham. *Collected Essays* (Bodley Head, 1969)

Greene, Graham. *A Sort of Life* (Bodley Head, 1971)

Greene, Graham. *The Honorary Consul* (Bodley Head, 1973)

Greene, Graham. *The Human Factor* (Bodley Head, 1978)

Greene, Graham. *Ways of Escape* (Bodley Head, 1980)

Greene, Graham. *Getting to Know the General* (Bodley Head, 1984)

Greene, Graham. *The Tenth Man* (Bodley Head, 1985)

Greene, Graham, and Greene, Hugh. *The Spy's Bedside Book* (Rupert Hart-Davis, 1957)

Holroyd, Michael. *Hugh Kingsmill* (Unicorn Press, 1964)

Howarth, T. E. B. *Cambridge Between Two Wars* (Collins, 1978)

Hunt, E. Howard. *Undercover: Memoirs of an American Secret Agent* (Berkeley Publishing Corp., 1974)

Hunt, E. Howard. *The Berlin Ending* (Knopf, 1972)

Hunt, E. Howard. *Bimini Run* (Knopf, 1948)

Hunt, E. Howard. *East of Farewell* (Knopf, 1942)

Hunt, E. Howard. *Limit of Darkness* (Random House, 1944)

Hunt, E. Howard. *The Hargrave Deception* (Stein & Day, 1980)

Hunt, E. Howard. *The Gaza Intercept* (Stein & Day, 1981)

Hunt, E. Howard. *The Kremlin Conspiracy* (Stein & Day, 1985)

Ingrams, Richard. *God's Apology* (André Deutsch, 1977)

Lewis, Peter. *John le Carré* (Frederick Ungar, 1985)

Mackenzie, Compton. *Greek Memories* (Chatto & Windus, 1932)

Mackenzie, Compton. *Water on the Brain* (Chatto & Windus, 1954)

Mackenzie, Compton. *My Life and Times, Octave V* (Chatto & Windus, 1966)

Mackenzie, Compton. *My Life and Times, Octave VI* (Chatto & Windus, 1967)

Mackenzie, Compton. *Extremes Meet* (Chatto & Windus, 1928)

Mackenzie, Compton. *The Three Couriers* (Chatto & Windus, 1929)

Marchetti, Victor, and Mark, John D. *The CIA and the Cult of Intelligence* (Jonathan Cape, 1974)

Maugham, W. Somerset. *Of Human Bondage* (Heinemann, 1915)

Maugham, W. Somerset. *Ashenden* (Heinemann, 1928)

Maugham, W. Somerset. *Cakes and Ale* (Heinemann, 1930)

Maugham, W. Somerset. *Collected Short Stories*, vols 1–3 (Heinemann, 1951)

Maugham, W. Somerset. *Selected Novels* (Heinemann, 1953)

McCormick, Donald. *Who's Who in Spy Fiction* (Elm Tree Books, 1977)

Merry, Bruce. *Anatomy of the Spy Thriller* (Gill & Macmillan, 1977)

Monaghan, David. *The Novels of John le Carré* (Basil Blackwell, 1985)

Monaghan, David. *Smiley's Circus* (Orbis, 1986)

Morgan, Ted. *Somerset Maugham* (Jonathan Cape, 1980)

Muggeridge, Malcolm. *Winter in Moscow* (Eyre & Spottiswoode, 1934)

Muggeridge, Malcolm. *Affairs of the Heart* (Walker, 1961)

Muggeridge, Malcolm. *The Thirties* (Collins, 1967)

Muggeridge, Malcolm. *Chronicles of Wasted Time: The Green Stick* (Collins, 1972)

Muggeridge, Malcolm *Chronicles of Wasted Time: The Infernal Grove* (Collins, 1973)

Muggeridge, Malcolm (ed. John Bright Holmes) *Like It Was* (Collins, 1981)

Page, Bruce, Leitch, David and Knightley, Phillip. *Philby: The Spy Who Betrayed a Generation* (André Deutsch, 1968)

Pearson, Hesketh, and Muggeridge, Malcolm. *About Kingsmill* (Methuen, 1950)

Pearson, John. *The Life of Ian Fleming* (Jonathan Cape, 1966)

Pearson, John. *007 James Bond* (Sidgwick & Jackson, 1973)

Philby, Eleanor. *Kim Philby: The Spy I Loved* (Hamish Hamilton, 1968)

Philby, Kim. *My Silent War* (MacGibbon & Kee, 1968)

Pincher, Chapman. *Their Trade is Treachery* (Sidgwick & Jackson, 1981)

Pincher, Chapman. *Too Secret Too Long* (Sidgwick & Jackson, 1984)

Powers, Thomas. *The Man Who Kept the Secrets: Richard Helms and the CIA* (Weidenfeld & Nicolson, 1979)

Quennell, Peter. *The Wanton Chase* (Collins, 1980)

Rees, Goronwy. *A Chapter of Accidents* (Chatto & Windus, 1971)

Seale, Patrick, and McConville, Maureen. *Philby: The Long Road to Moscow* (Hamish Hamilton, 1973)

Sinclair, Andrew. *The Red and the Blue* (Weidenfeld & Nicolson, 1986)

Snelling, O. F. *Double O Seven: James Bond, a Report* (Spearman Holland, 1964)

Spurling, John. *Graham Greene* (Methuen, 1983)

Sutherland, Douglas. *The Fourth Man* (Secker & Warburg, 1980)

Symonds, John. *The Great Beast: The Life and Magick of Aleister Crowley* (Macdonald, 1971)

Symons, Julian. *Bloody Murder: From the Detective Story to the Crime Novel: A History* (Faber & Faber 1967)

Symons, Julian. *The Detective Story in Britain, Writers and Their Work* series (Longmans Green, 1962)

Trevor-Roper, Hugh. *The Philby Affair* (Kimber, 1968)

West, Nigel. *A Matter of Trust: MI5 1945–72* (Weidenfeld & Nicolson, 1982)

West, Rebecca. *The Meaning of Treason* (Macmillan, 1949)

Wheatley, Dennis. *The Time Has Come: The Memoirs of Dennis Wheatley, 1897–1914: The Young Man Said* (Hutchinson, 1977)

Wheatley, Dennis. *The Time Has Come: The Memoirs of Dennis Wheatley, 1919–1977: Drink and Ink* (Hutchinson, 1979)

Wood, Neal. *Communism and British Intellectuals* (Gollancz, 1959)

Wyndham, Francis. *Graham Greene* (Longmans Green, 1955)

Young, Kenneth. *Compton Mackenzie, Writers and Their Work* series (Longmans Green, 1968)

INDEX

Index by Jenny Rudge

DATE DUE

GAYLORD			PRINTED IN U.S.A